TONY DEAR

The Story of Golf in 50 Tournaments

BACK NINE PRESS

Back Nine Press
Chicago, Illinois
www.back9press.com
Instagram and X: @backninepress

This book is in no way affiliated with Augusta National GC, the Masters tournament, or any professional golf tours.

9 8 7 6 5 4 3 2 1
First Edition

The Story of Golf in 50 Tournaments /
Written by Tony Dear

Back Nine Press (USA)
Pages cm
Printed in China

ISBN 978-1-956237-39-9 (hardcover)

For my long-lost father, who introduced me to golf and showed me how special a game it is.

For my wonderful kids, who haven't chosen golf… yet (that's cool, you do what you love).

But mostly for my incredible wife,
whose humor, patience, and quiet selflessness
are a very special combination.

CONTENTS

INTRODUCTION

Ten years ago in *The Story of Golf in 50 Holes*, I identified the most influential holes that had influenced the development of the game, either by being the scene of a memorable moment in a significant competition or because of their place in course architecture. Those holes had become well-known and had a story worth telling—stories that appeal to golfers who have a deep affection for the game they play. Some of the entries that made the cut (sorry, couldn't help myself) were/are so famous some readers probably knew a lot about them already but, among those 50, there were also holes they'd never seen or heard of before.

The same is likely to be true here. Even with 1,000+ tournaments contested each year across the world's professional tours and leagues—not to mention those at the highest level of amateur golf—only a handful can be truly memorable or influential. With all due respect to the great golfers who battle their peers to hoist a big trophy, don a custom jacket, or receive a purely minted medal, there's only so much room in our collective consciousness to recall all the great moments.

Not all tournaments can create legends. Not all victories can inspire a young boy or girl to take up the game. Not all finishes are reenacted by eager youngsters or seasoned veterans on the world's putting greens. Some, though, just stand out above the rest and are special, unique, larger than life ... sacred almost.

The reality is there's an elite few tournaments so important that what happens during tournament week can shape the future of the game—tournaments we'll always remember.

The goal with this book is to take your minds back to those truly significant events while introducing you to others you may not know much about but which definitely had a significant impact on the game. Some will be so familiar, you may already be able to rattle off the winner, the winning score, the venue, the weather, who else was in contention, and numerous other details your wife/girlfriend/non-golfing friends will think you strange for knowing. Then there will be those you've never considered before and had no idea were so important. Trust me, there were a few tournaments whose status rose during research from possible inclusions to must-haves.

Look at the Table of Contents and there will be entries at which you shake your head and wonder why they were included. For others, though, those same tournaments might already mean a great deal. You might have posters or reproduction flags on your walls from certain tournaments while those same events might be of no interest to some.

There are a lot of golfers you know—and might even play with—who have no idea what happened at Turnberry, Scotland in July 1977. They'll probably know Tiger Woods won the Masters in 2019, but have no idea how pulsat-

ing the final few hours of the 1999 and 2012 Ryder Cups were.

Most golfers won't see it this way, but there are people who think it weird to search for the 1977 Open Championship or 1986 Masters on YouTube and watch them repeatedly. Readers of this book, however, will know reliving either of them, or the 1991 Ryder Cup, 2016 Open Championship, or some Shell's Wonderful World of Golf (exhibitions, really, so not suitable for this book) is a pretty solid way for a golf junkie to spend some time.

Sure, even those who watched the '77 Open Championship and '86 Masters as they happened will still set aside time to see them again, just to ensure Tom Watson's second to the 18th in the final round at Turnberry, and Nicklaus' putt at the same hole, or his tee shot at Augusta National's 16th in round four of the '86 Masters, really did happen. And talking of shots you need to re-watch just to be sure ... did Seve Ballesteros' putt at the 18th in the final round of the 1984 Open Championship at the Old Course really go in? How about Tiger Woods' second shot to the 6th in the 2000 U.S. Open at Pebble Beach—does that still look as unbelievable today as it did then?

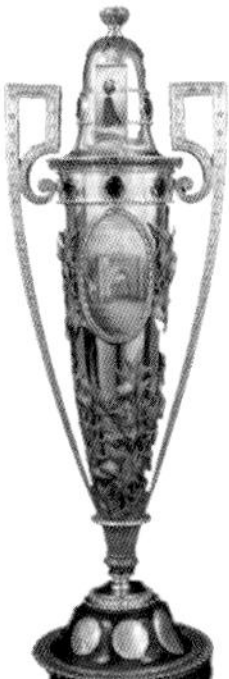

The hope is you see enough tournaments here you already know something about to realize we're singing off the same hymn sheet, but that you'll also see some you're eager to learn more about.

It's fair to say, this isn't the definitive list of the most exciting or important tournaments ever played. No list could be. Everyone has different factors that contribute to the worth and greatness of an event. What appealed and seemed significant to me might mean nothing to you.

It was important to remove bias as much as possible; I assure you if there was more bias, the book might have included an unreasonable number of events that Seve won. The aim was to include tournaments that really meant something to the sport and its followers, as measured by their effect on golf media and the sort of conversations golfers have—the fact we still read and talk about the 1930 U.S. Amateur and 1913 U.S. Open obviously indicates how important a part of golf's story they are.

It's possible, of course, that what happened to my friend, author Tim Gay, will also happen here. Almost as soon as Gay had submitted his excellent biography of Rory McIlroy—Rory Land—to his publisher, the Ulsterman went and won a thrilling Masters; I know Tim would've loved to include that sweet victory in his book (it did appear in the U.K. and Ireland editions, as well as the digital version in the U.S.), but books can't wait until the end of time to be written. No doubt an even more remarkable Masters, or the most thrilling U.S. Open in living memory will happen shortly after this book hits the shelves. So be it; c'est la vie.

An ideal starting point was obviously the first official golf competition that ever happened, while it seemed the 2025 Masters—Rory's Redemption—was an equally good place to finish. Relatively little time has passed since McIlroy completed the career Grand Slam—opening myself up to recency bias—but, using the same criteria that was applied to the other entries in this book, it's very likely that Masters will hold up as an extremely significant event moving forward. You don't really have to be a student of the game to appreciate how big a deal it was.

The golfer's ability to reminisce is strong. Sensational shots by the world's best players on the best courses at its biggest tournaments align with moments and phases in our lives. Just as many people know where they were when Neil Armstrong landed on the Moon; on September 11, 2001; or, more recently, when Taylor Swift and Travis Kelce announced their engagement, golfers will invariably remember where they were when Nicklaus won his sixth green jacket, Bernhard Langer missed the crucial putt at the 1991 Ryder Cup, Martin Kaymer holed his Ryder Cup-winning putt at Medinah in 2012, or when Tiger Woods outlasted the competition at the 2019 Masters.

Okay, they know they were in front of the TV (or at the venue), but they probably also know what Nicklaus, Langer, Kaymer, and Woods were wearing, what they themselves were wearing, and exactly what the commentator/announcer said at all the important moments. They'll remember who else was in the room when the final putt dropped, and how they felt about what they'd just seen.

The great English Romantic poet William Wordsworth called these distinct, vivid memories in our lives "spots of time" (though in the 1790s, he wasn't referring to professional sport). That's true of a lot of these tournaments for many of us. Others that happened before we were born, or became obsessed with the game, would also have been great to watch. But learning about them now adds to the never-ending and always colorful story of golf.

For those of us who make heroes of people that hit a little white ball with a metal stick, there really is nothing like watching our favorite players at an exciting tournament we know we're going to be talking about for years. I wonder what your next "spot of time" will be.

15 32 17 4

11 13 1

36

20 10

45

46 19

9

33 8

29

40

3 23

38

21

47 31

35 41

14

50 TOURNAMENTS

1744 Silver Club

First ever organized golf tournament.

DATE
April 2, 1744

LOCATION
Leith Links
Edinburgh, Scotland

PRIZE
The Silver Club,
Captaincy

IN THE FIELD
10 or 11 prominent
Edinburgh Gentlemen

In 1744, "several Gentlemen of Honour, skillfull in the ancient and healthfull exercise of Golf" asked the City of Edinburgh to provide a silver club as a prize for an annual competition to be held on the five-hole links (Braehead to Sawmill—414 yards; Sawmill to North Mid—461 yards; Sawmill to East—426 yards; East to South Mid—495 yards; South Mid to Thorntree—435 yards) at Leith, the city's port town about three and a half miles northeast of Edinburgh Castle. The City had earlier given The Silver Arrow for an archery competition so it agreed, donating a silver club that cost £17, 4 shillings, and 3 pence and adding it would not be responsible for any other expenses except for transporting the silver club to the links "on the day of the match" and to "intimate by Tuck of Drum through the City the day on which it shall be played for."

This obviously indicates there was an existing community of golfers in Leith (it has been said golf was actually played there as early as 1554). This community had no bylaws or official premises, but most believe it was actually formalized in 1744 when the Silver Club was first contested (plus, the Honorable Company of Edinburgh Golfers—HCEG—announced in the 1839 *Edinburgh Alamanack*, "The period at which the Company was formed cannot now be ascertained; but the first regular series of minutes, signed by Lord Duncan Forbes of Culloden (the Lord President, Scotland's most senior judge) bears the date 1744."

What the HCEG was actually called in 1744 is a little vague as it was referred to, in various places, as "The Leith Society," "The Golfing Company," "The Gentlemen Golfers of Edinburgh," "The Edinburgh Company of Golfers," and "The Gentlemen Golfers of Leith" before officially becoming "The Honourable, The Edinburgh Company of Golfers" (later shortened to "The Honourable Company of Edinburgh Golfers") on March 26, 1800. Initially, it used Luckie Clephan's tavern in Leith's Kirkgate as a meeting place but, in 1768, it built Golf House—the world's first Golf Clubhouse. The club shared Golf House with the Thistle Golf Club from 1815 and sold it in 1834 during a period of financial instability.

The first Silver Club competition was open to all golfers and would be held on April 2, the winner to be declared "Captain of the Golf" (each winner attached a silver replica golf ball to the club engraved with their name and the year they won). The scoring system appears to have been a curious affair: players were put in "parties of two—or three if their number should be so great" (not a great concern as only 11, possibly 10, showed up) that were drawn by lot, and competed against each other with the shorter player from the tee playing the odd and his opponent then playing the like. Whoever played the fewest strokes before holing out won the hole and the player with the most holes won the match. That part, at least, seems logical (even if we are unfamiliar today with the language and terms used), though it got odd when the player who won their match by the largest margin was declared the winner of the competition.

Two good players who halved (or tied) their match might therefore have to watch as a lesser player who beat an even worse player by three holes, say, won the trophy. You have to assume the tournament organizers would have realized the peculiarities of their scoring system were it not for the fact the golfers that did play were likely all fairly advanced and similarly competent, and that the same man—John Rattray, an Edinburgh surgeon who was also a member of the Royal Company of Archers and physician to Bonnie Prince Charlie (Charles Edward Stuart, the Young Pretender) during the Jacobite Rebellion—won the first two events, in 1744 and 1745—there was no event in 1746, due to the Jacobite Uprising. Rattray, having been pardoned for his role in it and after swearing an oath of allegiance to the British King George II won the Silver Club again in 1751.

The Silver Club, awarded in 1744

Because golfers from anywhere in Great Britain and Ireland were allowed to enter, the City Council stated that a common set of rules was to be drawn up for the tournament. At the time, golfers at the few other places the sport was played usually agreed the rules for their match before starting, and any disagreements tended to be ruled upon by elder players. But the elder players at one course might interpret a situation differently to those at another, so a universal set of rules seemed sensible.

The 13 "Articles and Laws in Playing at Golf" were drafted by the Leith golfers and approved by the City Council on March 7—just 26 days before the tournament was to be played (two rules were amended in 1758, and

The R&A's Silver Club

On May 14, 1754 (the date given for the formation of the Society of St Andrews Golfers which became the Royal and Ancient Golf Club of St Andrews—R&A—in 1834), 22 Noblemen and Gentlemen from the Society met to confirm the regulations for their own Silver Club competition. The rules would be very similar to those first used in Leith 10 years earlier.

The competition was held to help "the interest and prosperity of the City of St Andrews," and was open to all-comers with much of the field being comprised of East Coast lairds and aristocracy. The St Andrews Golfers also invited the HCEG to play, and even advertised its meetings in the Edinburgh newspapers.

Since St Andrews invited golfers from Leith/Edinburgh, had members in common, and adopted their rules, the two societies are thought to have been amicable toward each other. Local merchant William Landale won the first Silver Club at St Andrews, hung a silver ball from the Silver Club, and was appointed Captain of the R&A for a year.

In 1806, the club decided to elect its Captain (as the HCEG would 30 years later), so the competition ceased. As the HCEG would at Musselburgh, R&A captains continued to attach silver balls to the club, the second of which was first presented at the 1819 Autumn Meeting. This second club features four gold balls attached by monarchs—the Prince of Wales (later Edward VII) Captain in 1863; Prince Leopold in 1876, the Prince of Wales (later Edward VIII) in 1922, and the Duke of York (later George VI) in 1930.

The Prince of Wales (later Edward VIII) presented a third Silver Club at the end of his captaincy, in 1923, and the fourth was presented by Queen Elizabeth II in 2021, "in commemoration of her 70-year Patronage of the Club."

in 1775, a 14th rule—describing the route to be taken round the links at Leith—was introduced. This was also the first time a circuit of the holes was referred to as a 'Round.' And a new 15th rule stated that any disputes were to be resolved by the Captain if he happened to be present, and if he were absent, the most recent Captain who was present was to adjudicate.

Sketch of The Silver Club being paraded through the streets of Leith, 1744

In 1764, after 20 years of open competition, the Leith golfers that would become the HCEG and Edinburgh City Council agreed only members of the HCEG would be entitled to compete for the Silver Club.

The HCEG began paying for the Silver Club in 1811 even though it was still presented by Edinburgh City Council. In 1836, the competition stopped when the HCEG began electing its captains and moved from Leith to Musselburgh, five miles to the east (now Musselburgh Old Course), because the links at Leith had become crowded with archers, cricketers, football (soccer) players, and families enjoying the open space.

The Captain continued to add a silver ball to the club, however. Forty-four balls were attached to the first Silver Club before it was replaced (the second had 45 balls, the third 43, and the fourth 44). The tradition continued when the HCEG moved from Musselburgh to its third home—Muirfield, 13 miles farther east along the East Lothian coast in Gullane, where the Silver Clubs are now housed in display cases in the clubhouse dining room.

Today, an organization known as the Leith Rules Society, founded in 2003 to "increase the recognition of Leith Links as the home of the earliest recorded rules of golf and one of the game's prominent early locations" meets on Leith Links every July for a week of hickory golf on a five-hole, 848-yard course laid out by a local greenkeeper. The society raised funds in 2019 to erect a life-size statue of John Rattray—the first signatory of the 13 Rules of Golf—on Leith Links together with plinths inscribed with Rattray's biography and the 13 Articles and Laws in Playing at Golf.

Statue of John Rattray on Leith Links

1857 Grand National

Early Scottish inter-club tournament; a stepping stone to the Open.

DATE
July 29-31, 1857

LOCATION
St Andrews, Scotland

PRIZE
A silver claret jug

IN THE FIELD
Sir Hugh Lyon Playfair
Thomas Moncrieff
Mjr. James Ogilvie Fairlie
Robert Hay
Robert Clark
George Glennie
Lt. J. Stewart
Robert Chambers

Although the Silver Club tournaments at Leith and St Andrews existed, the vast majority of competitive play up to the middle of the 19th century was private money matches. Money games still happen nowadays, of course, but formalized competition on a much larger scale than that of the Silver Club events was about to happen. In his 1955 book *A History of Golf*, Robert Browning asserts that credit for the development of championship golf belongs almost entirely to Prestwick GC, which was founded in 1851.

On April 6, 1857, the club sent out a letter (see "The Letter that Changed the Game?") to six other Scottish clubs and one in England, proposing a foursomes team competition. Four members from each club was the original suggestion but, by the time of the competition, this had become one pair. Every club accepted with five others expressing a desire to compete. Carnoustie and the HCEG were unable to find a suitable pair, however, so a total of 11 clubs competed.

A four-man committee that included Major James Ogilvie Fairlie—the primary force behind the formation of the Prestwick club—organized the event, which—it was decided—would be held at St Andrews, with each match being played over 30 holes.

The tournament was won by George Glennie and Lieutenant J.C. Stewart of London's Blackheath Club, who beat the R&A by seven holes. You might expect the reaction to a club from London beating the home team from the R&A to have been a little contentious ... combative even. But, as the *Edinburgh Courant* reported, when the city's provost—Sir Hugh Lyon Playfair, proposed three cheers for the winners, they were "heartily given" by the large crowd that had gathered.

The 30 holes of the final match were played between noon and 4:15 p.m. *The Courant*'s reporter said Glennie and Lt. Stewart played a "beautiful game throughout with the greatest coolness." As their last names suggest, both men were from Scotland—each had learned the game at St Andrews. At the prize-giving ceremony, Rennie was handed the silver claret jug and made a "suitable reply," after which "the proceedings of this very successful meeting of golfers from throughout the Kingdom terminated."

The Letter that Changed the Game?

It is proposed to play a match at golf between the eight undermentioned clubs:

St Andrews, Perth, Musselburgh, Blackheath, Prestwick, Carnoustie, North Berwick, Leven, each Club to send four members to contend.

The Game to be played in double Matches, or Foursomes, drawing for opponents by lot before starting, and again after each game by the winners.

The remaining winning pair to be considered the champions. The Prize for this competition to be a Medal, or other piece of Plate purchased at the expense of the competing Clubs in proportion to the number of members in each. At the conclusion of the playing by pairs, the winning pair will compete for the prize in a single match, the Winner to become the Possessor.

The game to be played at St Andrews or Prestwick during the Summer Meeting.

If your Club consents to play in this Match will you be kind enough to inform me at your earliest convenience, at the same time naming which of the two links you prefer, as the Majority will decide.

Etc., etc.,

JOHN CUTHBERT, *Secretary*

Major James Ogilvie Fairlie

George Glennie

It was proposed, said *The Courant*, that the tournament would be repeated the following year. It was played in 1858, but with a different format. Club foursomes were replaced with an individual contest open to "all gentlemen players of any established club," and matches would be over 18 holes.

Twenty-eight players each paid £1 to enter (a significant amount in those days), and the final was played between the youngest competitor—20-year-old Robert Chambers (a member of the Edinburgh Bruntsfield Club, who donated a set of clubs to the winner and a dozen balls to the runner-up) and the eldest—D. Wallace (known as the "Knight of Balgrummo") of Leven, who was aged 60+, and according to the *Fife Herald*, enjoyed the majority of the support.

The two finalists had already met in the fourth and fifth rounds, as both players involved in a halved match advanced to the draw for the next round (we know how bizarre scoring methods and tournament protocol were in those days). Wallace was a notoriously slow player—the *Herald* said he took "half-an-hour every stroke" (words that appear to have been written without any hint of shock or distress)—but his frustrating habits didn't seem to bother Chambers, who is reported to have said, "Give me a novel and a camp stool, and I'll let the old chap do as he likes."

The final was, apparently, something of a dismal affair, with both players fatigued by the amount of golf they had played in so short a time. Chambers won by a single hole, collecting the silver jug and plate. The clubs and balls Chambers had donated went to Wallace.

At the third Grand National, in 1859, 49 players entered and the highly talented George Condie of Perth beat North Berwick's Sir Robert Hay in the final by six holes.

The Grand National tournaments were only partly successful. While they brought together the country's finest players for organized competition and did receive some press attention, they didn't settle on a consistent format and never really ignited a passion for championship golf. Nor did they reveal an unquestioned leading light. After Allan Robertson's death on September 1, 1859 (see pages 28-9), it was time for a proper championship to identify the game's true Champion Golfer.

Grand National golfers outside the R&A clubhouse

1860 Open Championship

First Open Championship; finding a successor to Robertson.

DATE
October 17, 1860

LOCATION
Prestwick GC
Ayrshire,
Scotland

PRIZE
The Challenge Belt

IN THE FIELD
Tom Morris
Willie Park
Andrew Strath
Robert Andrew

On a front page packed with requests, advertisements, and announcements, the October 11, 1860 edition of the *Fife Herald* incorporating the Kinross, Strathearn and Clackmannan Advertiser printed a message notifying readers that a golf competition proposed by Prestwick Golf Club was to be held on Wednesday, October 17th and contested over 36 holes—three rounds of the club's 12-hole links. Prestwick GC's archives show planning for a stroke-play competition that sought to identify the game's best professional golfer had begun in May.

The impetus for such a tournament was the widespread attention and press coverage matches between the big-name players of the day—Allan Robertson, Tom Morris, Willie Dunn, Willie Park, et cetera—were attracting. They were duels, in a sense. These money matches, financed by wealthy Golf Club members, were reported in much the same manner as prestigious horserace meetings and boxing bouts. They were a big deal and aroused the notion of a national competition.

Major Fairlie, a beneficiary of his father's will to the tune of £19,000, and a very talented golfer himself, was the instigator. Captain of the R&A in 1850, Fairlie was a Lieutenant Colonel-Commandant in the Ayrshire Yeomanry Cavalry, a co-founder of Prestwick Golf Club in 1851, and the man who convinced Tom Morris to move from St Andrews to the Ayrshire coast to take up a position at the newly founded club. Fairlie first began working on a national tournament in 1856, his efforts resulting in the Grand National Golf Club Tournament (see "1857 Grand National").

Support for Fairlie's national tournament seemed to be diminishing after the first three years, but he envisaged something very different—a singles strokeplay event contested by professionals rather than amateurs—and he was determined it should happen.

As it had previously, Prestwick GC sent letters to other prominent clubs—Aberdeen, Blackheath (in London), Bruntsfield, Carnoustie, Panmure, Dirleton Castle, Innerleven (Leven), Montrose, North Berwick, Perth, and the R&A, and made announcements in the national press. They stated each club in Scotland and England was to send its three best players, and that he who "succeeded in holing his ball in the fewest number of strokes" would be winner of the Challenge Belt: a red, leather, Moroccan-style belt with a silver buckle that anyone winning three years in succession would be allowed to keep and which was valued at £25—roughly $2,000 in today's money and, at the time, the equivalent of about 125 days of wages for a skilled craftsman.

"Cawdies, i.e. Professional Players, not Keepers of Links, must produce a certificate of respectability from the Treasurer of the Golf Club to which they are attached," the announcements said. At the time, anyone who carried clubs for gentlemen members was considered a professional. Some were capable players and some were clubmakers. And most of them had a reputation for indulging themselves to excess in local taverns.

The event was played during the week of Prestwick GC's Autumn meeting, and the first tee time would be at noon. Contestants were to assemble beforehand outside the Red Lion Inn—where, on July 2, 1851, Prestwick Golf Club had been founded by 57 professional men and gentry, a group gathered and led by Fairlie.

It's estimated that around 15 Golf Clubs and courses (fields of play) existed in Britain in 1860, which means that around 45 players could conceivably have teed it up and fought for the Challenge Belt, a fitting analogy as the belt was likely modeled on those awarded to winners of bare-knuckle prizefights gentlemen would organize for the purpose of making large wagers.

The Belt was indeed a handsome prize, but since Prestwick Golf Club owned it (the winner could pay a £25 deposit to keep it for the year following his win), and there was no accompanying prize money (first paid in 1863 to those finishing 2nd, 3rd, and 4th. The winner didn't receive cash, in addition to the Belt, until 1864), it's perhaps not surprising the entry list was rather short. In fact, only eight professionals deemed it worth their while to make the journey to Ayrshire; the famous Dunn brothers of Musselburgh decided not to go. It's not clear how long the intervals between tee times were, but it's possible all eight balls were in the air by 12:20 p.m.

The favorite for the Belt was undoubtedly Prestwick's professional, Tom Morris: a native St Andrean who had apprenticed under ballmaker Allan Robertson (his first cousin once removed) from his mid-teens. Four years after beginning as an apprentice, Morris became Robertson's employee, contributing to the creation of two, perhaps three, featheries a day. He also played exhibitions, and partnered with his boss in money matches ... none of which they lost.

At Fairlie's urging, Morris had left St Andrews for Prestwick in 1851, three years after he and Robertson had fallen out following an awkward moment on the links. Playing with an R&A member—Mr. Campbell of Saddell—Morris ran out of featheries whereupon

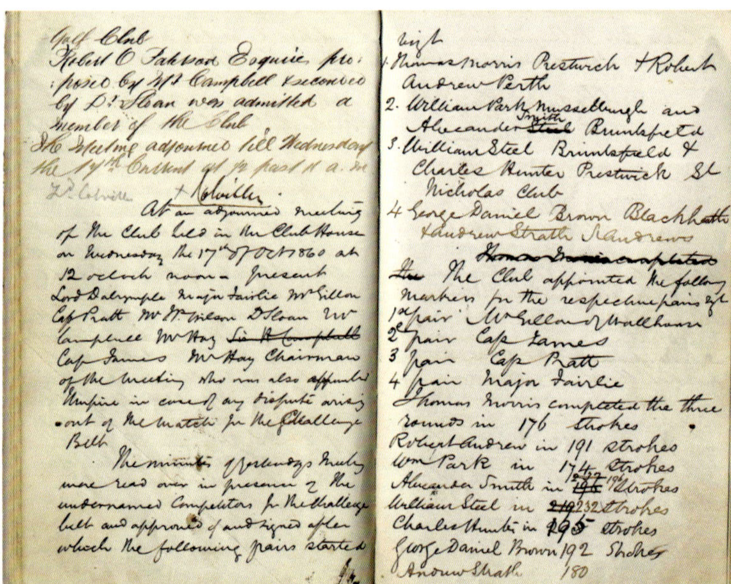

1860 entry from Prestwick GC's minute book

Campbell offered him a gutty. Robertson learned of Morris' use of the newly developed ball and clearly wasn't happy, the two "having words" in Robertson's shop. Their quarrel was not the fevered and prolonged feud it became in various accounts over the next 150+ years, but it was fractious enough, apparently, for Morris to leave Robertson's employ and open his own shop—with the address of 15 The Links road (the two remained friends, however, and continued playing matches together for years after Morris moved west, despite the fact 100 miles separated them).

Fairlie had engaged Morris as Prestwick's Keeper of the Green and club/ballmaker. He would design the original 12-hole course

Prestwick

The venue for the very first Open Championship (and 23 thereafter) originally had 12 holes, many of which criss-crossed, and covered 50 acres or so. Tom Morris laid out the course, using the site's best dunes and undulations to create what must have been a very interesting and enjoyable test. It measured 3,799 yards, and each hole was given a name. After Charles Hunter extended the course in 1882, James Braid made alterations to the stretch between the 7th and 11th in 1922 with contributions from Harold Hilton. Since then, the course has remained largely untouched.

Card of the Course in 1860

1st	Back of Cardinal	578 yards
2nd	Alps	385 yards
3rd	Tunnel (Red)	167 yards
4th	Wall	448 yards
5th	Sea Hedrig	440 yards
6th	Tunnel (White)	314 yards
7th	Green Hollow	144 yards
8th	Station	166 yards
9th	Burn	395 yards
10th	Lunch House	213 yards
11th	Short	132 yards
12th	Home	417 yards

Who Was Allan Robertson?

Born in St Andrews in September 1815, Robertson was something of a pioneer; very likely the first man to establish himself as a golf professional, partnering R&A members in matches, caddying for those same members, and being the head of a family that produced the finest quality feathery golf balls. Making a feather-filled ball was an arduous, and at times, dangerous task that basically involved stitching together strips of cowhide and filling the resulting hollow, ball-shaped sack with boiled goose feathers. The feathers would need to be squeezed into a small hole in the sack as tightly as possible before the ball was sewn up. It would then be hammered to level any bumps and given three coats of white paint. The maker stamped his name on it and left it to dry for two days, allowing the feathers to expand and fill any remaining voids.

Once complete, the ball was extremely hard but, unfortunately, would rarely last very long—the stitches bursting open and spraying a small collection of feathers over the ground. Since a skilled ballmaker might average making only three featheries a day, they were expensive, keeping Robertson in business and golf a sport mostly for well-to-do gentlemen and dignitaries.

Robertson took on Tom Morris (five years his junior) as an apprentice sometime in the mid-1830s (possibly following the death of Allan's father David in 1836), and Morris later became Robertson's journeyman employee. During that time, they formed a formidable pairing (billed as "The Invincibles"), though they played against each other on occasion. Robertson was an excellent golfer, regularly breaking 90 on a course where the people he caddied for seldom broke 100. He became the toast of the town in 1843 after beating Willie Dunn of Musselburgh convincingly in a 20-round match played over 10 days.

As previously mentioned, Robertson and Morris' relationship soured temporarily when Morris played a few holes with a gutta-percha ball (gutty) having lost his supply of featheries—the fairways at St Andrews were very narrow at the time and bordered by thick gorse bushes.

The new ball, made from the sap of a southeast Asian Palaquium tree, had been invented by Dr. Robert Adams Paterson, a clergyman who attended the University of St

Andrews but was unable to play golf because of the cost of featheries. While performing missionary work in Malaysia, Dr. Paterson found a statue he wished to send back to Scotland, and wrapped it in gutta-percha for safe transit. After arriving back in his homeland and removing the covering, Paterson suddenly became aware of how suitable this packaging material might be for making a golf ball. He heated it to make it softer, then molded it into a ball that, he discovered, performed remarkably well and lasted significantly longer than a feather ball. In *The Golfer's Manual*, H.B. Farnie wrote, "The first flight of the 'Guttas' was hailed with a burst of joy by everyone except the old monopolists of the feather manufacture."

Robertson in 1850

(The gutta-percha industry had grown rapidly in the West during the 1840s when manufacturers used it to make picture frames, cornices, brackets, card trays, inkstands, pen trays, biscuit trays, flowerpots, shells, platers, walking sticks/canes, whips, balls, window cords, and even surgical tools. Its greatest achievement, besides changing golf forever, of course, came in 1851 when it was used to insulate the electrical wire that was stretched across the English Channel to form a submarine telegraph, giving Britain instantaneous contact with Continental Europe.)

At first sickened and indignant about the introduction of the gutty (he is known to have burned them) which killed the feathery industry in less than five years, Robertson slowly came around to its benefits. He may even have made some and, on September 15, 1858, he used one to shoot an incredible 79 at St Andrews, becoming the first person to break 80 there.

He was, without doubt, the finest golfer of the time and when he died of jaundice on September 1, 1859, at the age of 43. He was mourned by all golfers and St Andreans, one saying, "They may toll the bells and shut up their shops in St Andrews for the greatest of them is gone."

and develop the practice of top-dressing playing surfaces after he had observed turf becoming stronger and the ground firmer when the wind covered it in sand.

Morris' main competition for the Belt would be Willie Park, a Musselburgh (East Lothian) professional 12 years younger than Morris. A confident, and by many accounts, somewhat brash individual, Park had first played Morris in St Andrews during the R&A's 1854 Autumn Meeting. In a two-round match for £50 per round, the first 18 was halved, but Park won in the afternoon by 5&4. Morris, who had been in Prestwick for three years, regained some honor the following morning beating Park over a single round, but that first encounter the day before (October 19th) was considered Park's coming-out party and the symbolic start of his impressive playing career.

The *Fifeshire Journal*, which had taken to reporting golf matches shot by shot, clearly admired Park's game, saying he was "Possessing all the requisites of a good golfer—neat style, long driver, cool as a cucumber whether playing a losing or a winning game, and equally handy with all the tools used in golf. He fully justified the confidence reposed in him by his backers."

In the quest for the Challenge Belt, Morris would be in the first group out, playing with Perth's Robert Andrew. Park and Bruntsfield's Alex Smith came next and were followed by William Steel and Charles Hunter (the professional at nearby Prestwick St. Nicholas GC, who would move to Prestwick GC in 1864 and expand Morris' 12-hole layout to 18 in 1882). George Brown from Blackheath in London and St Andrews' Andrew Strath were the final pairing.

Two rounds (24 total holes) would be played before lunch was taken at the Red Lion, after which the final 12 would be played

LEFT TO RIGHT: Feathery ball, hand-hammered gutty, machine-shaped gutty

before sunset fell at 5:16 p.m. Park led after a first-round 55 with Morris three shots behind. The reaction in Prestwick was, apparently, total astonishment and it hadn't abated after two rounds when Park stood at 114 and Morris 117.

Morris did win the third 12 by a shot—59 to 60—but it wasn't enough as Park holed a 30-footer across the bumpy final green to win by two, at 174. Strath was third at 180, with William Steel bringing up the rear on a fairly uncompetitive 232; 36 shots behind Alex Smith in 7th.

Though the event wasn't technically "open" as amateurs hadn't been allowed to play, the 1860 tournament is officially the first ever Open Championship. And though Morris had been expected to win and take over Allan Robertson's mantle as the game's best player and become the Champion Golfer, it was his bitter rival from Musselburgh that won the day.

In 1861, amateurs and indeed any golfer from around the world would be allowed to enter making the tournament genuinely "open." Two amateurs finished in the top 10: Major Fairlie was 8th, and Robert Chambers of Bruntsfield 10th.

The 12-hole course at Prestwick that hosted the first ever Open Championship has obviously evolved a great deal over the last 165+ years. It's now 18 holes, of course (extended by Charles Hunter in 1882), and the criss-cross fairways are gone. However, a few of the ancient holes cover the same ground as some of the current holes, most notably the 17th. Named 'Alps' for the large sand dune you hit over to get to the green (watch out for the Sahara bunker between the dune and the putting surface), the 17th is much the same as the original 2nd, and one of the game's most extraordinary holes which has to be seen/played to be believed.

Willie Park Sr. wearing the Challenge Belt

1867 Open Championship

Old Tom Morris wins for the fourth and final time.

DATE
Sept. 26, 1867

LOCATION
Prestwick GC
Ayrshire, Scotland

PRIZE
£7

IN THE FIELD
Tom Morris Sr.
Willie Park
Andrew Strath
Bob Kirk
Tom Morris Jr.

Born in St Andrews in June 1821, Morris grew up in a town experiencing significant growth, thanks to Sir Hugh Lyon Playfair's vision for it to become the "Metropolis of Golf." Morris began playing the game at the age of six or seven and—despite coming from a family of weavers (though his father caddied, too)—he quickly grew obsessed with the game becoming a ballmaker, keeper of the green, and brilliant player.

He moved to Prestwick with his wife Nancy and young son, Tom Jr., in 1851 to work at the newly founded golf club where he also assisted Major Fairlie in identifying other players that might compete for the Challenge Belt.

Morris would likely have been under tremendous pressure to win the inaugural tournament as he knew the course better than anyone. He was also well aware that Prestwick Golf Club members were watching, and he'd have desperately wanted to prevent Willie Park from taking the title of "Champion Golfer" back to rival Musselburgh. That he didn't win the 1860 event would have been deeply disappointing, not to say embarrassing, though he made up for it by winning the next two (by 13 shots in 1862, no less).

He lost to Park by two shots in 1863, meaning the pair shared the first four Challenge Belts. Morris then won in 1864, and Park in 1866 (Andrew Strath won in 1865) leaving them with three titles each. Morris would be the first to four victories, winning in 1867 at the age of 46 years, 3 months, and 10 days.

The field for the eighth staging of the event would total 14, made up of 10 professionals and four gentleman amateurs. Park and Morris were drawn together in the sixth match. For the first time ever, an amateur led after the morning's first round: William Doleman of Musselburgh, who shot 55. Three shots back and tied for 4th were Tom Morris Jr., Willie Park Sr., and Tom Morris Sr. "Old" Tom would take a one-shot lead after the second round following an excellent 54, and a third-round 58 was good enough for him to hold off Park.

Morris became the championship's oldest winner, beating the record he'd set himself in 1864: a record that was still intact 158 years later.

Second String

It's interesting to note the timing and positioning of reports from the 1867 Challenge Belt tournament in Scottish newspapers. The *Scotsman* and *Edinburgh Daily Review* ran stories on September 30, four days after it had taken place. And on October 3, the *Fife Herald* sandwiched a third of a column about the tournament between stories of Prestwick GC's Autumn Meeting and a slightly longer report from the R&A's annual meeting and Silver Club event which had been contested the day before.

Though the Challenge Belt was slowly gaining momentum and earning some credibility, it still seems to have been regarded as something of an inconvenience to Prestwick members, most of whom had traveled to the course from Glasgow to enjoy some golf with their fellow members.

The Challenge Belt

Only four of the 14 players competing for the Challenge Belt took home prize money. While Morris Sr. earned £7, Park won £5, Andrew Strath £3, and Tom Morris Jr. £1. Immediately after the Belt had been won, Morris Jr. challenged Park to a match, Park winning with a 54 to Morris Jr.'s 56. The following day, a competition called the "Consolation Stakes" was hosted by the Prestwick St. Nicholas Club (won by Bob Kirk, who pocketed £3), a group of artisans that included Tom Morris Sr. The St. Nicholas club was formed four months after Prestwick Golf Club and was originally known as Prestwick Mechanics Club. It relocated to its own course in 1877, moved to a new location shortly afterward, and settled into its present home on the coast, about half a mile south of Prestwick GC, in 1892.

Tom Morris Sr.—more affectionately known as Old Tom Morris and perhaps the most influential individual in the history of the game—would play in the Challenge Belt/Open Championship 26 more times. His final appearance came in 1896, just a few days short of his 75th birthday. The last of his 18 top-10 finishes (only eight players were in the field in 1860, 1862, and 1872) had been a tie for 10th in 1883, at the age of 62.

The approach to Prestwick's Alps hole

Tom Morris Sr. and Jr.

1870 Open Championship

Young Tom Morris wins third Challenge Belt in a row, gets to keep it.

DATE
Sept, 15, 1870

LOCATION
Prestwick GC
Ayrshire,
Scotland

PRIZE
£6

IN THE FIELD
Tom Morris Sr.
Tom Morris Jr.
Willie Park Sr.
Jamie Anderson
Bob Kirk
Davie Strath
William Doleman

You'll remember that Prestwick GC had decreed any player winning the Challenge Belt three years in succession would get to keep it. One can only speculate on whether the club expected someone to win it three times in a row but, with Tom Morris Sr. not yet 40 when the tournament was first staged, and Willie Park Sr. 12 years his junior, it surely would have been considered a possibility.

Indeed, Major Fairlie and his fellow Prestwick officials would likely have anticipated such an outcome in 1863, when Morris Sr. was going for three in a row in just the fourth playing of the event. Park beat Morris by two that year, however, preventing the Belt's early transfer of ownership. It wouldn't be long, though, before it did change hands.

The 1870 tournament was the 11th Challenge Belt/ Open Championship, and as it had in 1861 when it was made open to professionals and amateurs for the first time, the event attracted 18 players. The first twosome went off at 10 a.m. and every player (actually, only 17 finished 36 holes) had completed three rounds of the 12-hole course by 3 p.m.

The now 19-year-old Tommy Morris was a firm favorite and looking to three-peat. Sure enough, a spectacular round of 47 put him five clear after the first 12 holes. His day began perfectly when he holed his long third at the 578-yard 1st hole—'Back of the Cardinal." It's tough to imagine how monstrous a hole the 1st must have seemed in 1870, but it's easy to picture an excited and astonished crowd celebrating their hero's amazing shot and the resigned gloom every other player in the field must have felt when the cheer from the gallery went up.

Young Tom's score beat his own course record by two shots and was 13 better than the disappointing 60 returned by Park Sr. who must have known his chances were over for another year (he wouldn't win his fourth Open Championship until 1875). Morris Jr. followed with two rounds of 51 completing the 36 holes at 147—12 clear of Bob Kirk and Davie Strath who played another 12 holes to decide who finished 2nd and 3rd, Kirk winning 56 to 60.

Only three players had ever beaten 160 for the three rounds at Prestwick since the event began. Morris Sr. did it in 1868 finishing with 157, and Robert Andrew shot 159 that same year. Tommy Morris had now done it three times himself with his total of 149 beating his 1868 score by five.

The Belt was now Tommy's to keep. On Tuesday the 20th (five days after the championship), the *Dundee Courier* described Morris Jr.'s triumphant arrival back in St Andrews on Saturday evening. A large and buoyant crowd was waiting for him at the station where Morris' train arrived at 10 p.m. The hordes carried him on their shoulders to Mr. Leslie's Golf Hotel on Golf Road, where "his health was drank with every honour."

Sadly, Tommy Morris would be gone five years later. On September 4, 1875, he played a match with his father against Mungo and Willie Park at nine-hole North Berwick. They won the foursomes encounter 1-up in front of a large and unruly crowd but, as they stood enjoying the victory (which assuaged a big defeat they had suffered at the hands of the Parks the previous year), Tommy received a telegram saying he should return to St Andrews as quickly as possible as his wife, Margaret Drinnen, was experiencing a difficult labor. The journey home would be long, but they accepted the offer of a boat ride across the Firth of Forth. Tragically, Margaret and the baby died while the Morrises were en route, and when he was told the news after docking in St Andrews around midnight, Tommy was understandably heartbroken. In early December, he reluctantly played a challenge match at St Andrews, the weather so harsh it could have contributed to the pulmonary hemorrhage he suffered on Christmas Day. That was given as the official cause of Tommy's death, but the shock of his young wife (they had been married for less than a year) and son's passing and the profound grief he suffered could also have been partly to blame.

The swirl of excitement surrounding his exceptional talent and competitive years, and the tragedy of losing his wife and child followed by his early death, are depicted superbly in the 2016 movie *Tommy's Honour*, directed by Jason Connery. Golf history enthusiasts usually have a hard time getting through the film without shedding a tear, or without imagining what young Tom might have achieved in the game had he lived as long as his father.

Young Master Morris

Thomas Morris Jr. was born in St Andrews to Tom and Agnes Morris (née Bayne and who went as "Nancy") on April 20, 1851. His parents had already had a son named Thomas (whom they called "Wee Tom") who tragically died shortly before his fourth birthday, in April 1850.

In July 1851, just three months after the birth of their second son, the Morrises packed up everything they owned and made the arduous trek across the country to Prestwick where Tom Sr. had been offered a job at the new GC.

Tom Morris Jr. (also known as Young Tom Morris and Tommy Morris) would become the eldest of four siblings—Elizabeth was a year younger; James Ogilvie Fairlie Morris (named in honor of Morris' boss and mentor, and known as "Jof") was born in 1856, and John arrived in 1859—and attended the prestigious Ayr Academy, a private school three miles to the south, where the young Morris would likely have felt a little uncomfortable (at first at least) among the children of wealthy industrialists and land-owners.

Tommy quickly became adept at the game, which his father taught him on the newly laid-out links at Prestwick. By 12, he was regarded as a prodigy, winning a well-chronicled match in Perth against another young player, after he had been banned from playing in both the professional and amateur events, and where his winning score would have won the professional event. In 1865, he played in his first Open Championship at the age of 14. After respectable rounds of 60 and 57—which put him just one stroke behind his father but nine behind Park Sr., who led with a round to go—Tommy inexplicably withdrew. Whether he was upset at being so far behind Park or didn't want to finish ahead of his father isn't clear, but as Stephen Proctor wrote in *Monarch of the Green* (2019), it was an "inglorious moment in one of the most glorious careers in the history of golf."

A year later, Tommy would finish 9th and he improved to 4th in 1867, completing the 36 holes at 175—just five shots behind his father, who won his fourth and final Challenge Belt (see "1867 Open Championship," pages 24-7).

The week before the 1867 Open, Tommy and 31 other professionals had played for a prize of £10 at 10-hole Carnoustie, on the other side of the Firth of Tay from St Andrews. That the winner earned £3 more than what Morris Sr. would win at the Open Championship seven days later, and that the size of the field was more than double what it would be at Prestwick, shows that the Open was taking its time to become established as the premier event, so Tommy's win on the Angus links—his first professional victory—was a huge stepping stone to stardom.

Tom Morris Jr. with the Challenge Belt

He would win the Challenge Belt for the first time in 1868 when he shot an impressive 154 (eight shots better than anyone else had shot in the previous seven years of the tournament) for the 36 holes—beating his father by three and finishing five ahead of Robert Andrew in 3rd. Park was 4th at 162. Strangely, the £6 Tommy won was £1 less than what his father had earned for winning the year before.

In 1869, Tommy won again, finishing with 157—11 shots ahead of Bob Kirk in 2nd. His prize was £6.

1873 Open Championship

The Open goes to St Andrews for the first time, and the Claret Jug makes its debut.

DATE
October 4, 1873

LOCATION
St Andrews, Scotland

PRIZE
£11

IN THE FIELD
Tom Morris Sr.
Tom Morris Jr.
Davie Strath
Jamie Anderson
Tom Kidd
Bob Kirk

When Tom Morris Jr. won the Challenge Belt three years in succession (1868, '69, and '70), it apparently threw the organizers of the Open Championship for a loop, as they were unable to organize an event for 1871. They did eventually come to an arrangement the following year, however, and on August 22, 1872, the *Glasgow Herald* reported that the venue for the Challenge Trophy would henceforth rotate between Prestwick, the Royal and Ancient GC of St Andrews, and the Honourable Company of Edinburgh Golfers, then playing over the links at Musselburgh. Additionally, each of the three clubs would contribute £10 for the purchase of a new trophy.

The arrangement wasn't confirmed until September 11, however, two days after the 12th Championship was played at Prestwick. The 21-year-old Morris won again and received £8 and a gold medal as the new trophy obviously wasn't ready yet.

To avoid a similar situation as that which had happened with the Belt, officials decided the new trophy, a claret jug created by Edinburgh silversmith Mackay Cunningham, would forever remain the property of the three clubs that had commissioned it.

The Field magazine wrote that "this trophy can never become the absolute property of any winner but, along with custody of it for one year, he gets a medal to be specially retained and also a money prize. It will be observed that the Championship competition is now thoroughly established which will tend to increase the popularity of this elegant and healthy pastime."

The Claret Jug was completed in time for the 1873 Championship which, in accordance with the three-club agreement, would be played in St Andrews for the first time. As the event was still conducted over 36 holes, two rounds of St Andrews' 18-hole course would be played instead of three rounds over Prestwick's 12 holes.

The course at St Andrews was going through changes implemented by Tom Morris Sr. who had returned to the town from Prestwick in 1864. In 1856, the 17th green had effectively been made into a double green with the 1st positioned to the immediate east (closer to the R&A clubhouse). Then, in 1871 or 1872, as women who had done their laundry in the Swilcan Burn for decades began vacating the area, the 1st green moved about 50 yards to the north and adjacent to the burn (its current location), with a new 2nd tee being built to the right of the 1st green.

The Claret Jug

The 1873 championship was held on Saturday October 4, at the end of the Royal and Ancient GC's Autumn Meeting. A disappointing 26 players showed up for the event, with only three players from outside of St Andrews making the effort to get there: Bob Pringle from Musselburgh, William Thomson from Edinburgh, and Jack Morris (Tom Morris Jr.'s cousin) from Hoylake in England. It isn't clear why Willie Park Sr. of Musselburgh didn't make the trip. Perhaps he had fallen ill, was otherwise engaged, or just didn't want to play in St Andrews.

Heavy rain had fallen for most of the week prior, inundating the sandy soil and leaving pools of water scattered throughout the course. At the time, dropping your ball behind casual water resulted in a shot penalty, and that, combined with the total lack of run, led to the highest scores in the Championship's short history. Well, that and what the *Glasgow Herald* reported as "indifferent play."

A view of Holes 1 and 18, from the 17th hole, late 1800s.

Going for his fifth win in a row, Morris Jr. was obviously the favorite especially as he was on home soil (the Morris family had been back in St Andrews for nine years). He shot a disappointing 94 in the morning round, however, going into lunch two behind Walter Gourlay and three back of a trio of players—Tom Kidd, Jamie Anderson, and Bob Kirk.

In the afternoon, Morris Jr. improved to 89 (one of just three sub-90 rounds in the championship), but it wasn't enough to catch Kidd, a fellow St Andrean, who shot a best-of-the-tournament 88 to win the championship by a stroke from Anderson. The 52-year-old Morris Sr. shot 93-96 to finish 7th.

Kidd, 25, therefore became the first player to lift the Claret Jug (though Morris Jr. was the first name engraved on the trophy as he had won in 1872 when there was no trophy). The *Fifeshire Journal* did its best to applaud the victor, but the compliment it compliment it paid Kidd (who had cut grooves into his irons the night before) was somewhat backhanded. "Tom Kidd has distinguished himself in many singles and foursomes, and the honour thus gained will consequently be grudged him the less, although he has won it with so high a score."

It's a good thing Prestwick GC, the HCEG, and R&A decided anyone winning the Open Championship three times in a row couldn't take possession of the new trophy, as Young Tom Morris had with the Challenge Belt. Just four years after the Claret Jug debuted, Jamie Anderson began a three-year run of victories, and as soon as his reign was over, Bob Ferguson won the first of his three successive titles.

Tom Kidd

1892 Open Championship

First Open Championship contested over 72 holes.

DATE
Sept. 22-23, 1892

LOCATION
Muirfield,
East Lothian,
Scotland

PRIZE
£35

IN THE FIELD
Hugh Kirkcaldy
John Ball
Harold Hilton
Horace Hutchinson
Willie Park Jr.
Sandy Herd
Freddie Tait
Tom Morris Sr.

Not surprisingly, the early years of the Open Championship (also known as The Open, British Open, Challenge Belt, Challenge for the Belt, and so on) featured a lot of firsts:

1860—First playing of the event;
1861—First time event is genuinely open (amateurs as well as professionals);
1864—First three-time winner: Tom Morris Sr.;
1870—First three-time consecutive winner: Tom Morris Jr.;
1871—First time since the event started that it wasn't played (no trophy; World War I, World War II, and the Covid-19 pandemic would cause future cancellations);
1873—First time not played at Prestwick, First time played at St Andrews, First time Claret Jug awarded;
1874—First time hosted by the Honourable Company of Edinburgh Golfers, at Musselburgh;
1890—First amateur winner: John Ball.

And the 1892 Open, the 32nd playing of the Championship, had a few firsts of its own. Most significantly was the fact it was the first championship played over 72 holes. That's a lot of golf for a field of 60 (66 had registered—six didn't show up—and 52 made the cut) to finish in one day so, consequently, the event was the first to be held over two days, something that had been suggested (no, demanded) in golf magazine articles and letters following the previous year's Championship.

Though the winner was an amateur, it wasn't the first time an amateur had won—that was John Ball Jr. in

1890 at Prestwick. And though the winner was English, that too had happened before (John Ball Jr. in 1890 at Prestwick). It was, however, the first time an amateur lead after each round. And it was the first time that amateurs finished 1st and 2nd (Ball was tied for 2nd, admittedly). It was also the first time the event had been played at Muirfield, the HCEG's third home.

Though considerably larger (117 acres) and more private than the course it had shared with other golfers at Musselburgh, Muirfield was far from ideal as much of it was restricted by stone walls. It opened only nine months before it staged its first Open Championship, and as well as the walls, its lower parts were apt to fill with water during periods of heavy rain. Indeed, the acid-tongued Andrew ("Andra") Kirkaldy labeled it "nought but an auld water meadie."

The *Edinburgh Evening News* was, likewise, somewhat scathing of the course, saying it "leaves a lot to be desired," that its artificial hazards could "never rival the formidable natural difficulties of other courses" and that it failed to "exercise the judgement as do many courses of lesser note, not to mention St Andrews, Prestwick and Carnoustie." The reporter did, however, say that "time will tell its tale," "golf courses are not made in a day," and that Muirfield might, in time, "come to be one of the best Scottish courses" (how right he was. Thanks to a later expansion—50 acres were added in 1923—and a reworking from Harry Colt and, to a lesser extent, Tom Simpson, plus the passage of time, it is now widely regarded as one of the top 10 courses in the world).

The course was originally laid out by Old Tom Morris whose original 16 holes were extended to 18 in time for the Championship. It began early on a warm, sunny Thursday with Willie Park Jr. (son of the four-time Open champion) attracting the largest gallery.

The leader after the first round was an English amateur by the name of Horatio ("Horace") Hutchinson. An Oxford graduate and prolific author of golf books

Horace Hutchinson

and magazine articles as well as articles on other sports, Hutchinson had won the Amateur Championship twice—in 1886 at St Andrews and 1887 at Hoylake where he defeated the home club's John Ball Jr. in the final. He was a member at Royal North Devon, another course designed by Old Tom Morris. His opening 74 gave him a one-stroke lead over Ball, and though his second round was four shots higher, Hutchinson was three shots clear of Ball, Park Jr., and Sandy Herd.

Hutchinson fell out of the running after a dismal 86 in Friday morning's third round, however, losing his lead to Ball, whose steady 74 gave him a two-shot cushion over Harold Hilton. Another English amateur, Hilton had lost to Ball—a fellow Royal Liverpool GC member, in the final of the Amateur Championship four months previously, and had arrived at Muirfield the day before Thursday's first round having been unsure if he could get time off work. On the first day, he'd shot a fairly uninspiring 159 for the 36 holes that had put Jones in a tie for eighth. He began the third round with a 2 and six consecutive 4s, however, leading to an impressive outward half of 35. An inward 37 gave him a round of 72 that was the best of the Championship, and an afternoon 74 saw him win by three shots over Ball, Herd, and defending champion Hugh Kirkaldy.

As an amateur, Hilton couldn't receive the 1st-place prize money of £35 but he did take home a gold medal. The winner's share of the purse was actually withheld to the dismay of the pros. Herd and Kirkaldy shared the 2nd and 3rd-place money, each earning £15.

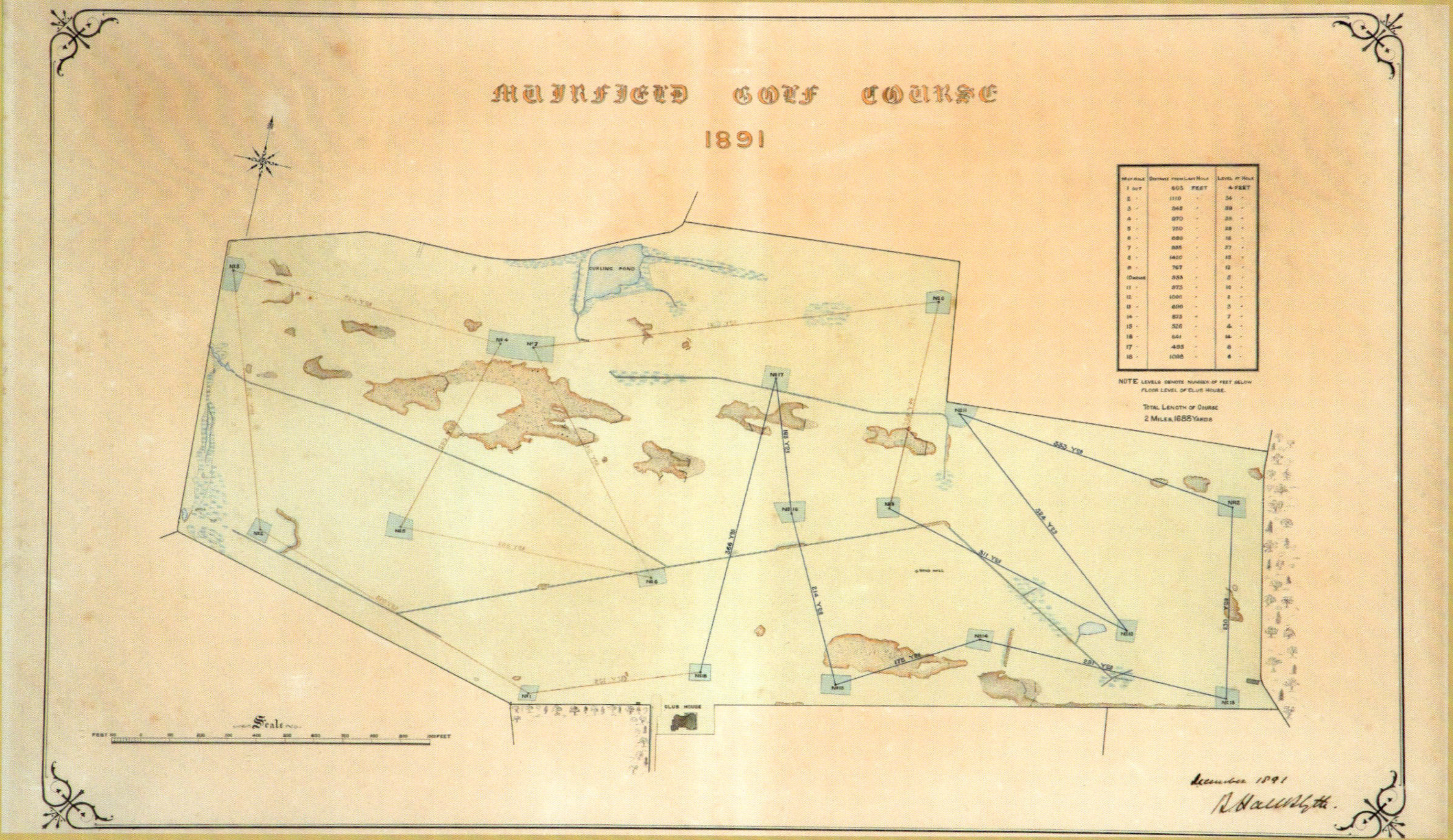

Map of original Muirfield layout

Portrait of Harold Hilton, and his medal

Despite the fact its report spoke first of the HCEG's excellent organization of the event and commented extensively on the performance of the Scottish players in the field, the *Edinburgh Evening News* described Hilton's victory as a "popular" one with the spectators "giving the Englishman his due meed of praise."

The *Glasgow Herald* had been generous in its praise of John Ball following his win at Prestwick two years previously, saying "The champion exponent of the national game of golf is neither a professional nor a Scotchman, but an amateur and an Englishman. Mr. Ball is all the more to be congratulated upon his victory." Still, his win must have come as something of a nasty shock to many Scottish golfers. Hilton's victory at Muirfield was further evidence the game was spreading beyond Scotland, and that the auld Scottish pros could no longer expect to win. Indeed, only eight of the next 20 Open Championships were won by Scots.

The Musselburgh Tournament

Because it had been the home course of the HCEG, the Bruntsfield Links Golfing Society, the Edinburgh Royal Burgess Golfing Society, and the Royal Musselburgh Golf Club (plus 60 or so smaller clubs and societies that used the links for their various events), as well as three members of the Park family who had all won the Belt or Claret Jug, Musselburgh was obviously a very significant golf town in the mid-late 1800s (it is also thought to have been the site of the world's first ever women's tournament—on New Year's Day, 1811, when the wives and daughters of the town's fishermen competed for a skull and creel. Local historians think the "skull" was a headscarf or bonnet, while a creel is a wicker basket used to catch and carry fish, predominantly lobsters.)

So it was seen as a serious snub, one that might negatively affect the town's finances and reputation, when the HCEG decided to hold the 1892 Championship at Muirfield rather than in Musselburgh. A largely working-class town, especially in the 19th century, Musselburgh was so upset that its townspeople and golfers organized an alternative event to the official Open Championship to be held on exactly the same dates. The town offered a much larger purse—£95—to that on offer at Muirfield, enticing the game's top players to play at Musselburgh. The HCEG, R&A, and Prestwick responded by raising the official Open purse to £110, and a major imbroglio was avoided when the Musselburgh event was moved forward one week.

Fifty-eight players competed, and after two days and eight rounds on the nine-hole course, Willie Park Jr. triumphed in front of the 1,000 or so people who had arrived by train from Edinburgh. Park Jr., who had contributed to organizing the event, shot rounds of 41, 40, 39, and 38 on the first day, and 35, 39, 37, and 36 on the second to finish 72 holes on 305, five shots clear of Tom Vardon. He won £30 and a gold medal, awarded by the town's provost before he was swept up and carried on the shoulders of the large crowd.

1895 U.S. Amateur

Charles Blair Macdonald wins the inaugural U.S. Amateur.

DATE
October 1-3, 1895

LOCATION
Newport CC
Newport, RI
USA

PRIZE
N/A

IN THE FIELD
C.B. Macdonald
Charles Sands
Charles Claxton
F.J. Amory
Findlay S. Douglas
Lawrence Curtis

The history of how golf started in the USA is tangled, complex, unconfirmed and largely undocumented, but there is credible evidence—unearthed by the University of Edinburgh's Dr. David Purdie, together with a researcher at the National Archives of Scotland-suggesting it was being played in Charleston, South Carolina in 1739. A gentleman named William Wallace had some clubs and balls delivered to him, and though it's unclear where he played (possibly his backyard as there was nowhere else for him to go), the evidence of the shipment is clear. A golf club—the South Carolina GC—is known to have been founded at Harleston Green on the Charleston Peninsula, but that wasn't until 1786—47 years after Wallace's clubs arrived. A club in Savannah, Georgia was established in 1794, but the course the club plays on today didn't open until 1899.

There were a handful of other courses/clubs that existed in the country before the game experienced its first major milestone in America in the last decade of the 19th century. These included Oakhurst Links in West Virginia, Murchison Ranch in Nebraska, Quogue Field Club in New York, Shinnecock Hills GC in New York, Chicago GC in Illinois, Dorset Field Club in Vermont, Foxburg CC and York CC in Pennsylvania, Sarasota CC in Florida, The Country Club in Massachusetts (founded in 1882 but golf wasn't played there until 1893), Newport CC in Rhode Island, and Saint Andrew's GC in Yonkers, New York, which was founded in 1888 after Scottish expat, John Reid, and a few friends played a little pasture "gowf" (Saint Andrew's is the oldest continuous golf club in the U.S.).

In 1894, each of the last two clubs mentioned here—Saint Andrew's and Newport—held an amateur tournament to identify a national amateur champion. Newport's event was held on September 1 and called the "Championship of America" while the Saint Andrew's tournament took place on October 4-5 and was the "Championship on the United States" (see "Charles, the First" for more on this).

This disorganization couldn't go on, so delegates from the two clubs, together with others from Shinnecock Hills GC, Chicago GC, and The Country Club, were invited by a Mr. H.O. Talmadge, secretary of the Saint Andrew's GC, to meet at the Calumet Club in New York City on December 22, 1894 and form an organization that would stage national championships and administer the game's rules.

Businessman Theodore Havemeyer, a co-founder of the Newport CC, was chosen as the organization's first president, but there was some controversy over where the new national championships—one amateur, one open to both professionals and amateurs—would take place. "Golf, like religion, is really a question of geography," said one of those present to the *New York Sun*'s reporter. "It makes a great difference in a man's play whether he is playing on his own links or not."

The *New York Sun*'s story referred to the man speaking as "one of the officers" and went on to say that he thought Chicago's Charles Blair Macdonald, who had lost in the final at both events, was a far better player than the men he had lost to and that he was beaten simply because the victors had been practicing on their home links all summer. "This is clearly all wrong," the officer continued, "and the association, wherever they may hold their tournaments will endeavor to correct this evil either by arranging a special course at Newport, Shinnecock, or Saint Andrew's or by making special championship links at some spot yet to be selected." "No two links are alike," he added, "so it is manifestly unfair to hold a tournament on a particular club's links as a local player would always have a decided advantage."

Theodore Havemeyer

It seems the unnamed person was advocating for the construction of an entirely separate course to be used only for the new national championships. That's an intriguing—if highly impractical—thought, but it didn't happen, as it was decided that Newport would host the first national Amateur and Open to be held during the same week in October of the following year.

Though he did allow that Charles E. Sands showed some promise and that, if he was to stick to golf, he might do better the following year, the *New York Times*' reporter was pretty scathing of Sands' performance in the 36-hole final of the 1895 U.S. Amateur Championship. A member of the Saint Andrew's GC, Sands had, the report said, "utterly failed to push his opponent to any great extent" and that, for Macdonald, the final "amounted to a practice game." Sands "foozled" his opening two drives, and after more "erratic" play, was 5-down at the end of the morning's 18 (two rounds of the nine-hole Newport course).

After lunch, the match was "entirely without feature," and after taking seven holes in succession, Macdonald ran out a 12&11 winner. The *New York Times* writer finished his report with one last disdainful pass ... "Sands did about as well as he was expected to," which, judging from the general tone of the report, wasn't much. "Stronger men fell earlier in the tournament."

The report was, however, highly complimentary of Macdonald saying that, among American amateurs, he was "in a class alone," and that he had been the overwhelming favorite in the 32-player (all invited) tournament. He beat USGA president-to-be Laurence Curtis 7&6 in the first-round, then Gerald Bement in the second 8&6. On the following day, he dispatched William Rutherford 5&4; there was some controversy here, as Macdonald had a professional, James Foulis, on his bag coaching him—an argument that didn't really get off the ground, as Rutherford had a pro on his bag, too. And then Macdonald beat Charles Claxton in the semi-finals 8&7. All of these matches had been played over 18 holes, while the final was contested over 36, of which Macdonald needed only 25. It was a convincing victory.

The original Havemeyer trophy

Charles, the First

Charles Blair Macdonald was born in 1855 in Niagara Falls, Ontario, Canada, but grew up in Chicago, Illinois. At the age of 16, his parents sent him to St Andrews in Scotland to attend the university there. He would live with his grandfather (his father's father, William), a professor at the University of St Andrews and an R&A member who thought the boy should learn golf so took him to Old Tom Morris' shop to get kitted out. Macdonald wasn't terribly keen on the game at first—"It seemed to me a form of Tiddly-Winks, stupid and silly," he wrote in his 1928 book *Scotland's Gift—Golf*. "For never in my life had I known a sport that was not strenuous or violent."

It wasn't long before he began enjoying its challenge, though, and he played the links often with David Strath, Tom Kidd, Tom Dunn, and Tom Morris Jr., becoming more than competent and a hardened match player. He soon became utterly besotted with the game and developed strong opinions on how, where, and why it should be played.

He left Scotland in 1874 and endured nearly two decades of mostly golf-less life back in Chicago. In 1888, he did, however, lay out a basic 7-hole course for a friend in Lake Forest and then, in 1892, a 9-hole course in Belmont, Illinois (extending it to 18 in 1893). It became the Chicago Golf Club and moved again, in 1894 (because of surging popularity), to rolling farmland in Wheaton, about 25 miles west of downtown Chicago where Macdonald designed an 18-hole course that was redesigned by his protégé, Seth Raynor, in 1923.

C.B. Macdonald

Macdonald would move from Chicago to New York City in 1900, becoming a partner in a financial company on Wall Street. His obsession with golf continued; though, by now, he was far more interested in designing courses than winning tournaments on them. In 1908, he got a group of wealthy friends to invest in a course/club he was building on Long Island called National Golf Links of America which opened in 1909.

A number of excellent designs, built using Raynor's expertise, followed and included Mid Ocean, Yale, The Creek, Piping Rock, Deepdale (the club relocated to its new Dick Wilson-designed course in 1955), St. Louis, and The Lido on Long Island.

1895 U.S. Open

Horace Rawlins wins the inaugural U.S. Open.

DATE
October 4, 1895

LOCATION
Newport CC
Newport, RI
USA

PRIZE
$150

IN THE FIELD
Horace Rawlins
Willie Dunn
Willie Davis
Willie Campbell
James Foulis

As had been the case at the inaugural Open Championship/Challenge Belt in Scotland 35 years before, the list of players registering for the first ever U.S. Open wasn't terribly long: 14 entered but only 11 of them teed it up, and 10 were professionals—the lone amateur being Andrew Whyte Smith from Canada who finished tied for 3rd. And, likewise, the U.S. Open attracted about the same level of attention as the Open Championship had (i.e., very little). The inaugural U.S. Amateur Championship that had finished on the same course the day before was a far bigger story, and the U.S. Open considered something of an afterthought.

Among the pros, Willie Dunn, Willie Campbell, and James Foulis were probably the favorites, but unknown and unheralded Horace Rawlins used his local knowledge to defeat them all, having become an assistant professional at the host club just a few months before. The club's head professional, William Davis, had also been highly favored, but obviously didn't use what experience he had gained as effectively as Rawlins; Davis finished five shots behind in 5th.

Rawlins was born in 1874 in Shanklin on the Isle of Wight, England, and learned the game at the long-gone Royal Isle of Wight GC. He played in a professional event in London in 1894, but it appears that was the extent of his competitive experience prior to setting sail for America in January 1895. In July, by which time he had been hired as an assistant at Newport CC, he played an event at Shinnecock Hills and finished 4th—16 shots behind the man in 3rd.

Newport Country Club was home to one of the game's newest and grandest clubhouses which had replaced the more humble Pond Cottage. Financed by a syndicate led by Theodore Havemeyer, who had first encountered the game in Pau, France, in 1889 and made a fortune in sugar before becoming the USGA's first president, the building was designed by well-known Gilded Age architect, Whitney Warren, and originally had three wings, one being lost to Hurricane Carol in 1954.

Willie Dunn Jr.

The U.S. Open was played over 36 holes, which meant four trips around the nine-hole course (it was expanded to 18 in 1897). Dunn, an Englishman who'd been involved in the early design of Shinnecock Hills and was the club professional, led after the first nine, shooting 43. Rawlins, meanwhile, was two back. By the end of the first 18, only three players—Dunn, Foulis, and Campbell—were sub-90, while Rawlins was on 91 following a second-nine 46.

Newport CC's clubhouse, designed by Whitney Warren, was built in 1894-95.

In the afternoon, however, Rawlins passed everyone with a couple of 41s—scores which, given the difficult conditions (the *New York Times* said that "half a gale was blowing"), must have been pretty impressive. His total of 173 gave him victory over Dunn by two and earned him $150 plus a gold medal valued at $50. The club got to keep the Championship trophy.

Charles Blair Macdonald, who had won the first U.S. Amateur the day before, withdrew from the Open. The *New York Times* said he "watched the professional players with great interest," adding that he was "warmly congratulated on his victory (in the Amateur) by all present."

In its report of the day's play, the *New York Tribune* not only got Rawlins' name wrong by calling him "John," but also said he was "about nineteen years old" when, in fact, he was 21.

The following day, a grand money match between the players that had finished 2nd, tied 3rd, 5th, and 6th was staged, with Campbell and Davis beating Dunn and Foulis 3&2. The winners shared $100, and the match attracted far more interest than the U.S. Open had. None of the New York newspapers could explain why poor Horace Rawlins was left out of the proceedings, while his boss played. He may have won the U.S. Open, but Rawlins wasn't nearly as famous as the other four ... and wouldn't be for many years. Even now, relatively few people would be able to name the first winner of the U.S. Open.

The first U.S. Open winner, Horace Rawlins

Englishmen and Scotsmen in America

For the first 16 years of the U.S. Open golf championship, players from the old (auld) country dominated. After Rawlins won the first, James Foulis would claim the second, in 1896. Englishman Joe Lloyd—the professional at Essex County Club in Massachusetts during the summers between 1895 and 1909—won in 1897.

James Foulis with U.S. Open trophy

Scotland's Fred Herd took the title in 1898, the first year the U.S. Open was played over 72 holes, then countryman Willie Smith was the victor in 1899. Jerseyman Harry Vardon won at Chicago Golf Club in 1900, before a string of eight Scottish victories. North Berwick's Willie Anderson won the U.S. Open four times in five years (1901-1905), the last three in succession. In 1909, George Sargent became the third English player to win the U.S. Open, and a year later, Alex Smith made it 12 victories for Scotsmen.

A U.S. born player would not win until 1911 (see pages 70-1). Since then, there have been just 21 victories by overseas players in 118 U.S. Opens.

LEFT: Fred Herd in 1898

RIGHT: Willie Anderson and Alex Smith

1904 Olympics

Canada's George Lyon wins golf's Gold.

DATE
Sept. 17-24, 1904

LOCATION
Glen Echo CC
St. Louis, MO
USA

PRIZE
Gold Medal

IN THE FIELD
Chandler Egan
Walter Egan
George Lyon
Robert Hunter

On the morning of Saturday, September 24, 1904, the *St. Louis Republic* opened its preview of the Olympic Games golf tournament final with the somewhat cryptic "It will be the Land of Our Lady of Snows against the City of the Ladies with Large Feet in the final round of the Olympic Golf Championship at Glen Echo Links today."

That's not something you read every day, but a little digging tells us that the "Land of Our Lady of Snows" was originally a name given to Brazil by Portuguese explorers in the 16th century, but that it also came to represent Canada. And, it was said, the ladies of Chicago—a largely industrial, working-class city—had big feet on account of their being taller and stronger than ladies from "more refined cities like New York or Boston." It's not clear how these opening lines went down, but, one assumes, the writer didn't expect many ladies from Chicago to be reading newspapers in St. Louis that weekend.

Whatever the words were a reference to, the two finalists were George Lyon, a 46-year-old Canadian and 20-year-old Chicago native, Harold Chandler Egan.

The two had made their way to the gold medal match via a 36-hole strokeplay qualifier (which 77 players—72 Americans, 3 Canadians, and 2 from Britain—had entered), then four rounds of match play, with each match being contested over 36 holes. The strokeplay qualifier took place on September 19, with the top 32 players advancing. Anyone, literally anyone, was welcome to enter as long as they paid the $5 entry fee. The secretary of their golf club made the official entry on behalf of the member, while those who weren't members of a club had to prove their amateur status "to the satisfaction of the committee."

Players who didn't advance to match play, and those who lost in the first round, were entered into a consolation tournament, with 64 players separated into four flights with 16 players in each. An 18-hole strokeplay qualifier and five rounds of 18-hole matches then decided the consolation prize-winner.

A putting contest was held by "electric light" at 8 p.m. on Saturday the 17th, with a prize to the winner, and likewise, a prize was awarded in a long-drive competition the previous afternoon.

A Weak Field?

Golf was first played at the Summer Olympics in Paris in 1900, and even though it would be included for a second time in 1904, the event hadn't yet built much of a reputation. Calling the 1904 Olympic golf competition the "greatest golf tournament ever held in America" and "the championship of the world" might suggest, in fact, the sports writer for the *St. Louis Globe-Democrat* wasn't a specialist golf writer and hadn't attended m(any) golf events.

Even though the St. Louis press was clearly trying to embellish the significance of the Games, which were part of the Louisiana Purchase Exposition (or St. Louis World's Fair), the fields for both the team and individual competitions were rather light on star players. A devoted golf fan of the time might recognize only three names among the 77 golfers that competed—the two Egans (Chandler and cousin Walter) and Robert Hunter who had assisted famed course architect Alister MacKenzie on his California designs. Even George Lyon, the gold medalist, was virtually unknown outside of Canada where he had won three Canadian Amateur Championships (despite taking up the game at the age of 38!), and where he also excelled at cricket, tennis, hockey, and rugby.

A handful of early U.S. golf tournaments carried more weight than that year's Olympic golf competition—primarily the U.S. Open and U.S. Amateur, but also the Western Open, Trans-Mississippi Amateur, and North and South Amateur.

And, as if the week's events didn't resemble a member-guest tournament or corporate pro-am enough already, a team Nassau and individual handicap event—with a prize going to the net winner—were also held the day before.

In the matchplay rounds leading to the final, Lyon had beaten Willard, Smith, Egan (Walter), and Newton, while Egan (Chandler) had defeated Lambert, Semple, Maxwell, and McKinnie. The climax to the serious part of the week eventually got underway at 11:20 a.m. on the 24th, following a torrential downpour that left the course extremely wet. Lyon got off to a great start by driving the 270-yard 1st to win the hole and go 1-up. The Canadian was 4-up after five, but Egan won a hole back by the turn. A seesaw back nine saw Lyon leading by a single hole after the first 18 that concluded at 2 p.m.

Gold medalist, George Lyon

After an hour for lunch, Lyon got off to a fast start in the second round, getting back to 4-up through 24 holes. The lead was two as they arrived at the 34th hole (16th), but Lyon won it to go 3-up and claim what the *St. Louis Globe-Democrat* called the golf competition "the championship of the world." The USGA, which had staged 10 U.S. Opens and a similar number of U.S. Amateurs by this point, might suggest that the Olympic Games certainly weren't then the spectacle they have become (580 of the 650 "athletes" at the 1904 St. Louis Games were from the host country).

The gallery for the final—about 100-strong at the start of the day—grew steadily as the match went on, and obviously favored Egan. But it generously applauded Lyon, whose formidable long game was the telling difference between the two players. "I attribute my success to my long drives," Lyon told the *St. Louis Dispatch*. "I outdrove Egan and it was mainly through this that I won."

The 1904 Olympic Gold Medal

Egan, who was clearly tired after playing numerous tournaments that summer, described himself as "stale and over-golfed", but was magnanimous in defeat. "My opponent was the better player," he said simply, "and, consequently, he won."

The individual event was preceded by a team event on Saturday the 17th, in which golf associations could enter a team of 10 amateurs. The competition was held over 36 holes of medal play, with all 20 scores (10 players each playing two rounds) from each team counting. Despite the fact every golf association in the world (admittedly there weren't many in 1904) had the chance to compete, only six registered. And of those six, only two—the Western Golf Association (WGA) and the Trans-Mississippi Golf Association (TMGA)—showed up with enough players. However, it was discovered that, among the entrants for the individual competition, there were enough players that weren't part of either the WGA or TMGA to create a third team, which would represent the USGA.

The WGA won gold with a score of 1,749. The TMGA finished 21 shots behind, while the USGA came in 3rd (good for a bronze medal) 69 shots further back. The apparent lack of organization and nugatory extra events seem almost comical compared with the gravity of today's Olympic golf competitions.

Is Olympic Golf Here to Stay?

Golf was scheduled to be played at the 1908 Olympic Games in London, but the tournament, planned for Royal St. George's Golf Club in Kent, was abandoned two days before it was scheduled to start. It turned out that a number of leading British golfers had voiced their disapproval, saying it was unnecessary and against the spirit of the game, as the Open Championship and one or two other prestigious events were already well-established in the United Kingdom.

Following London in 1908, there was little inclination to re-establish golf at the Olympics, as the professional game was fast becoming the sport's highest standard. Indeed, 112 years would elapse between 1904 and the year golf made its popular return to the Games—at Rio de Janeiro in Brazil.

Because of its fast-growing global appeal, golf was considered for inclusion in the 2016 and 2020 Games during the 121st Olympic Committee Session, held in Copenhagen, Denmark in October 2009.

Ty Votaw, then chief marketing officer of the PGA Tour and vice president of the International Golf Federation (IGF), and Peter Dawson, president of the IGF and chief executive of the R&A led the move to have golf reinstated, and they were joined during the Olympic Committee Session presentation by golfers Padraig Harrington of Ireland, Matteo Manassero of Italy, Michelle Wie of the USA, and Suzann Pettersen of Norway.

On October 9, 2009, the IOC voted to have golf be part of the 2016 and 2020 Olympics.

2016

The tournament was held at a Gil Hanse-designed course built specifically for the Games in Barra da Tijuca, about 20 miles west of downtown Rio. Forty one nations participated in the men's and women's tournaments, both of which would be strokeplay events played over 72 holes.

In the men's competition (60 players), England's Justin Rose won the gold medal, Sweden's Henrik Stenson took silver, and the U.S.'s Matt Kuchar claimed the bronze. In the women's tournament (also 60 players), Inbee Park of South Korea won gold, New Zealand's Lydia Ko took the silver, and Shanshan Fang of China won bronze.

2020

Tokyo was the host city in 2020 (though the games were actually held in 2021 because of the Covid-19 pandemic) and the golf tournament was held on the East Course of the historic Kasumigaseki CC, about 35 miles northwest of the city center. The format was the same as it had been in 2016, and Americans won gold in both the men's (Xander Schauffele) and women's (Nelly Korda) events. Slovakia's Rory Sabbatini and C.T. Pan of Chinese Taipei took the silver and bronze, respectively, in the men's competition, while the other medal-winners in the women's event were Japan's Mone Inami (silver) and Lydia Ko (bronze).

2024

Golf was played again at the 2024 Olympics—in Paris. Le Golf National—a regular stop on the DP World Tour and venue for the 2018 Ryder Cup—was selected as the venue. The U.S.'s Scottie Scheffler, #1 in the world rankings, won the men's gold, while England's Tommy Fleetwood (silver) and Japan's Hideki Matsuyama (bronze) also made it on to the podium. In the women's competition, Lydia Ko won gold (meaning she had won a medal of each color), Germany's Esther Henseleit took silver, and China's Lin Xiyu claimed bronze.

Gold medalist in 2024, Scottie Scheffler

2028

The 2028 Summer Olympics will take place in Los Angeles. Riviera Country Club will host the golf competitions.

1907 Open Championship

Frenchman Arnaud Massy becomes the first overseas player to win the Claret Jug.

DATE
June 20-21, 1907

LOCATION
Royal Liverpool
(Hoylake)
Wirral, England

PRIZE
£50

IN THE FIELD
Harry Vardon
J.H. Taylor
James Braid
Ted Ray
George Duncan
Sandy Herd
John Ball
Ben Sayers
Andrew Kirkaldy
Willie Park Jr.

For the first time in its 47-year history, a foreigner/overseas player/non-Brit claimed the Claret Jug. Frenchman Arnaud Massy completed the four rounds in 312 strokes—two better than England's J.H. Taylor. Massy had traveled from France to Britain the day after winning the French Open, arriving three weeks before the championship in order to prepare. It was a significant victory for the Frenchman, as it would be another 72 years before the next Continental European, Spain's Seve Ballesteros, won the title.

The venue, Hoylake—home of the Royal Liverpool Golf Club (RLGC)—was a strong test, revered by the pros and described by the great golf writer Bernard Darwin as a "breeder of mighty champions." The course had hosted the championship twice before—in 1897 when amateur and RLGC member Harold Hilton won, and in 1902 when Scotsman Sandy Herd finished a stroke ahead of Harry Vardon and James Braid.

The weather for the qualifying rounds had been glorious, but a fierce wind rolled in for the first two Championship rounds on Thursday the 20th, making scoring difficult. Massy carded a 76 in the morning, a round equaled only by England's Walter Toogood who had played in the previous 12 Open Championships with a top finish of T15. Three strokes back, Willie McKewan and J.H. Taylor were tied for 3rd. Scotland's James Braid, winner of the previous two years and who started the 1907 event as the bookies' firm favorite at 4 to 1, finished with a disappointing 82 that put him in a tie for 9th.

Massy's afternoon 81 was good enough to give him a one-shot lead at the end of the first day. Toogood struggled to an 86 and was no longer a factor, eventually tying for 13th. Moving into a tie for 2nd—just a shot behind Massy—were local pro Tom Ball and Taylor, already a three-time champion. Braid's 85 put him 10 shots back and needing something special on Day 2 to have any chance.

The wind was a good deal weaker the second day, and the scoring consequently much better. Braid improved to 75, and only Harry Vardon could go any lower: his sweet swing taking him to a best-of-the-week 74. That pushed him into a tie for third, five strokes out of the lead now held by Taylor, whose morning 76 meant he was now the only player in the field to have beaten 80 in all three rounds.

In the fourth and final round, Taylor reached the turn in 41, having holed a 12-foot putt for a 7 at the par-five 3rd. Massy began the final round at 4 p.m. and still had nine holes to play when Taylor finished the 72 holes at 314 after carding a final-round 80. Despite finding a couple of deep bunkers on the way home, Massy did enough to finish in 77, good for a two-stroke victory. Some of his fellow competitors rushed the green and held Massy aloft, with the 4,000-strong gallery giving him a hearty cheer.

Earning your place

With the number of entries increasing every year, this would be the first time players had to qualify for the championship proper. The 193 golfers who had submitted their applications were each assigned to one of two groups. The first group would play 36 holes on the Tuesday of tournament week, the second on Wednesday. The top 30 players and ties from each day earned the right to compete for the Claret Jug, with a total of 67 players advancing. The eventual winner, Massy, was also the best player in qualifying, shooting excellent rounds of 73 and 74 to qualify with ease.

Arnaud Massy

Before 1907, the Open Championship field had been populated somewhat randomly. Basically, all that an interested player had to do was fill out the application and send in his entry fee. Previous winners, high finishers, and players with a good reputation whose clubs had endorsed them were certainly given preference, but there was no formal qualification process as such. Ten of the 46 Open Championships had been won by non-Scots before 1907, but Massy became the first golfer from overseas to win the Claret Jug.

Vive La France

Arnaud Massy was born in 1877, in the town of Biarritz on France's southwest coast. The golf club there, Biarritz Le Phare, was laid out by British expats and opened in 1888. During his teens and young adulthood, Massy worked as a fisherman and supplemented his income by caddying for club members and the occasional British pro golfer who would travel to Biarritz to practice during the winter.

Through connections he made with the British golfers, Massy traveled to North Berwick, Scotland in 1898 and benefited greatly from his association and friendship with Ben Sayers. He became a clubmaker and regularly played the town's famous West Links, which had expanded to its current size in 1895 (Sayers made significant alterations to the course, along with C.K. Hutchison, in 1932).

A natural golfer and something of a quick study, Massy won the inaugural French Open in 1906 at La Boulie, outside Paris. He won again the following year, beating a strong field that included Harry Vardon, James Braid, and J.H. Taylor—the Great Triumvirate. Massy beat all three of them again a few weeks later at Hoylake, with a victory that the *London Evening Telegraph and Post* said was "well-deserved and not unexpected."

Postcard of Biarritz le Phare GC

Taylor was quoted as saying that the Frenchman had won on his merits alone, adding he had all the characteristics of a great player, and that his style was pleasant to watch. "There is nothing forced or cramped about his methods," Taylor noted. "Five years ago, Sandy Herd observed to a friend that Massey [sp] was a champion in the making, and his forecast has turned out as he prognosticated. Massey [sp] is the undisputed sovereign of the links for a twelvemonth at least, or until a greater than he arises."

Massy's victory raised awareness of golf in France, as did the fairly regular exhibition matches he played throughout western Europe. He won the first ever Belgian Open in 1910, the inaugural Spanish Open in 1912, and amassed a total of 20 wins during a career that had been stalled somewhat by World War I (he was injured at the Battle of Verdun in 1916). Thankfully, Massy was able to continue playing following the War and won his fourth French Open in 1925, at the age of 48. He then claimed his second and third Spanish Opens in 1927 and '28. Massy also finished in the top 10 at the Open Championship 10 times, losing in a playoff to Vardon at Royal St. George's in 1911.

Though he died in France in 1950, Massy spent much of his life in Scotland after marrying North Berwick native, Janet Henderson, in October 1907. Janet gave birth to their daughter the same week as Arnaud won the Open, which influenced the baby girl's name: Margot Lockhart Hoylake Massy.

1912 (British) Amateur

John Ball wins his eighth British Amateur title.

DATE
June 3-8, 1912

LOCATION
Royal North Devon
Devon, England

PRIZE
Gold Medal

IN THE FIELD
Harold Hilton
Fred Herreshoff
Abe Mitchell
Harry Colt
Bernard Darwin

John Ball Jr. was 50 years old when he arrived at Royal North Devon GC for the 1912 Amateur Championship. Though probably not the outright favorite for the event, he was still obviously a threat having won two years previously at his home club—Royal Liverpool GC, where the inaugural Amateur Championship was played in 1885.

Ball Jr. was born in 1861, eight years before the first nine holes at what would become Royal Liverpool GC were laid out on and around the local race-track. He grew up at the adjacent Royal Hotel where his father (also John) was the proprietor. Something of a prodigy, a 16-year-old Ball finished tied for 4th in the 1878 Open at Prestwick GC: he and Bob Martin played off for 4th place, Martin winning with a 55 to Ball's 64. Ball would return to Prestwick 10 years later to claim his first Amateur Championship, in 1888.

At Royal North Devon (RND), Ball received a bye into the second round and, in reaching the final, he defeated former Irish Amateur Champion H.M. Cairnes, RND member F.S. Bond, and Angus Hambro, a member of parliament from South Dorset. In the championship match, he faced the 25-year-old Abe Mitchell.

Early on in the morning round, it looked like Mitchell might run away with the match. Three-up after eight holes, and 4-up through 16, Mitchell was taking advantage of an out-of-form Ball who chose not to carry a niblick—likened to today's wedge—thinking it an ugly, modern contrivance.

Ball was playing so poorly, in fact, that the *Daily Telegraph's* special correspondent said he was "doing a lot of slack things about this time," adding that he was "whistling quietly to himself as though he had wearied of his struggles in recalcitrant bunkers and wanted to treat the affair with a light heart." Perhaps he was being patient, knowing there was a lot of golf left. Ball got one hole back before lunch, ending the morning round 3-down. He came out much stronger in the afternoon, however, buoyed by the fact the constant rain was taking 20-30 yards of run off Mitchell's long drives. The match was all-square after 23 holes, and Ball edged one hole clear for the first time at the 32nd (14th).

Mitchell won the 33rd, then the 34th was halved after Mitchell had laid a nasty stymie (his fifth of the match), but Ball dealt with it by "applying a lot of cut spin, the ball creeping in on the right side of the hole." Mitchell won the 35th hole to retain his slender lead, but he missed a four-footer for a half on the 36th hole; if he had holed it, it would have won him the championship.

On the first extra hole, Mitchell found a ditch but recovered well to earn a half. However, after topping his tee shot into another ditch at the 38th hole, Mitchell pulled his third into a nasty spot left of the green and was all but dead. His next shot flew almost straight up, and he caught it before the ball landed, thus conceding the match.

Ball had won the Amateur Championship for the eighth time: a record that will likely remain in place as long as golf is played. (Michael Bonallack is second with five wins.) Mitchell turned pro the following year and ea victories (including one in America, where he played in three U.S. Opens), with eight top-10 finishes, and four top-fives, in the Open Championship.

John Ball

How Good was John Ball?

Besides winning eight Amateur Championships, Ball became the first Englishman (and amateur) to capture the Open Championship, when he beat Willie Fernie and Archie Simpson by three shots at Prestwick in 1890. This was the same year that Ball won his second Amateur; he and Bobby Jones remain the only players to win the Amateur and Open Championships in the same year. Twelve years earlier, Ball had finished 5th at the Open Championship as a 16-year-old, and he came in 2nd to Harold Hilton at Muirfield in 1892. He won four Irish Amateur titles, four St. George's Challenge Cups (a prestigious amateur event played at Royal St. George's GC), and numerous club events.

Though he held the club tightly in the palms of both hands, Ball had a graceful, balanced swing. Bernard Darwin of *The Times* in London, said he "derived greater aesthetic and emotional pleasure from watching John Ball than from any other spectacle in the game."

Fellow Royal Liverpool GC member Harold Hilton said Ball's game "couldn't be imitated, just admired," while many years later, the *Sunday Telegraph* golf correspondent and course architect Donald Steel insisted that no other golfer was "more of a legend in his own lifetime." Of all the golfers who remained amateurs throughout their careers, John Ball was surely second only to Bobby Jones.

Whither the Stymie?

Golf's first official rules—drawn up in 1744 by the Gentlemen Golfers of Leith (later the Honourable Company of Edinburgh Golfers) ahead of an "open" competition to be played over the Leith Links—dictated that a ball could only be moved if it was touching another. This means that if another player's golf ball was in the way between your ball and the hole, you would have to play around it. Being in this prickly predicament was called being "stymied," and it was considered an important part of competition.

Thirty-one years later, the Leith gentlemen added that a ball within six inches of another could be moved. When the six-inch rule was a part of the game, a measure was often printed on putter shafts or scorecards; some cards were made precisely six inches long on one side for proper measurement.

For most of the 1800s, the ruling bodies of the game made adaptations and amendments, and reversed decisions regarding the stymie. In 1812, the R&A decided that a ball lying directly between the hole and another ball must be lifted. And 18 years after that, the rules used at Montrose Links, 40 miles north of St Andrews, stated the stymie would no longer be used in medal play, but was permissible in match play. The R&A abolished the stymie altogether in 1831 but reinstated it the following year, and then in 1891 removed the stymie from medal play.

Though British golfers considered the stymie a legitimate, sometimes skillful, means by which to hinder your opponent—Harry Vardon, J.H. Taylor, and James Braid all offered advice on how to chip a ball over another or put cut-spin on it with the putter in order for it to find the edge of the hole and topple in—the stymie was never particularly popular in the U.S., where it was regarded as too flukey or unsportsmanlike. It did have its supporters in America, though. Bobby Jones said, "With the stymie in the game, matchplay becomes an exciting duel in which the player must always be on guard against a sudden, often demoralizing, thrust."

"More than anything else," Jones continued, "it points up the value of always being the closer to the hole on the shot to the green and after the first putt. The player who can maintain the upper hand in the play up to the hole rarely suffers from a stymie. I think it merits a respected place in the game, and I know a return to it would greatly enhance the interest and excitement of match play golf for player and spectator alike."

In the U.S., the USGA originally recognized the stymie as part of the game. In 1920, it began a one-year trial in which a player who had been stymied was allowed to concede his opponent's next putt. In 1941, the organization made it legal to lift any ball lying within six inches of the hole and, in 1944, the PGA of America banned the stymie in all its competitions. The USGA abolished it in 1950, though the R&A would continue to allow it in match play until 1952, when the Joint Rules of Golf (approved by both organizations) were adopted, thus eliminating the stymie altogether.

1913 U.S. Open

Ouimet beats Vardon and Ray, igniting American interest in golf.

DATE
Sept. 18-20, 1913

LOCATION
The Country Club
Brookline, MA
USA

PRIZE
$300

IN THE FIELD

Harry Vardon
Ted Ray
John McDermott
Walter Hagen
Macdonald Smith
Jerome Travers
J.H. Taylor
Francis Ouimet

Movies about golf typically don't enjoy the greatest success at the box office, though that's not to say they can't be positively reviewed. Indeed, Bill Paxton's adaptation of Mark Frost's historical-fiction book, *The Greatest Game Ever Played*, which dramatized the amazing story of the 1913 U.S. Open, was highly rated. But if there was ever a movie about a golf tournament that didn't require "Hollywood-ifying," it was surely the story of how a humble, disadvantaged 20-year-old amateur who grew up across the street from where the event was played beat two of the game's greatest players to become a major champion.

Born in 1893 to a French-Canadian father and Irish mother, Francis Ouimet grew up relatively poor in a house on the wrong side of the fence, across from the prestigious CC, established in 1882 and one of the USGA's five charter clubs. The young lad began caddying there at the age of 11 and was very keen on the game, teaching himself how to play with his brother's clubs, and balls he found on the course. He practiced in the field adjoining his house and was soon the best player at Brookline High School, where he organized the team.

He dropped out of school—at his father's insistence—and was forced to find a job to earn desperately needed money for his family. He began working at a dry goods store but soon found a position more to his liking: working in Boston at a sports equipment store co-owned by the famous baseball player George Wright, who played for the Boston Red Stockings and Red Caps in the 1870s.

It was here that Ouimet met the head of Wright & Ditson's golf department, an elder Scotsman named

Alexander Findlay, who helped spread golf across America by laying out courses and leading Harry Vardon on a highly publicized tour of the U.S. He's now known as the "ambassador" of American golf—a position the young Ouimet would soon find himself in as well.

Ouimet continued caddying and practicing, and—because he was a likable young man as well as a talented golfer—he was occasionally allowed to play the course at Brookline.

In the summer of 1913, he won the Massachusetts Amateur and, in early September, played in the U.S. Amateur at Garden City Golf Club on New York's Long Island. There, he qualified for match play but lost in the second round to defending champion Jerome Travers, who would go on to win his fourth U.S. Amateur there, and also win the U.S. Open in 1915.

Ouimet's win at his state amateur championship, a decent showing in the national amateur two weeks before the U.S. Open, and his connection to the host venue, convinced USGA President Robert Watson that he warranted a special invitation to play in the Championship. The tournament had actually been postponed three months so Vardon could play in it: the five-time Open Championship winner and 1900 U.S. Open champion had been in the U.S. since August on an exhibition tour tour, this time alongside 1912 Open Championship winner and fellow Isle of Jersey

Turn-of-the-century postcard of the Brookline clubhouse

native Ted Ray, and the English pro Wilfred Reid, who had won the 1904 French Open and 1911 German and Belgian Opens.

Having taken time off work to play in the U.S. Amateur, however, Ouimet politely declined the invitation. Watson, though, was eager that he should play, and Ouimet's employer allowed him the time off.

Ouimet, Vardon, Ray, and Reid were among the 49 players to advance through 36-hole qualifying early in the week, Vardon showing he would probably be the man to beat in the championship proper, shooting rounds of 75 and 76. Determined not to let Vardon have it all his own way, though, was the two-time defending champion, John McDermott, who had become the first American-born winner of the U.S. Open, in 1911, at Chicago GC.

Four weeks before the U.S. Open, McDermott competed against the visitors from the British Isles at the Shawnee Open, beating Vardon and Ray in the process, he won by eight shots. During the prize-giving ceremony, however, he made some unflattering remarks directed at the overseas guests (see "Johnny Be Not-So-Good" on pages 70-1).

Despite his excellent U.S. Open record—he had finished 2nd after an 18-hole playoff in 1910, before winning back-to-back titles—and obvious desire to keep the U.S. Open trophy in America, McDermott would ultimately finish in 8th place.

Brits Shine on Day 1

The first two rounds of the championship were played on Thursday, September 18, with the first six places on the leaderboard at the end of 36 holes taken up by players from England, Scotland, and the Isle of Jersey. Reid and Vardon shared the lead at 1-over 147, with Ray two shots back in a tie for 3rd after shooting a 3-under-par 70—the best round of the tournament—in the afternoon. Also tied for 3rd was Herbert Strong, who was born in Kent, England, but who had emigrated to the U.S. in 1905. Tied for 5th were Jim Barnes, born in Cornwall, England, but a resident of the U.S. since 1906 (he remained in America for the rest of his life but never became a U.S. citizen), and Macdonald Smith, a Scotsman who had emigrated in 1908. A shot further back were Ouimet, England's George Sargent, Scotland's Alec Ross (who emigrated to the U.S. in 1900, won the 1907 U.S. Open, and was the younger brother of famous course architect, Donald Ross), and a 20-year-old Walter Hagen, who was just six months older than Ouimet but already the club professional at The Country Club of Rochester in New York. Hagen's bosses at the club had only reluctantly agreed to letting him play in the championship, as he had no tournament experience and would be a total unknown.

The Amateur Rises in the Rain

For the second and final day's play, the heavens opened and dropped nearly two inches of rain on a course that became so sodden that balls plugged in the fairways and the bunkers became ponds. Encouraged by his 10-year-old caddie Eddie Lowery, Ouimet shot a 74 to jump into a tie for the 54-hole lead with Vardon (78) and Ray (76).

Conditions were still bad for the final round in the afternoon. Ray would be the first out among the leaders, followed by Vardon. Ouimet was several groups behind and was actually playing the 5th when Vardon putted out on 18.

LEFT TO RIGHT: Vardon, Ouimet, and Ray

Vardon and Ray both shot fairly poor 79s, but no one else was prospering in the downpour: the best scores in the final round were two 76s. Ouimet would need a 78 to win but reached the turn in 43. He then double bogeyed the short 10th, meaning he'd have to play the last eight holes in 1-under-par to tie—a pretty tall order given how bad the weather was and how badly he was playing.

But somehow Ouimet found his game and, after bogeying the 12th to fall to +8 for the round, he made two birdies—at the 13th and 17th—and three pars, before rolling in a four-footer for another par at the last. Home in 36 and round in 79, he tied both Vardon and Ray.

Well-known American amateur Fred Herreshoff, who had finished runner-up at the 1904 U.S. Amateur as a 16-year-old, finished down the field in a tie for 16th but had a few words to share with the press about Ouimet, with whom he had been greatly impressed: "He goes about his work as though it were a business he had pledged himself to go through with, and his indifference to the results of his play is very strongly modeled on that of Vardon. He is undoubtedly the coming American player."

Ouimet in Extra Holes

The weather for the 18-hole playoff the next day was mercifully better, and with no rain in the air and the work week behind them, an estimated 20,000 people left the city bound for Brookline to watch a young local go up against two of the world's best golfers for the biggest prize in American golf. They were there for the 10 a.m. starting time and watched all three players reach the turn in 38. It could have gone all wrong for Ouimet at the 420-yard 5th, where he hit his second out-of-bounds. But, with the penalty for going OB just distance—not stroke and distance as it is today—he hit a marvelous third shot and came off the green with a 5—the same as his opponents.

The back nine went Ouimet's way, as both Vardon and Ray bogeyed the 10 and 12th holes and then made disastrous double bogeys—Ray at the 15th, Vardon at the last. Ouimet, however, was solid as a rock over that final nine, carding eight pars and a birdie (famously on the 17th) for a superb round of 72. Though it probably never felt like he could stop focusing and simply cruise home, Ouimet beat Vardon by five and Ray by six.

Ouimet never turned professional, becoming a successful businessman in the sporting goods business. In 1914, the year after his famous victory, he traveled to England to play in the (British) Amateur Championship at Royal St. George's, where he was beaten in the fifth round by Robert Harris. During his stay in Britain, he spent many enjoyable evenings with Vardon and Ray, who also showed him around some of London's famous sights. On his return to the U.S. that summer, Ouimet won the U.S. Amateur at Ekwanok CC in Vermont, where he beat Jerome Travers in the final, 6&5. He won the U.S. Amateur again—in 1931 at Beverly CC in Chicago, where he beat Jack Westland in the final, also by 6&5. He played on the first eight U.S. Walker Cup teams, three as a playing captain, and was the non-playing captain for the next four. In 1951, at the age of 58, he was made Captain of the Royal and Ancient GC of St Andrews: an honor that overwhelmed him according to his daughter, Barbara.

He died in 1967 in Nelson, Massachusetts, about six miles from where he had changed American golf forever. He was 74 years old. To better understand the impact his 1913 U.S. Open victory had on the country: there were approximately 350,000 golfers in the U.S. in 1913, and just 10 years later, there were six times that many. And when Ouimet won at Brookline, there were roughly 700 courses in the U.S., but by the end of the 1920s, there were over 5,500.

Post-victory Ouimet on shoulders, with caddie Lowery in front

Johnny Be Not-So-Good

While this chapter celebrates the amazing feat of Francis Ouimet, it would be wrong to leave it without giving John McDermott his due. The feisty young American was born in Philadelphia, and like Ouimet, he dropped out of school to make his way in the world. He caddied at the famous Aronimink GC and became a pro, working at Merchantville Field Club (now the Merchantville CC) in Cherry Hill, New Jersey. From there, he moved to the Atlantic City CC, and he played his first U.S. Open in 1909, aged 17, finishing 49th.

The following year, he lost in a playoff to Alex Smith at Philadelphia Cricket Club and, in 1911, he beat George Simpson and Mike Brady in a playoff to become the first U.S.-born winner of the Championship and its youngest ever champion at 19 years 10 months and 14 days. In 1912, he won again, this time defeating Tom McNamara by two strokes at Country Club of Buffalo in New York, and becoming the first player to complete the four rounds under par (294, -2).

In 1911, he had won three straight $1,000 challenge matches in Philadelphia; the following year, he finished 5th at the Open Championship at Royal Liverpool GC: the best finish by an American to that point. He won the 1913 Western Open, three Philadelphia Opens (1910, 1911, and 1913) and the 1913 Shawnee Open. He was also making good money from endorsements and appearance fees, so everything seemed to be going well for McDermott.

But sinister forces were at play in the markets and in his mind. Many of his financial investments failed in 1912, and somewhat bizarrely, following his victory at the Shawnee Open where he had won by eight shots—beating Vardon and Ray in the process—he seemingly badmouthed the British players, saying "We hope our foreign visitors had a good time, but we don't think they did. And we are sure they won't win the National Open." One newspaper reported that the reigning U.S. Open champion jumped on a chair and said the visiting English golfers may as well go back home as their quest for the American championship would get them "nowhere in particular."

It was a strange outburst to be sure and McDermott was forced to apologize (though it seems Vardon and Ray soon forgot about the whole thing). It's possible his failing finances were causing McDermott distress, or an innate disagreeable nature might have been to blame. Whether it was meant as a joke or if he had been misquoted as he claimed, it clearly caused McDermott significant distress.

In 1914, he traveled to Britain again to play in the Open Championship but arrived too late, owing to travel complications. On the voyage back to the U.S., the ship he was traveling on hit another in the foggy English Channel and he had to be lowered onto a lifeboat. Apparently, this had as negative an impact on McDermott's mental health as the Shawnee incident had, and the combined effects resulted in serious mental illness.

McDermott played only occasionally in local events for the next 15 years or so and lived the rest of his life in mental institutions or with family, shunned by society and forgotten by the game.

In 1971, at the age of 79, he attended the U.S. Open at nearby Merion, with the hope of spending some time with the players. However, because of his appearance, he was asked to leave the pro shop. As he was turning to leave with his care workers, McDermott was recognized by Arnold Palmer, who greeted him, spoke with him, and made him his guest for the rest of the week. Six weeks later, McDermott died in his sleep.

The photograph taken by Tillinghast at the 1913 Shawnee Invitational, only 15 minutes after the "incident." LEFT TO RIGHT: Wilfrid Reid, Ted Ray, Alex Smith, Harry Vardon, and a distant, dejected McDermott.

1914 Open Championship

Harry Vardon wins his sixth Claret Jug.

DATE
June 18-19, 1914

LOCATION
Prestwick GC
Ayrshire,
Scotland

PRIZE
£50

IN THE FIELD
Harry Vardon
James Braid
J.H. Taylor
Ted Ray
Arnaud Massy
Francis Ouimet
George Duncan
Sandy Herd

After 54 holes of the 54th Open Championship, it looked like defending champion J.H. Taylor would be the one to break out of the three-way tie for most Claret Jugs won, and become the first to reach six titles. The four-round championship was held over two days—36 holes on Thursday and 36 on Friday to enable players to be back at the Golf Clubs that employed them for the weekend—and, by lunch-time on the second day, the 43-year-old Englishman from Devon was two clear of another five-time winner, Harry Vardon, who'd shot a disappointing 78 in the third-round. James Braid—the third player with five Open Championship victories—was eight back of Taylor in a tie for 7th.

The Prestwick course, now hosting the 23rd of the 24 Opens it would ultimately stage, was running hard and fast thanks to a heatwave that saw temperatures soar into the 90s (Fahrenheit)—25-30 degrees higher than the seasonal norm. "The turf of the fairway has been ripened into the tinge of waving, yellow corn," the *Glasgow Herald* reported. "And the ball runs a very long way off a well-hit tee stroke." With the course playing 512 yards longer than it had in 1908, when Braid had shot a superb 72-hole total of 291 to win by eight shots, the newspapers were saying that longer hitters ought to have an advantage. "Though (long-hitting) will avail them of nothing unless the driving is straight," the Herald warned, "for the margin of safety is not too generous, and the course is now severely bunkered."

With the two leaders playing together in the final round, Taylor went three clear after Vardon made an ugly six on the 1st hole. The Jerseyman would claw one back with a birdie four on the famous par-five 3rd hole, named "Cardinal" for the huge bunker that crosses the fairway about 230 yards out. And he regained the lead he had held after the first and second rounds, when Taylor found the Pow Burn off the tee at the 4th and ended up carding a miserable seven to Vardon's four. Taylor dropped more shots at the 5th and 8th and would complete the first nine holes in 44 strokes.

Taylor's two-shot lead had become a three-shot deficit. And when Vardon picked up two more shots at the 10th and 11th holes, the contest was all but over. Taylor made up two strokes with a birdie three at the short par-four 16th, but it was too little too late. Both players would par the famous 17th (Alps) and short par-four 18th, Vardon eventually signing for a 78 and Taylor an 83.

High Scores

Vardon's four-round total of 306 was 15 strokes higher than Braid's 1908 total of 291, and only one better than what he had shot in 1898 at the same venue. The heat and length of the course—third longest in Open history to that point—both played their part in pushing scores up, as did the size of the galleries that had made the 35-mile journey south from Glasgow that week.

Even with a leaderboard packed with golfers from south of the border—though a proud Jerseyman, Vardon was recognized as English—the Scots turned out in large numbers. On the final afternoon, over 10,000 spectators jockeyed noisily for position hoping to see 3rd-place James Jenkins—an amateur and member at nearby Troon Golf Club who had won the Amateur Championship at Royal St George's just a few weeks before—salvage some pride for the home nation.

The last time a Scotsman had claimed the Claret Jug was four years earlier, when James Braid won the last of his five titles, hoisting the trophy at St Andrews. Three different Englishmen won the following three years, and—to be fair—it was asking a lot for the local man to pass both Vardon and Taylor, four and six shots ahead respectively.

Indeed, Jenkins had as tough a final round as Taylor, crumbling to an 83 of his own and finishing back in a tie for 8th.

The Morrises were golf's first superstars, but their fame really didn't extend far past Scotland's coastline and southern border (course design work saw

Vardon putting on the 9th green at Prestwick, during the 1914 Open

Old Tom's renown and reputation spread throughout much of England and, late in his life, Ireland). Arnaud Massy achieved a degree of acclaim in Great Britain and western Europe when he won the Open Championship in 1907. Vardon, meanwhile, was the game's first genuinely international icon. Along with winning six Open Championship titles, the man known as 'the Stylist' played some tournaments and exhibitions in Continental Europe and made three tours of North America (1900, 1913, 1920) playing a total of 220 or so exhibition matches and competing for the U.S. Open in which he finished 1st (1900), 2nd (1913), and T2 (1920). J.H. Taylor also made a much shorter U.S. Tour in 1900, but he wasn't the celebrity Vardon was.

The Great Triumvirate

Harry Vardon's win at Prestwick marked the end of the Great Triumvirate's extraordinary run in the game's oldest major. Between 1894 and 1914, Vardon, J.H. Taylor, and James Braid won 16 of the 21 championships with Vardon earning six titles (still the record), and Taylor and Braid five each. Vardon's first win came at Muirfield in 1896, when he beat Taylor in a playoff. He then won twice at Royal St. George's (the first time in 1899, before the club had been awarded its "Royal" designation) and three times at Prestwick. Taylor won at St. George's in 1894 and then defended the title at St Andrews a year later. Back at the Old Course in 1900, he beat 2nd-place Vardon by eight shots, and he then won at Royal Cinque Ports in 1909 and Royal Liverpool in 1913. Braid, meanwhile, won twice at St Andrews, twice at Muirfield, and once at Prestwick.

LEFT TO RIGHT: J.H. Taylor, James Braid, and Harry Vardon

1916 PGA Championship

The first ever PGA Championship, a matchplay event until 1958.

DATE
Oct. 10-14, 1916

LOCATION
Siwanoy CC
Bronxville, NY
USA

PRIZE
$500

IN THE FIELD
Walter Hagen
Jim Barnes
Jock Hutchison
Mike Brady
Tom McNamara

Lewis Rodman Wanamaker was an interesting man, one of several layers, competencies, and interests. His father John was also a bit of a polymath; he had served as U.S. Postmaster General, was involved in politics, religion, and philanthropy, and built a hugely successful department-store business that Rodman (he dropped the "Lewis") worked for and eventually inherited in 1922, six years before he died.

Rodman was also involved in religious activities, and a Special Deputy Police Commissioner in New York City during World War I. He commissioned photographic projects to document Native American life and conceived of a national monument to native tribes (though it was never built). He was a huge promoter of aviation, co-owned a Philadelphia newspaper and, in 1908, founded the Millrose Games: a prestigious indoor athletics event that still takes place every year.

Most importantly, though—for the purposes of this book anyway, and for tens of thousands of golf club professionals—he was responsible for the formation of the Professional Golfers Association of America.

Modeled on the original PGA in Great Britain which had been established in 1901, the PGA of America was officially founded on April 10, 1916. Four months prior, on January 17th, Wanamaker had hosted a luncheon at New York City's Taplow Club for 35 leading golfers and other industry representatives, during which the organization's administration and goals were discussed.

Motivated by what an esteemed and regulated body of club professionals might do for club sales in his stores, Wanamaker put forward the idea of a pro-only championship. It was agreed upon and led to the inaugural event being played in October at Siwanoy Country Club in New York.

Entrants had to be a member of the newly formed PGA of America, and each of its seven sections—Pacific, Southeastern, New England, Metropolitan, Middle West, Central, and North and Southwest—held a qualifying event in September (Central Section event in October):

Pacific—Olympic Club, San Francisco, CA
Southeastern—Wilmington CC, Wilmington, DE
New England—Worcester CC, Worcester, MA
Metropolitan—Inwood CC, Inwood, NY
Middle West—Glen View Club, Glenview, IL
Central—Algonquin GC, St. Louis, MO
North and Southwest—The Country Club, Cleveland, OH

Matches were played over 36 holes, and 32 qualifiers advanced to the national tournament. The size of each section determined its number of qualifiers:

Metropolitan	12
Middle West	7
Southeast	5
New England	3
Central	2
N & SW	2
Pacific	1

Rodman Wanamaker

One of the two qualifiers from the North and Southwest Section withdrew, but rather than his place going to the next in line from the N&SW Section, it went to one of the three players who had finished tied for 13th in the Metropolitan Section qualifier.

On October 4, Jack Dowling, Clarence Hackney, and Macdonald Smith were due to compete for the remaining spot at Englewood GC in New Jersey, but Smith arrived too late to play. Dowling then trounced Hackney by 18 shots over the 36 holes. Then Mike Shearman—the player who had qualified from the North and Southwest Section—along with Fred Clarkson of the Central Section, withdrew leaving a field of 30 players.

The players Shearman and Clarkson had been due to meet were given byes. Among the 14 first-round matches that did go ahead were a number of lopsided wins. William Macfarlane (a Scottish immigrant who would go on to win the 1925 U.S.

Open) beat Robert McNulty 10&9, and Jock Hutchison repeated his 11&9 defeat of Joe Mitchell in the first round by beating William Brown by the same scoreline the following day. Hutchison was also a native of Scotland and would win the PGA Championship in 1920 and the Open Championship in 1921, becoming the first U.S.-based player to win the Claret Jug.

Scotland vs. England Final

Even though Hutchison had been in the U.S. for 12 years and Barnes for 10, it's likely there was a little cross-Hadrian's Wall needle between the Scot and Englishman when they teed off on that Saturday morning in 1916. Having said he was "fiery" the day before, the *New York Times* was now calling Hutchison "picturesque," and reporting that he had the lion's share of the support from a sizable gallery—if only because Barnes had won so often already that year that he was "laying in a stock of trophies and medals that rival(ed) a court jeweler's collection." All Barnes needed to win a golf tournament, the *New York Times* continued, was "a golf course, a putter, and the liberal supply of clover leaves he carries in the corner of his mouth."

It was Hutchison who made the better start, however, going 4-up after just eight holes. Barnes got three back on the inward half and, though both players had gone around in the equivalent of 77 strokes, Hutchison led 1-up at the break.

After winning the 21st and 25th holes in the afternoon, Barnes took the lead for the first time, and he went 2-up after a birdie at the 10th. Though certainly exciting, the final eight holes were fraught with mistakes. Barnes made most of them and was 1-down again through 15 holes. The 16th was halved (tied) leaving Hutchison 1-up with two to play. Hutchison admitted afterward that he thought he had his opponent at this point, but the match was by no means over. The "long, lean, and lanky" Cornishman won the 17th with a par and, following four mediocre shots each down the last, both players had four-foot putts for fives. After the referee had adjudged him away, Hutchison missed, and from an inch or so closer, Barnes holed out to secure the $500 winner's check, a diamond-studded gold medal, and the large, 27 lb. Wanamaker Trophy.

In the semi-finals, Macfarlane would meet England native Jim Barnes who had enjoyed a fairly easy passage through to the final four, winning his matches 8&7, 8&7, and 3&1. And, in the other match, Hutchison would play Walter Hagen, who'd had an easy time of it himself, demolishing his opponents 7&6, 3&2, and 10&9. Suffice to say, the 18th hole saw limited action that week.

With his strange, very wide putting stance—he also leaned forward on his left leg, the ball positioned midway between his feet—Barnes overcame Macfarlane 6&5, while Hutchison, described by the *New York Times* as "the fiery laddie from the land of the heather," came through in the end to beat Hagen 2-up.

The final would, therefore, be between two of the five qualifiers from the Southeast Section: Barnes, the pro at Whitemarsh Valley near Philadelphia, against Jock Hutchison, representing Allegheny Country Club near Pittsburgh.

In November 1957, the PGA of America's Board of Directors voted unanimously to make what was then the only remaining match play event in U.S. professional golf a stroke play tournament, starting the following year. Match play had become unpopular with the players and unprofitable for the PGA of America. In an August 1957 *Sports Illustrated* article, however, revered golf writer Herbert Warren Wind lamented the probable loss of match play: "It is high time the PGA stopped talking about turning the championship into a 72-hole stroke-play affair ... there is probably nothing more exciting in golf than to watch a head-on contest between two top shotmakers played over a dramatic layout with true shot values."

Jim Barnes in the first PGA Championship

The idea of a return to match play comes up in the golf press from time to time, but given the economics and TV demands, there's probably next to no chance of that ever happening.

1922 Open Championship

Hagen becomes first U.S.-born player to win the Claret Jug.

DATE
June 22-23, 1922

LOCATION
Royal St. George's
Kent, England

PRIZE
£75

IN THE FIELD
Walter Hagen
Jim Barnes
Jock Hutchison
Harry Vardon
J.H. Taylor
George Duncan

For the last two days of the 1913 U.S. Open—and certainly for a long time after it—the golf spotlight had shone squarely on Francis Ouimet. This was hardly surprising given his age, his background, and whom he had beaten in the playoff. Golfers with a knack for spotting young talent, however, might also have paid a scrap of attention to the player who quietly finished in the tie for 4th, three shots out of the Ouimet-Vardon-Ray playoff.

Walter Hagen made his U.S. debut in that year's U.S. Open, and though he played well, he complained that he hadn't really enjoyed the experience as the elder pros has been disrespectful. "They pushed me off the tee and told me I could practice when they got through," he said, before adding "I'm going back next year and will win that tournament."

In 1914, the U.S. Open was held at Midlothian CC, southwest of Chicago. Hagen was due to try out for the Philadelphia Phillies baseball team but chose to play in the golf tournament instead and, after opening with a championship-record 68 (4-under-par) and following it with rounds of 74, 75 and 73, he did indeed win, fulfilling his promise from the previous year. Hagen won it again in 1919, by which time his position as the pro at The Country Club of Rochester had been terminated, and he had moved to the pro shop at Oakland Hills Country Club north of Detroit. After a year there, he would leave to become the game's first touring professional. In 1920, he played in his first Open Championship in Great Britain, finishing tied for 53rd at Royal Cinque Ports Golf Club in Kent, 26 shots behind the winner, George Duncan.

The following June, Hagen finished tied for 2nd at the U.S. Open, nine shots behind Jim Barnes and, in his second appearance in the Open Championship, finished 6th having grown significantly more comfortable on links terrain—something that must have seemed very foreign and unfamiliar to him the year before. Three months after the Open Championship, Hagen won the first of his five PGA Championship titles, beating Barnes 3&2 in the final at Inwood CC.

The 1922 Open Championship was played at a 6,616-yard Royal St. George's GC, three miles north of Royal Cinque Ports GC on the Kent coast. With two U.S. Open victories, a PGA Championship, two Western Open wins, three Metropolitan Open titles, and a North and South Open win, Hagen was regarded as one of the world's three or four best players and was a firm favorite for the Open, with Barnes, Hutchison, and Australia's Joe Kirkwood also among the players expected to contend.

Before the championship proper, though, every player had to advance through 36-hole qualifying—the case until 1963 when exemption criteria were used for the first time—on the Monday and Tuesday of championship week, with 18 holes at Royal St. George's and 18 at nearby Prince's. The day after qualifying was left open for players to rest, practice, or enter a long-drive contest in which each player was allowed six drives—three with rules-conforming balls and three with whatever they liked. The only big name to enter was Hagen, whose two counting drives measured 250 and 252 yards. The winner was an amateur by the name of Smith, whose longest drives were 260 and 271 yards. A total 53 players took part, and among the observers was a 20-year-old Joyce Wethered, a hugely talented golfer and future Hall of Famer (see pages 92-5).

Walter Hagen at the 1922 Open Championship

Ted Ray and the 51-year old J.H. Taylor were

joint leaders after the opening round on Thursday morning, each shooting 73. Hagen, who opened with a 76, jumped into a two-shot lead by the end of the day, however, with an afternoon round of 73. Tied for 2nd were Taylor, Duncan, and Barnes. Meanwhile, Ray had an ugly 83 and, with subsequent rounds of 85 and 80, would drop into a tie for 46th.

On Friday morning, Hutchison rose to the top of the leaderboard after a 73 and looked a good bet to defend the title he had won at St Andrews the previous year. Hagen shot 79 and fell into a tie for 4th, but he would come storming back in the afternoon with a 72 that saw him finish on an even 300, which no one was subsequently able to match.

Hagen may have become the first U.S.-born player to win the Open Championship, but the toast of the galleries and press was George Duncan. After a morning 81 that seemingly took him out of it, the Scot finished with a gutsy 69 to end up just one shot adrift. "Hagen won, but I think, without disparagement of the American golfer, I can say that the figure of the day was Duncan," said the Scotsman. "Altogether it was the drama of a game on a high plane, and the scene will live long in the memory. The result before us tonight was not unexpected, and has been reached in such a day of thrilling golf as may be paralleled but not surpassed in the annals of the game. Hagen will be hailed in the United States and he has, I think, routed the view that he is a fair-weather golfer and ineffective in a seaside wind. His victory was acclaimed by a large crowd here."

Hagen at Royal St. George's

Quite the Character

Walter Hagen had earned his reputation for being something of a showman long before the 1922 Open Championship. Since professionals were still seen almost as second-class citizens, they usually weren't allowed to enter the clubhouse unless invited by a member. Hagen didn't think much of this and, at the 1920 championship, he arrived at Royal Cinque Ports Golf Club in a luxury, chauffeur-driven Daimler which he used as his dining room, feasting on smoked salmon, caviar and champagne, and as his personal dressing room, changing outfits between morning and afternoon rounds. The 1920 U.S. Open at the Inverness Club in Toledo, Ohio was played six weeks after the Open Championship, and Hagen, the defending champion, had told the USGA he was going to use the locker room. If denied access, he warned, he would find alternative arrangements. Concerned what Hagen's "alternative arrangements" might be, officials wisely permitted him and all the professionals to enter the locker room. The pros recognized the significance of the gesture—it was the first time they'd been allowed to do this—and, led by Hagen, they presented the club with a large grandfather clock, on which a brass plaque had been attached. It bore the inscription:

> God measures men by what they are
> Not what in wealth possess
> This vibrant message chimes afar
> The voice of Inverness

Hagen in 1914

Revered golf writer Herbert Warren Wind wrote of Hagen: "On and off the golf course, the ex-caddie and sandlot hurler comported himself in such a manner as imperial as a king or a Hollywood star. He loved the high life ... Walter broke eleven of the Ten Commandments and kept on going. He knew how to take care of himself. He had the right words and the right tie for every occasion."

1922 Walker Cup

The first official match between the USA and GB & Ireland.

DATE
Aug. 28-29, 1922

LOCATION
National Golf Links of America
Southampton, NY
USA

PRIZE
The Walker Cup

IN THE FIELD
Francis Ouimet
Jesse Guilford
Bobby Jones
William Fownes Jr.
Chick Evans
Max Marston
Cyril Tolley
Willis MacKenzie
Robert Harris

The first ever official team matchplay event featuring teams from the United States and Great Britain & Ireland/Europe was played by male amateur golfers competing for the Walker Cup. The competition was named in honor of George Herbert Walker, a St. Louis/New York banker and golf enthusiast who served as president of the USGA in 1920. Walker was the maternal grandfather of U.S. President George Herbert Walker Bush and great grandfather of U.S. President George Walker Bush.

An international match had been played between male amateurs from the U.S. and Great Britain in 1921, ahead of the Amateur Championship at Royal Liverpool Golf Club (Hoylake). Gershom Stewart, a parliament member for the nearby Wirral Peninsula and chairman of Royal Liverpool GC, arranged the event involving eight-man teams representing their respective countries. The U.S. team included the great Bobby Jones, 1913 U.S. Open champion Francis Ouimet, and 1916 U.S. Open winner Chick Evans. They won 9-3, and therefore entered the first official match the following year at National Golf Links of America (NGLA) as firm favorites.

Tommy Armour and Ernest Holderness—two prominent players on the 1921 British team that had played at Hoylake—were unable to play in 1922: Armour because wounds he had suffered in World War I were still a problem, and Holderness because he was a civil servant and unable to get adequate time off work.

The initial choice of captain, England's Angus Hambro, was also unable to make the trip because of "private affairs." Scotland's Robert Harris replaced Hambro, which meant another reserve needed to be found in case one of the players fell ill en route to New

York. They chose writer Bernard Darwin, who was traveling with the team as golf correspondent of *The Times* in London. And when Harris was "bitten by a giant sand-fly" prior to the first day's play, Darwin suddenly found himself on the team: the only alternate player they had on site. Darwin was a fine golfer who had reached the semifinal of the (British) Amateur Championship in 1909 and would go on to play in the event 26 times.

The two-day event would consist or four 36-hole foursomes (alternate shot) and eight 36-hole singles, with all eight players involved on both days. The British team (no Irish players were chosen to play) arrived in New York on August 10th aboard RMS Carmania.

Bernard Darwin

Cyril Tolley beat teammate Charles "Chubby" Hooman in an invitational event at the National Golf Links of America (NGLA) before the Walker Cup got underway, but both players would be beaten in the first day's foursomes. Partnering with Darwin, Tolley was given an 8&7 drubbing by Jesse Guilford and Francis Ouimet, while Hooman and William Breck Torrance lost to Bobby Jones and Jesse Sweetser 3&2. Giving the U.S. team its third point was playing captain William Fownes Jr. (son of Henry Fownes, who founded and designed Oakmont CC), and Philadelphia investment banker Max Marston, who beat the Scottish pairing of Willis MacKenzie and John Caven 2&1. The visiting team's only point was won by the pairing of Oxford graduate Roger Wethered and golf club secretary Colin Aylmer, who beat Chick Evans and Robert Gardner 5&4.

Cyril Tolley

In the second day's singles matches, Guilford beat Tolley 2&1 before Jones beat Wethered 3&2. Evans beat Caven 5&4, then Ouimet thrashed Aylmer 8&7. Torrance

Chick Evans

had a similarly tough time, losing 7&5 to Gardner. The British team had the consolation of winning the final three matches: Hooman beating Sweetser at the 37th, MacKenzie beating Marston 6&5, and Darwin beating Fownes Jr. 3&1, making the final score 8-4.

The British team would return to Southampton on September 19th, its members having played in the U.S. Amateur at The Country Club in Brookline, September 2-9 (none advanced past the third round). Sweetser won the championship, beating Evans 3&2 in the final after taking down Jones 8&7 in the semi-final.

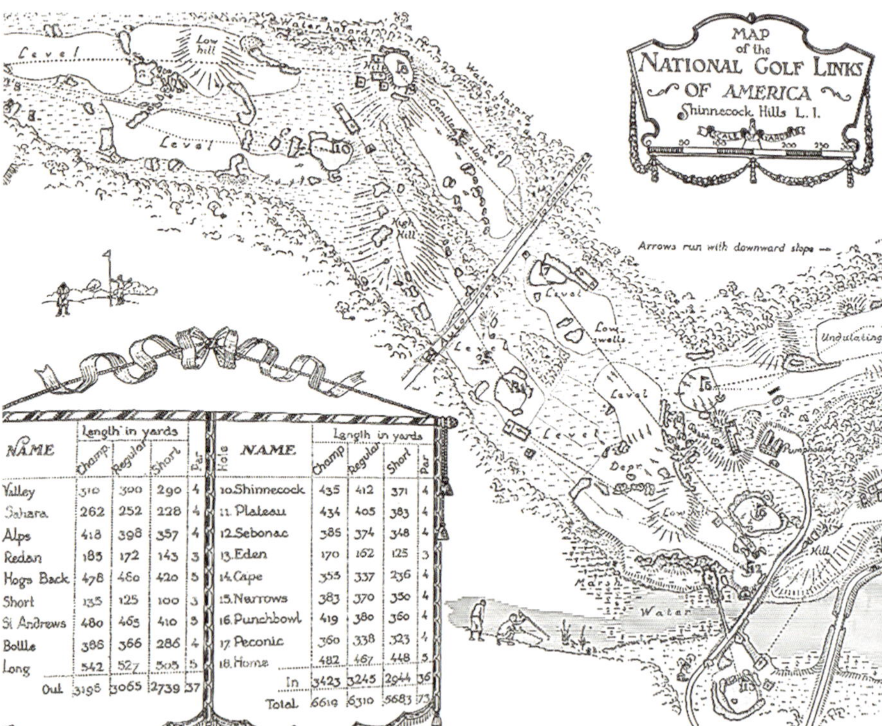

Map of NGLA from the 1920s

The Walker Cup was played again the following year and in 1924, after which it became a biennial event. GB & Ireland didn't win until the 10th playing—in 1938 at St Andrews.

Though eligible from the beginning, no player from the island of Ireland played until 1924, when Major Charles Hezlet of Northern Ireland was chosen for the match at Garden City GC. Hezlet played again in 1926 and 1928. The first golfer from the Republic of Ireland to appear in the Walker Cup was John Burke, who played at The Country Club in 1932.

The Walker Cup

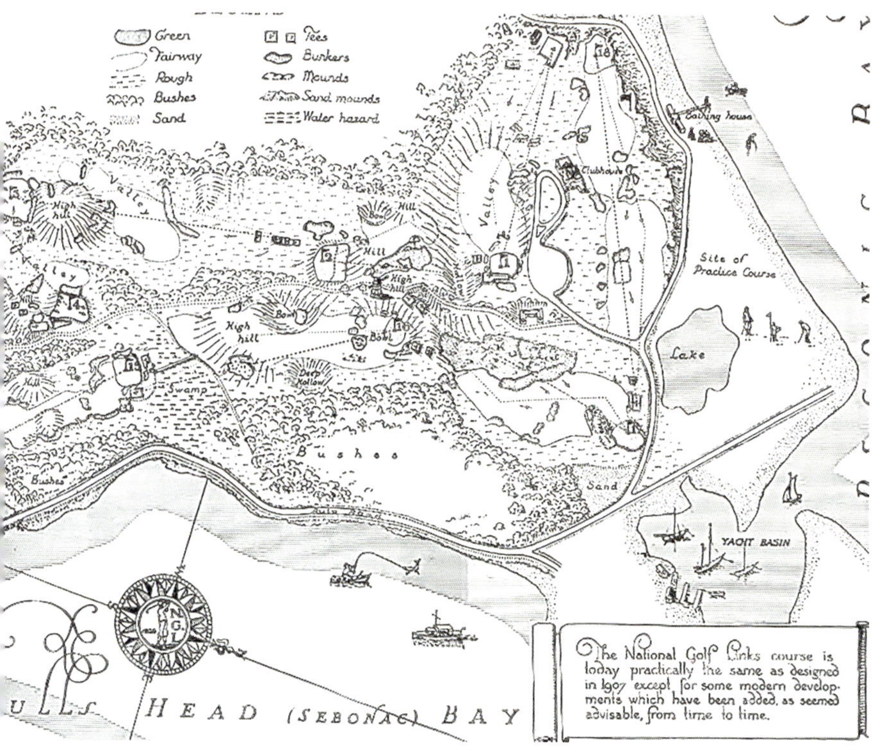

1927 Ryder Cup

The first ever Ryder Cup.

DATE
August 28-29, 1922

LOCATION
Worcester CC
Worcester, MA
USA

PRIZE
The Ryder Cup

IN THE FIELD
Walter Hagen
Leo Diegel
Gene Sarazen
Joe Turnesa
Ted Ray
Arthur Havers
George Duncan

The Ryder Cup may have become one of the world's greatest and most highly anticipated sporting occasions, but it was terribly slow in getting off the ground in the 1920s. Whereas the Walker Cup—a matchplay team competition between amateur teams from the USA and GB & Ireland—had one dry run before slotting into the schedule relatively easily the year after the "rehearsal," the professional version would need two previews before getting underway. Seven years elapsed between the initial idea being circulated and the first official shot in a Ryder Cup being played, in fact.

One of the very earliest seeds was planted by an American by the name of James D. Harnett who worked as the circulation manager for *Golf Illustrated*, a New York-based magazine founded in 1914. Harnett was able to convince the publication's editorial staff that, because American athletes had excelled in other sports around the world, it was high time they won the "British" Open golf championship, too. The magazine, therefore, penned a letter, dated September 27, 1920 and addressed to PGA of America President George Sargent, saying it would pay for a team of 12-20 American professionals to cross the Atlantic in order to play in the Open—the money being raised through the "British Open Championship Fund" to which the magazine's readers could donate $1.

Alex Pirie, Secretary of the PGA of America, said in October that the Association accepted *Golf Illustrated's* proposal, that the PGA would select the team, and that the magazine could "be assured of our hearty co-operation in every way."

The financial assistance enabled 11 Americans players (there was money for 12, but Detroit's Harry

Hampton had, according to the *New York Times*, "decided at the last minute that it would be impossible for him to make the trip.") to go to Britain in 1921—typically, only a couple of players would cross the Atlantic each year—to play in the Open at St Andrews. But it may not account for the match between American and British professionals that occurred two weeks before the Open.

That may be down to a Toledo, Ohio businessman by the name of Sylvanus Jermain, who was a huge promoter of golf in his home city; he developed, or was a consultant at, several Toledo-area golf courses/clubs including the famed Inverness Club, and also served as president of the Ohio, Central States, and Western Golf Associations while simultaneously serving four terms as president/chairman of Toledo's Board of Parks Commissioners and two years as its director of welfare. He had conceived the idea of a contest between American and British professionals and put it to Sargent who told the *Toledo News-Bee* in 1921 that Jermain had "suggested the scheme to me, and I tried to put it across without success."

Also involved was former St Andrean Jock Hutchison, who emigrated to America in 1904 and became a U.S. citizen in 1920. Hutchison and his friend, Laurie Ayton, often spoke of a trans-Atlantic duel between the best players of each country.

Whoever it was, the 11 American professionals set sail for Britain on May 24th. They left a month before the Open as they were scheduled to play in a warm-up event—the "*Glasgow Herald* 1000 Guinea Tournament" on the King's Course at Gleneagles beginning on June 7th. The day before the tournament started, however, U.S. and British professionals met in a match that would feature five foursomes in the morning and 10 singles in the afternoon.

Samuel Ryder

The home side won nine of the matches, the visitors three, and three matches were halved. It was certainly a convincing win for the British golfers, but not altogether surprising when you consider who was included on the team: Harry Vardon, James Braid, J.H. Taylor, Ted Ray, and George Duncan.

Everyone who played received a medal, on which "First international golf match at *The Glasgow Herald* tournament, Gleneagles, 6 June 1921" was inscribed, and the event was deemed a success. Weeks later, three members of the American team would finish in the top 10 at St Andrews: Walter Hagen tied for 6th, Tom Kerrigan was 3rd, and Hutchison won, becoming the first American to win the Claret Jug.

Given how well the match had gone down, it is odd nothing similar happened until 1926. That said, the *Golf Illustrated* funding only happened in 1921, and for the next few years, only Hagen, Hutchison, Macdonald Smith, and Jim Barnes would cross the Atlantic for the Open.

In 1926, however, a larger group of Americans committed to the Championship, and Hagen tried putting another international match together. In February, he planned a contest between two four-man teams but, by the time summer arrived, the scheme had been through a couple of changes, and a seed merchant from St Albans in England had offered to put up a cup for an annual competition. Ultimately, the event would be contested at Wentworth GC, 25 miles west of London, involving two 10-man teams.

U.S.A.	Great Britain
Walter Hagen	Ted Ray
Leo Diegel	Aubrey Boomer
Al Espinosa	Archie Compston
Johnny Farrell	George Duncan
Johnny Golden	George Gadd
Bill Mehlhorn	Arthur Havers
Gene Sarazen	Herbert Jolly
Joe Turnesa	Fred Robson
Al Watrous	Charles Whitcombe

Again, the British side ran out handy winners, taking the match 13-1, despite the fact none of the Great Triumvirate participated. Though most of the press seemed happy to call the event the "Ryder Cup"—after Samuel Ryder, the seed merchant from St. Albans—Ryder actually withdrew his support on the grounds that a large-scale strike in support of British coal miners and the American team's lack of practice time had resulted in a less than satisfying encounter. It was also pointed out that Hagen himself had selected the U.S. team, rather than the PGA of America, and a handful of the U.S. players were born outside the U.S.

Regardless of the outcome, though, enough interest had been created for the matches to become official in 1927. The British PGA and PGA of America settled on the contest's rules creating a Deed of Trust, and arranged the first official match for Worcester Country Club in Massachusetts (venue for the U.S. Open a couple of years before). To accommodate the travel schedules of the British players, the match would take place 10-12 days before the U.S. Open at Oakmont CC. The British edition of *Golf Illustrated* created a similar fund as the American version had in 1921, in order to send a British team to the U.S.

Walter Hagen and Home Advantage

The first Ryder Cup was played over two days, with four 36-hole foursomes matches on Day 1, and eight 36-hole singles matches on Day 2. Each team consisted of nine players, including playing-captains—Walter Hagen for the U.S. and Ted Ray for Great Britain.

Harry Vardon, James Braid, and J.H. Taylor selected the British side which originally included Abe Mitchell—Samuel Ryder's golf instructor and the player whose figure is atop the gold cup. Mitchell had beaten Jim Barnes 8&7 in the singles at Wentworth in 1926 and partnered George Duncan in beating Hagen and Barnes 9&8 in the foursomes. Unfortunately, he was suffering from appendicitis around the time the 1927 team set sail for America, and the 50-year-old Ray replaced him. The Jerseyman raised his team's average age significantly—the nine British players averaged 36.2 years, the Americans 29.1.

The U.S. got off to a quick start on Friday, winning the first three matches. Johnny Farrell and Joe Turnesa played the best golf, defeating the highly favored pair of George Duncan and Archie Compston 8&7. Duncan was an Open champion, and Compston was regarded as a fine match player, having beaten many top players in exhibition matches and winning the British PGA Matchplay Championship in 1925. The only point the British team earned was won by Aubrey Boomer and Charles Whitcombe, who beat Leo Diegel and Bill Mehlhorn 7&5.

The home side, therefore, led 3-1 at the end of Day 1, and they were similarly impressive the next day winning six of the eight singles matches. Duncan was the only British winner, beating Turnesa on the 36th hole, while Whitcombe and Sarazen halved their match (Mehlhorn beat Compston 1-up). Four of the Americans played two and won two, including Hagen who beat 1923 Open Champion Arthur Havers 2&1 in the singles. Whitcombe, who would win the British PGA Matchplay Championship in 1928 and 1930, was the top points-earner for the British with 1½.

In stark contrast to the level of interest the event generates today, the Associated Press' report following the event filled just seven thin lines of newspaper copy.

1929 British Women's Amateur Championship

Joyce Wethered and Glenna Collett meet in a famous final.

DATE
May 27–June 1, 1929

LOCATION
Old Course
St Andrews, Fife
Scotland

PRIZE
Championship
Trophy

IN THE FIELD
Joyce Wethered
Glenna Collett
Enid Wilson
Molly Gourlay
Edith Guedalla
Doris Park

In May 1920, a 19-year-old Joyce Wethered traveled to the English Ladies Amateur Championship at Sheringham Golf Club on the Norfolk coast—about three hours northeast of London, primarily to cheer on her friend, Molly Griffith. Before leaving Surrey for Norfolk, however, she decided that she, too, would probably enter and five days later, Wethered found herself playing in the final against the formidable Cecil Leitch. Leitch had won the British Ladies Amateur Championship in 1914 and again in 1920, and also the English Ladies Championship in 1914 and 1919.

At 6-up after 20 holes of the 36-hole final at Sheringham, Leitch was clearly destined to stop Ms. Wethered's spirited effort and add a third English title to her résumé. Wethered was a very determined young lady, however, and put together a string of birdies over the following holes, finally winning the match 2&1.

The victory would prove not to be a fluke. Wethered won the next four English Ladies Amateur Championships too, and she was almost as dominant at the British championship (established in 1893 by the Ladies Golf Union which merged with the R&A in 2017. Two years later, the event became the Women's Amateur Championship), beating Leitch 9&7 in the 1922 final, and winning again in 1924 and 1925.

Wethered, whose older brother Roger won the (British) Amateur Championship in 1923 and played on the GB & Ireland Walker Cup team five times, stepped back from championship golf following her victory in 1925 at Troon Golf Club (the club received its "Royal" designation in 1978). She rarely competed thereafter, perhaps because she had accomplished so much so quickly and didn't feel a need to continue.

Wethered's decision coincided with the continued rise of Glenna Collett in America. Wethered's junior by 17 months, Collett was born in Connecticut and grew up in Rhode Island. She took up golf at the age of 14 and was playing in the U.S. Women's Amateur Championship a couple of years later. She won it for the first time in 1922, and would claim the USGA's beautiful Robert Cox Trophy five more times in her illustrious career; she also played in, or captained, the U.S. Curtis Cup team on six occasions.

In 1929, Collett entered the British Ladies Amateur Championship, to be played at St Andrews, and Wethered felt similarly compelled to compete, having never played a tournament on the Old Course. The two had met in the third round at Troon in 1925 when Wethered won 4&3. Collett would later say she had met "the finest woman golfer in the world."

Because America's male golfers were beginning to assert a level of dominance at the Open Championship, Bobby Jones was clearly the best player in the world, and the U.S. side had won the first five Walker Cups, the possibility of Collett taking another prized golf trophy back across the Atlantic was an unsavory thought for British golfers. Though Wethered recognized the implications of being in the same tournament as the ascendant Collett, she always maintained that she played because she dearly wanted to experience the Old Course, where she had watched her brother play in the 1923 Walker Cup.

There was surely some truth to that. Wethered wasn't an obnoxious, chest-beating patriotic type, and she always held Collett in high-esteem saying, "Her charm, to my mind, as a golfer and a companion lies in a freedom of spirit which does not make her feel that success is everything in the world."

The British Women's Amateur Trophy

The two would meet in the final, with Wethered the firm favorite. She hadn't been taken past the 15th hole all week (18-hole matches before the 36-hole final), while Collett had struggled with her putter and hadn't given any indication she might give Wethered much of a match.

Roles were very much reversed in the morning's play, however. Though unable to putt with any confidence in the run-up to the final, Collett began holing putts from "all parts of the green." The *Glasgow Herald* stated, "she played the first 11 holes without a single flaw," and Wethered had been "made to look very ordinary."

Collett was 5-up after the first nine holes, played in just 34 strokes. Recalling the match, Wethered wrote in *Golfing Memories and Methods* (1934): "Glenna's first nine holes of the match was the finest sequence of holes I have ever seen a lady play."

The Englishwoman played better over the back nine, reducing Collett's lead to just two holes by the end of the first 18. And then, in the afternoon, Wethered came out and played like the golfer she had been all week, winning six of the first nine holes. After 27 holes, Wethered had turned the earlier five-hole deficit into a 2-up lead. She closed out the match on the 17th green, winning 3&1 to record her fourth British Ladies Amateur title—in front of 5,000 rowdy fans.

Wethered retired from golf again, although she did play (and captain) in the 1932 Curtis Cup at Wentworth Golf Club outside London, beating Collett (who had married in 1931 becoming Glenna Collett-Vare) 6&4 in the singles. Also, during the Great Depression, she worked in the golf department of the Fortnum & Mason store in London. And she would tour North America in 1935, playing 200 exhibition matches with the likes of Bobby Jones, Walter Hagen, Gene Sarazen, Francis Ouimet, Jess Sweetser, Tommy Armour, and Babe Zaharias. During the tour, she broke 34 course records, impressing everyone who watched. Jones always regarded Wethered's swing as one of the best he ever saw, once noting, "I have not played golf with anyone, man or woman, amateur or professional, who made me feel so utterly outclassed."

In 1937, Wethered married Sir John Heathcoat-Amory, becoming Lady Heathcoat-Amory. She moved to her husband's family estate—Knightshayes Court in Devon, and lived there for the rest of her life. In 1951, she became the first president of the English Ladies Golf Association, and in her later years, she developed into an expert and renowned gardener.

Glenna Collett (left) and Joyce Wethered (right) at St Andrews

1930 U.S. Amateur

Bobby Jones wins the "Impregnable Quadrilateral."

DATE
Sept. 22-27, 1930

LOCATION
Merion GC
Ardmore, PA
USA

PRIZE
Havemeyer Trophy

IN THE FIELD
Bobby Jones
Eugene Homans
Jess Sweetser
Max Marston
Jimmy Johnston

In 1916, Bobby Jones played at Merion Golf Club in Philadelphia for the first time. He had won the inaugural Georgia State Amateur Championship a few weeks before and had been invited by the USGA to the U.S. Amateur—which was remarkable, given that he was just 14.

Barely into his teens, Jones was playing against seasoned competitors twice his age. He qualified for match play and then beat his first two opponents—1906 champion Eben Byers 4&2 and Frank Dyer by the same scoreline—before going out in the third round (quarter-finals) 4&3 to Robert Gardner, the defending champion who had also won in 1909. Jones had gotten a taste of big-time golf and seen first-hand a course that was to play a huge part in his golf career.

Robert Tyre Jones Jr. was born on March 17, 1902 in Grant Park, Atlanta. A sickly child, he wasn't able to eat solid foods until he was five, but still won his first golf tournament at East Lake—the Atlanta Athletic Club's original golf course—at the age of six. He was encouraged to play by his doctor and his father, a fine athlete and lawyer known as the "Colonel," and he modeled his swing on that of Stewart Maiden, the club's professional who had emigrated from Carnoustie, Scotland in 1908. Jones never had a formal lesson but learned the game by watching professionals Maiden, Willie Ogg, and J. Douglas Edgar.

Jones spent teenage summers at a boarding house across the street from the golf course so he could avoid the daily journey from downtown Atlanta and get as much golf in as possible.

In 1917 and 1918, he toured the U.S. with fellow East Lake players Alexa Stirling and Perry Adair, playing large exhibitions to raise funds for World War I relief—an experience that surely helped him feel comfortable in front of the large galleries he would attract as his star continued to rise.

Later in 1918, he began a degree in mechanical engineering at Georgia Tech, and the following year, at the age of 17, he made it to the final of the U.S. Amateur at Oakmont CC. In 1920, he qualified for his first U.S. Open, finishing tied for 8th at Inverness Club, four shots behind winner Ted Ray.

At Georgia Tech, he played on the Varsity team, lettering all four years, and also met his future wife, Mary Malone, whom he'd marry in 1924. After graduating in 1922, he studied English literature at Harvard, and in August, he played in the first of five Walker Cups (he was on the winning side all five times, twice as playing captain.)

After tying for 5th in 1921 and 2nd in 1922, Jones won his first U.S. Open in 1923 at Inwood Country Club on Long Island. He defeated Bobby Cruikshank, a Scot who had emigrated to the U.S. two years before, in a playoff. A year later, he completed his undergraduate degree at Harvard and celebrated his return to Merion GC by winning the U.S. Amateur, defeating George Von Elm 9&8 in the final—an impressive victory over a respected opponent. (Utah's Von Elm would win the U.S. Amateur in 1926, have three top-five finishes at the U.S. Open and a tie for 3rd at the Open Championship, and won five times on the PGA Tour—twice as an amateur and three times after turning professional in 1930.)

At 22, Jones had earned two undergraduate degrees, and was already a U.S. Open and U.S. Amateur champion. He'd won other prestigious amateur titles and had represented the U.S. in international matches against Canada and in the Walker Cup. Really though, he was only just getting started.

A successful defense of the U.S. Amateur title came in 1925, after beating fellow East Lake member Watts Gunn, 8&7, in the final at Oakmont CC. And in 1926, he won both the U.S. Open (Scioto CC) and the Open Championship (Royal Lytham & St Anne's)—the first of three Open Championship titles. And, in case you thought he was beginning to stray from academia in favor of pursuing golf, he enrolled at Emory University's School of Law, passing the Georgia Bar exam after just three semesters, and subsequently joined his father's law firm.

Thankfully, the "Colonel" and the company's other partners gave Jones time off work to play golf, and he surely repaid the gesture by continuing to gather trophies and attract nothing but positive publicity. In 1927, he won his third U.S. Amateur in four years, plus the Open Championship on the Old Course at St Andrews, where he had won his singles match against Cyril Tolley, 12&11, in the previous year's Walker Cup, and where he had played for the first time in 1921. That was the year it is often said he tore up his scorecard and stormed off the course after failing to escape the "Hill" Bunker at the 11th hole in the third round. In reality, he actually just picked up his ball, thus intentionally disqualifying himself, and continued playing. It was the impetuous move of a 19-year-old still prone to moments of on-course anger, but it wasn't quite the meltdown many think he had.

Next came two of his most lopsided victories—a 10&9 win over England's Phil Perkins in the final of the 1928 U.S. Amateur (Brae Burn CC) and, in 1929, a 23-stroke victory over Al Espinosa in a 36-hole playoff for the U.S. Open (Winged Foot).

By the age of 28, therefore, Bobby Jones had toured the U.S. raising money for the U.S. war effort, been married for six years and had two children (a third would arrive in 1931), earned two degrees and passed the Georgia Bar exam as a student at Emory, worked as a lawyer for two years, won four U.S. Amateur Championships and three Southern Amateurs, and had three U.S. Open trophies on his shelf as well as two Claret Jugs.

Jones receives the trophy

And then 1930 happened.

In May, he played in the Walker Cup at Royal St. George's GC in England, where he won his foursomes match with partner Oscar Willing

8&7, and his singles 9&8 over Roger Wethered. Being in Britain, he was able to enter the Amateur Championship at St Andrews, the first leg of a four-Championship goal he'd first conceived in 1926: winning the Open and Amateur Championships of both the U.S. and Britain.

Back at the Old Course for the first time since winning the 1927 Open Championship, Jones beat Cyril Tolley in the fourth round, reigning U.S. Amateur champion Jimmy Johnston in the fifth, and Wethered, again, in the final to win the Championship for the first and only time. Having disliked the Old Course on his first visit, Jones had come to love and respect it as he did the town and its inhabitants; decades later in 1958, he was awarded the Freedom of the Burgh of St Andrews in an emotional ceremony, during which he said, "I could take out of my life everything except my experiences at St Andrews and I'd still have a rich, full life." Three weeks later, he won the Open for a third time, beating Leo Diegel and Macdonald Smith by two at Royal Liverpool.

Returning to the U.S., he was given his second ticker-tape reception in New York City (the first was in 1926) and, after a few weeks of rest in Atlanta, he was on his way to Minneapolis for the U.S. Open at Interlachen CC. There, he endured 100+-degree heat—he lost 17lbs—but won the Championship with a score of 287. He was the only player to finish the tournament under par.

Incredibly, Jones was three-quarters of the way to his ambitious target—something that *Atlanta Journal* golf writer and Jones' great friend O.B. Keeler had coined, "The Grand Slam."

Jones traveled back to Atlanta the day after the U.S. Open and was greeted by 125,000 fans who lined the city's streets to celebrate—a parade that culminated at Georgia Tech, where a number of speeches were given. Jones rested at home for four weeks preparing for the U.S. Amateur—the final event on his 1930 "to do" list, and which was to be played at a familiar venue: Merion.

As he had done five times before at the U.S. Amateur, Jones began the event by taking medalist honors, shooting 71, 73, which equaled his own record for lowest qualifying score. In the matchplay section (18-hole matches in the first two rounds, 36 the rest of the way), he was similarly dominant, never once being taken past the 14th or 32nd hole.

In the first round, he beat Canada's Charles Ross Somerviille (1932 U.S. Amateur winner), 5&4. In the Round of 16, he faced fellow Harvard graduate Fred Hoblitzell, whom he also beat 5&4. Fay Coleman was his quarter-final victim, going down 6&5, and then in the semi-final, Jones met his friend Jess Sweetser, to whom he had lost heavily in the semi-final eight years previously (Sweetser was the first American to win the British Amateur Championship—1926—and played on four Walker Cup teams alongside Jones.) This time, however, Jones was more or less unbeatable, winning 9&8. The *Philadelphia Inquirer* stated that "Built around Jones is the legend that you can beat him once, but never twice."

The victory put him in the final, where he would meet New Jersey's Eugene Homans. Described as "bespectacled, slim, and scholarly looking, even a bit anemic," Homans wasn't given much of a chance, despite his spirited play in getting to the final.

Not surprisingly, perhaps, Homans found himself 7-down to Jones after the morning 18. Jones was steady—if unspectacular—when play resumed, and he eventually took the match 8&7. It was his fifth U.S. Amateur title and fourth major of the season (Amateur Championship, Open Championship, U.S. Open, U.S. Amateur). He had won O.B. Keeler's Grand Slam, and as George Trevor called it in the *New York Sun*, the "Impregnable Quadrilateral."

It was the great sportswriter, Grantland Rice, who summed up Jones' achievement the best: "It was doubly interesting to recall the 14-year-old kid of 1916 who started on this course [Merion] making his all-time Championship stand at the age of 28. He had traveled over 120,000 miles to reach this spot. He had fought from St Andrews to Pebble Beach, from the North Sea to the Pacific, but he had piled up a record this generation will never see equaled."

Rice's prediction was right, and no one has equaled the feat since. Ben Hogan came very close in 1953 winning the Masters, U.S. Open and Open Championship in the same season (see pages 132-5), and Tiger Woods won what was labeled the "Tiger Slam" across the 2000-01 seasons (see page 204-9), but Jones remains the only player to have won the Grand Slam in one season.

Made Merion

Merion Golf Club is one of America's most historic Golf Clubs and home to one of its greatest courses. The club was formed in 1896 by members of the Merion Cricket Club, two miles from where the cricket club is now located.

Merion's golf club became a separate entity in 1941 and has hosted five U.S. Opens—1935 (Olin Dutra), 1950 (Ben Hogan), 1971 (Lee Trevino), 1981 (David Graham), and 2013 (Justin Rose). Merion will host the championship again in 2030, 2040, and 2050.

There were originally nine holes, but thanks to gaining access to new land (provided by Clement Grissom, owner of the Red Star Line that owned the Titanic) and a significant increase in play, the club decided in 1910 that it needed two new courses. It chose club member and Princeton graduate, Hugh Wilson, to design them.

The East Course—the stage for the U.S. Open—opened in 1912 on a tight 126 acres formerly occupied by the original course. Wilson had no experience as a designer, so he spent seven months in Great Britain studying the great courses and his Merion designs were inspired by what he saw overseas. To create a championship course—one invariably ranked among the 10 best in the U.S. on so small a site, and with no prior experience—was a huge achievement.

Because it's situated on a small acreage and because the U.S. Open was becoming so big an event, the club didn't host the Championship in the 1990s or 2000s as the course was considered too short and the property too small for crowds and infrastructure. The hope that it would one day host the U.S. Open again never disappeared altogether, however, and thanks to a committed effort by the club and USGA, it did so again in 2013. It's anyone's guess how it will survive in 2030, '40, and '50 with further technological advancements to equipment; one hopes suitable regulations will be in place before the U.S. Open returns.

Wicker basket pin at Merion

The club's outdoor patio sits right alongside the East Course's 1st tee, and the course's flags are wicker baskets (thought to have something to do with the sheep herders Wilson encountered in Britain. Their staffs had wicker baskets at the end, in which they kept their lunch). The West Course, separated from the East by half a mile and, likewise regarded very highly, opened in 1914.

1934 Masters

Inaugural tournament at Bobby Jones' Augusta National GC.

DATE
March 22-25,1934

LOCATION
Augusta National
Augusta, GA
USA

PRIZE
$1,500

IN THE FIELD
Bobby Jones
Walter Hagen
Macdonald Smith
Leo Diegel
Johnny Farrell
Joe Turnesa
Al Espinosa
Craig Wood
Denny Shute
Bobby Cruikshank

After retiring from competitive golf following his incredible Grand Slam in 1930, Bobby Jones did not have to look hard for things to do. He worked with the Spalding company to produce a set of steel-shafted clubs—the irons would have thicker heads than virtually every other blade on the market, giving them a softer, less brittle feel. Though not a born adversarial courtroom lawyer, he continued working intermittently for his father's law firm. He had business interests in Coca-Cola bottling plants in the U.S., Scotland, and South America. He made 18 instructional golf films for Warner Brothers that were shown in movie theaters throughout the U.S. He continued to write for the Jack Wheeler Bell Syndicate, which distributed his columns to over 200 newspapers (previously, the USGA had allowed him to make money from writing despite being an amateur, and his hugely successful book, *Down the Fairway,* was published in 1927.) And then there was the project that appealed to him the most: there were no guarantees it would work, especially with the nation's economy in such turmoil, and he certainly had no experience in anything like this, but he relished the idea of establishing a private golf club with a first-rate course in the South.

Jones' fame and appeal would help attract the sort of wealthy investors and attention his vision required to get off the ground, but he'd also need a driven, no-nonsense businessman to deal with the details, preferably someone who cared more about getting things done than making friends along the way.

The Man Behind the Curtain

Born in Iowa in 1894, Clifford Roberts left school at the age of 15 to work on the family farm. He held numerous other short-lived jobs before becoming a traveling menswear salesman, covering an area that spanned much of the Midwest.

At 23, he enlisted with the Army Medical Corps and spent a year or so toward the end of World War I driving ambulances in Paris. On his return to the U.S., he continued to sell suits and did so with such success his employer let him spend extended periods in California with his grandfather.

Because he hadn't gone to college, Roberts devoured his grandfather's extensive book collection, paying particular attention to biographies of the rich and famous. A successful salesman with a head full of knowledge, he started speculating in oil leases. In 1921, almost four years after returning from Europe and seeking a new life in New York, one of these enterprises came through, earning him $50,000—an enormous amount of money at the time. The windfall enabled Roberts to acquire a 1/6 share (17%) in the brokerage firm of Reynolds & Company, and he opened an office on Broadway.

Roberts had first encountered golf caddying as a teen in California, and now—seeing the potential playing the game had in furthering his career—he became a member at Knollwood CC, 30 miles north of Wall Street, where he could befriend wealthy New Yorkers who'd become his clients. At Knollwood, he met Walter Marshall who ran Vanderbilt hotels, a group of properties that included the Bon Air Vanderbilt in Augusta, Georgia.

Through Marshall, Roberts would visit Augusta for the weather, the golf, and because it was an easy, overnight train ride from New York. He played at Augusta CC, where he met other wealthy individuals, and would be introduced to Bobby Jones, who was a regular guest at the Bon Air for many years.

They became friends—though Roberts was as much an idolizing fan as he was a pal and confidant—and throughout the late 1920s, Jones often mentioned how he'd like to build a great course in the South. The two of them committed to making it happen.

In January 1931, the Bon Air paid $5,000 for an option to buy a 365-acre tract a few miles northwest of downtown Augusta. And in June, a group consisting of Roberts, Marshall, Augusta businessmen Fielding Wallace and Thomas Barrett (future mayor of the city), and Bobby Jones' father created a real-estate company called Fruitland Manor Corporation, which paid $15,000 in cash and took on

$60,000 of the previous owner's debt to purchase the property. The plan was that the golf club Bobby Jones hoped to create—Augusta National GC—would lease about half of the land, while the Fruitland Manor Corporation would sell or develop the rest.

Roberts became the chairman of the Golf Club and handled the task of attracting new members—an arduous job during the Great Depression. The initial plans for the club (two courses, a palatial clubhouse, lots for grand residences, etc.) were far more extravagant than what was eventually built. And the hope was that 1,800 individuals from all over the country and overseas would sign up. Howver, it took a few years before the club's membership roster included 100 names.

Roberts tried all manner of ways to find members, including sending introductory letters to 13,000 past guests of the Bon Air Vanderbilt, with precious little success. Just about the only people who could persuade people to join were Jones himself and Grantland Rice—the country's most prominent sportswriter, a great admirer of Jones, and one of the club's earliest members.

In February 1933, shortly after the course opened, Prescott Bush played Augusta National twice. A Wall Street attorney and the chairman of the USGA's Championship Committee (and

Early ANGC aerial shows original 9th (now 18th) green [left], and 18th (now 9th) green [right].

also the father of George H.W. Bush who would become the 41st U.S. president), Bush was obviously in a position of some power within the game and was seriously considering Augusta National as host site for the 1934 U.S. Open. Jones and Roberts invited him to the club hoping he'd go ahead with the idea, as the coverage would show Augusta National in a positive light and no doubt attract new members.

They were desperately disappointed, therefore, when the USGA wrote to say that, though it liked the idea of Augusta National hosting, 1934 was perhaps too soon.

Roberts came up with a possible solution—Augusta National could host its own tournament. And if Jones—still the most famous golfer in the world despite having retired from competition—could be persuaded to play, the event would certainly bring the club the attention it so badly needed. Jones liked the idea and decided it would be a fairly small invitational to which he would invite friends he had made during his competitive years.

To cut a long story short, the tournament survived the 1930s and '40s, despite the continuing economic crisis (which, according to most financial commentators, lasted from 1929 to 1940), several years of bad weather, Jones' deteriorating skills, and the strain of World War II, thanks largely to Roberts' efforts. He may have come across as something of a stern misanthrope who ruled the club and tournament with an unsmiling severity, but there's no question the Masters would look very different today were it not for his sacrifices, wisdom, and devotion.

MacKenzie's 1932 plan

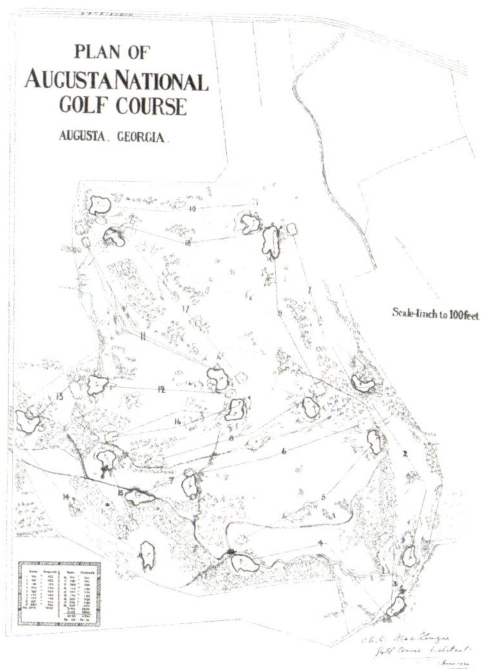

Fruitland

In 1853, Irish-born indigo farmer Dennis Redmond purchased 315 acres outside of Augusta, where he grew fruit trees as well as indigo plants—source of the dark-blue dye used to color fabrics. He also began construction of a magnificent house he called Fruitland Manor. Four years later, Redmond sold a 50% stake in the business to Belgian horticulturalist Louis Berckmans and his son, Prosper. In 1858, the Berckmanses became the sole owners, completed work on the manor house, and established Fruitland Nurseries where they grew many plants suited to the Georgia climate, including azaleas, magnolias, and camellias.

Following Prosper Berckmans' death in 1910, the family struggled to maintain the nursery, which eventually closed

MacKenzie's the Man

An *Augusta Chronicle* article on July 15, 1931 announced Jones' intention of building his ideal course, and it included a photograph of golf course architect Alister MacKenzie with a set of plans. Jones explained in his statement in the newspaper, "I am not having this dream alone or without expert collaboration. Dr. MacKenzie is the man who will actually design the course. His name needs no presentation to the American golfing public or the golfers of the world."

Though it's thought Jones might have met MacKenzie during the 1926 Walker Cup in St Andrews, no such meeting was ever chronicled. What certainly is known, however, is that Jones got his first taste of MacKenzie's architectural talents in September 1929, after losing in the first round of the U.S. Amateur at Pebble Beach. It may have been a fortuitous early exit, as Jones' shocking defeat to Johnny Goodman gave him the opportunity to check out a new private club a mile away: Cypress Point Club had been designed by MacKenzie.

MacKenzie had been hired by Marion Hollins, the 1921 U.S. Women's Amateur champion who worked for Del Monte Properties. While working on Cypress Point, Hollins had been looking for her own California property to develop and found it 50 miles to the north, in Santa Cruz. Again, she called on MacKenzie to design its doors in 1918. The land went unused for a few years before businessman, J. Perry Stoltz, purchased it in early 1925. Stoltz owned the successful Fleetwood Hotel in Miami, and he devised plans to build a second Fleetwood hotel on the Augusta land, as well as a golf course. In September, however, shortly after the foundations for Stoltz's new, $2 million hotel project had been laid, a hurricane all but demolished the original Fleetwood in Miami Beach, and Stoltz would wind up going bankrupt. The land again went undeveloped until July 1931, when it was announced it had been purchased by the group that intended to build Bobby Jones' ideal golf course.

Thomas Barrett had alerted Clifford Roberts to the property, knowing he was seeking somewhere suitable for Jones' course, and recognizing what the benefits of building it in Augusta

the golf course. She named it Pasatiempo (Spanish for 'pastime'), and on opening day, September 8, 1929, she played an exhibition match alongside British Amateur champion Cyril Tolley, reigning U.S. Women's Amateur champion Glenna Collett, and Jones, who had been extremely impressed with the design of Cypress Point and would be similarly smitten with Pasatiempo. Having enjoyed both courses immensely, Jones was certain MacKenzie was the right man to design his course in Georgia. MacKenzie first visited the site in July 1931 to stake out the holes. He returned in the fall to finalize the routing and construction got underway in February 1932.

Building the Augusta National course took little time, as good weather prevailed, and construction manager Wendell Miller had an army of local workers at his disposal. Due to the hard economic times, plenty of men were looking for employment and willing to work for as little as 25 cents a day. A lot of the elements required to build a course—topsoil, equipment, seed, and so on—were donated or sold to Miller at a discount, because it was Bobby Jones' course.

After MacKenzie returned to the Augusta site in March/April 1933 to ensure the last of the greens were built to his specifications, the course was seeded, then mown for the first time in June. Jones played his first round in August, and afterward he cabled Roberts in New York to share how pleased he was.

might be. Jones had reluctantly agreed the site should be in Augusta, and not his hometown of Atlanta, as Augusta's winters were significantly milder owing to a 1,000-foot drop in elevation, and there was a chance he'd find a modicum more privacy there.

Jones had no doubt been aware of the property when playing at Augusta Country Club on the other side of the boundary fence, but he hadn't seen it all and hadn't been down the magnolia-lined lane that led to the manor house. When, at last, he did in 1931, he was struck by its beauty. "The rare trees and shrubs of the old nursery were enchanting," he'd write in his 1960 book, *Golf is My Game*. "But when I walked out on the grass terrace under the big trees behind the house and looked down over

It's In the Hole!

One important player missing from the field in 1934 was Gene Sarazen, who—with six major championship victories and seven other top-three finishes in the Grand Slam events—was at the time probably considered the best player in the world. He initially accepted an invitation to play in the first Augusta National Invitational from club member Alfred Bourne, but Sarazen had to withdraw shortly before the event due to a prior engagement to which he had committed. One wonders if Sarazen would have played had the invitation come from Jones.

Sarazen and Australian professional Joe Kirkwood gave lessons at the Miami Biltmore Hotel during the winter, becoming good friends. Sarazen suggested they tour South America together to play in exhibitions, and Kirkwood made the arrangements. Unfortunately, the trip's dates coincided with the Augusta National event, and the South American plans couldn't be changed.

Sarazen always regretted not playing in 1934, and made absolutely sure he would be available the following year. After three rounds of the 1935 tournament, Sarazen was in 4th place, three shots behind leader Craig Wood. Since the leaders didn't necessarily go out last in those days, Wood played the final round a few groups ahead of Sarazen, and after a few early bogeys, it looked like he was giving the tournament away. But he came back strongly on the second nine and finished with a birdie three to post 6-under 282. Back on the 14th, Sarazen and his playing partner Walter Hagen heard the roar from the 18th and Hagen remarked that, at three shots back with just four holes to play, Sarazen's chances had probably gone. Sarazen is reported to have replied, "Oh I don't know, they might go in from anywhere."

Gene Sarazen

But he needed something good to happen quickly. At the 485-yard par-five 15th, he hit a fine drive down the middle and, with about 230 yards to the hole, chose a 4-wood. He struck the ball cleanly and watched as it bounced a yard or two in front of the green before rolling unerringly into the hole for an albatross (double-eagle) two. Immediately, Sarazen drew level with Wood. And he parred the last three holes to finish tied with Wood at 6-under-par. They would meet for a 36-hole playoff the following day—a playoff Sarazen won by five shots with rounds of 71 and 73. Sarazen's second to the 15th became known as "the shot heard around the world," and it helped put the tournament on the map and secure its future.

The debate over how many people actually witnessed it has continued for over 90 years. O.B. Keeler said in the *Atlanta Journal* that a "huge" gallery followed Sarazen that day, while the syndicated Grantland Rice wrote that a "gallery of 2,000 was banked back of Sarazen and packed back of the green." Sarazen, however, later said only 50 or so were there—quite a difference from Rice's estimate. Knowing Rice was a great friend of Bobby Jones and a hugely influential member of Augusta National, who would have desperately wanted the tournament to succeed, one could be forgiven for thinking his number was a little ... padded.

Sarazen's win was the seventh and last of his major victories, and it made him the first player to win the career Grand Slam—though he wouldn't have known it as that, of course. This was only five years after Jones' "Impregnable Quadrilateral," and the four majors that we know today—the Modern Grand Slam—weren't yet regarded as the Grand Slam events.

the property, the experience was unforgettable. It seemed that this land had been lying here for years waiting for someone to lay a golf course upon it."

Despite the fact everyone besides Jones thought the tournament should be called The Masters—numerous newspapers actually referred to it as the "Masters Open"—its official name until 1939 would be the "Augusta National Invitational." Jones thought "The Masters" sounded a little big-headed, preferring to go with something more understated.

The first tournament would be held in late spring (1934 was the only time it was played entirely in March. In 1935, it moved to April. In 1939, it began at the end of March and finished in April) partly to avoid any latent winter chill. It would be a strokeplay (medal) event, contested over four rounds, and the field would be kept relatively small to ensure members could get out before the tournament's first tee time and that there was no great rush to get everyone around. Jones would personally invite players, making it harder for them to skip the event—the club needed as many well-known golfers to attend as possible in order to maximize ticket sales—and who would turn down an invitation from Jones himself?

Seventy-two players teed it up in the 1934 event, including Jones who attracted the largest galleries of fans (patrons) who had been starved of seeing their hero play competitive golf for four years. Though the vast majority of people wanted to see him win again, not many expected him to contend. In a syndicated column for United News, player Paul Runyan, who had already won three times that year and had claimed nine titles in 1933, said the game had passed Jones by, and that he stood little chance of competing: "Playing the tournaments now are youngsters capable of far more brilliant golf than that shown by the men whom Jones defeated with such regularity when he was an active player," Runyan wrote.

It seemed he might have a point after Jones began with a 4-over-par 76 on the 6,700-yard course that put him in a tie for 33rd. Conditions hadn't been great, admittedly, but still it wasn't what the galleries were hoping for. Three players led after 2-under 70s: Horton Smith, Jimmy Hines, and Emmet French. Walter Hagen, now 41, shot 71 and was tied for 4th. In the second round, the club's professional, Ed Dudley, shot 69 to climb into a tie for 2nd, just one shot behind Smith. Meanwhile, Jones shot 74, and Hagen had a 76.

A 25-year-old from Chicago, Smith maintained his one-shot lead in Round 3 with another 70, while Jones shot 72. Billy Burke was in 2nd, and Hagen got back into contention.

In the final round, Smith, who had beaten Jones by a shot at the 1930 Savannah Open, shot another steady 72 to win the tournament with a 4-under score of 284. Craig Wood finished a shot back in 2nd, and tied for 3rd were Burke and Runyan. Hagen tied Jones and Densmore Shute for 13th at 6-over-par, 10 shots back of the winner.

Jones didn't seem dissatisfied with his performance. "I would have enjoyed myself more if I had got a few more of those short putts down," he said. "But I had a good time anyway, and hope the rest of the fellows did."

Since the club was still having a hard time with its finances, a hat had to be passed around the wealthiest members to meet the $5,000 purse, and only the top 12 finished in the money.

As we watch the Masters today, it's hard to imagine the club once suffered relatively hard times. The glorious course conditions we've become accustomed to seeing each year, the tournament's enormous purse ($21 million in 2025), the size of the merchandise 'tent' and the huge range of items available, and numerous other aspects of the tournament don't exactly suggest it's suffering any hardship or that the club is having trouble persuading people to join. Masters enthusiasts recognize Bobby Jones' popularity as contributing significantly to the survival of both the club and tournament, but our sincerest thanks should perhaps go to Clifford Roberts, whose tenacity was largely responsible for getting Augusta National and the Masters through the Great Depression and World War II.

Clifford Roberts and Bobby Jones at the Masters

1945 Glen Garden Open

Byron Nelson wins his 18th title of the season.

DATE
Dec. 14-16, 1945

LOCATION
Glen Garden CC
Fort Worth, TX
USA

PRIZE
$2,000

IN THE FIELD
Byron Nelson
Ben Hogan
Sam Snead
Jimmy Demaret
Jug McSpaden
Dutch Harrison
Joe Kirkwood

Between March 8 and August 4, 1945, Byron Nelson teed it up on the PGA Tour 11 times. Having already won three tournaments and finished 2nd at five more throughout January and February, he was in quite a rich vein of form already that season, and would certainly have been expecting a successful run through spring and summer. Winning all 11 of those tournaments—a stretch that included his fifth and final major (the PGA Championship)—was somewhat unexpected, though.

The final victory in the unlikely sequence was a four-stroke win at the Canadian Open played at the Thornhill Club in suburban Toronto. But, though his run had come to an end, he would still win four more times in 1945, making a grand total of 18 tournament victories that season.

In September, Nelson finished 2nd at the Portland Open, 14 shots behind Ben Hogan, who set the PGA Tour scoring record with 261. Asked how long that record might last, Nelson said, "Well, you don't know in this game. It could be forever, it could be a week." Actually, it was two.

Nelson would win the Seattle Open at Broadmoor Golf Club (his 17th win of the year) two weeks later, with rounds of 62, 68, 63, and 66, to establish a new scoring record of 259 which would stand for 10 years.

Nelson's 18th win of his epic season came nine days before Christmas, in biting cold at the Glen Garden Open in Fort Worth, Texas. The eight-stroke victory (the 45th of his 52 PGA Tour wins) was obviously extremely satisfying for Nelson, who beat Sam Snead by 13 shots and Hogan by 14, but the fact it had come at the course where he caddied as a youngster made it extra special.

Born in 1912, Nelson had moved with his family to Fort Worth when he was 11 and, the following year, he began carrying bags at Glen Garden G&CC six miles south of downtown. There, at the age of 14, he beat another young boy named Ben Hogan in a caddie tournament. And 19 years later, Nelson would cap off a sensational season by shooting 11-under-par 273 for four rounds, giving him a scoring average for the 120 competitive rounds he played that year of 68.33. His final round average of 67.68 was even more remarkable.

There are those who put an asterisk next to Nelson's accomplishments that year, saying fields were still slightly weak due to World War II—the war in Europe officially ended in May, while the conflict in the Pacific and Asia dragged on until September. Nelson was unable to join the military owing to a condition that caused his blood to clot four times slower than normal. "It wasn't hemophilia," he wrote in his 1993 autobiography *How I Played the Game*, "but what was called free-bleeding. ... After I failed the physical the second time, they didn't call me anymore. So there we were [Nelson and his friend Jug McSpaden who also failed the physical], looking as healthy as could be but not in uniform like the rest of the boys. It was an uncomfortable feeling, believe me." Nelson and McSpaden contributed as best they could, however, crisscrossing the U.S. four times between the end of 1942 and 1944, putting on 110 exhibitions for the Red Cross and USO.

As for the asterisk, there probably is a modicum of justification for it; but, in his book, Nelson said he thought his 68.33 scoring averge spoke for itself. Additionally, the average winning margin in the 16 individual strokeplay events he won was an astonishing 6.25 strokes. "Despite the fact some of the boys were in uniform for part of the year," he wrote, "most of them were playing at least part of the time. Snead played in 26 events, Hogan 18, Dutch Harrison at least 13, and so forth."

Ranking Nelson's Year

Was Byron Nelson's 1945 season the greatest ever in the history of professional golf?

It's certainly in the conversation, but there's some stiff competition. Bobby Jones' 1930 Grand Slam season would be many people's choice; as would Ben Hogan's in 1953 when he won the Masters, U.S. Open, and Open Champioship ; or Tiger Woods' 2000 year—the U.S. Open by 15 shots, Open Championship by eight, the PGA Championship in a playoff, six other PGA Tour victories, and 17 top-fives in 20 tournaments.

Other phenomenal seasons include Jack Nicklaus' in 1972, when he won the Masters and U.S. Open, finished 2nd at the Open Championship and had five other PGA Tour victories; Woods' in 2006 (Open Championship, PGA Championship, two World Golf Championships, and four other PGA Tour events); Arnold Palmer's in 1962 (Masters, Open Championship, playoff loss at U.S. Open, and six other PGA Tour wins), and Hogan's in 1948 (U.S. Open, PGA Championship, and eight other PGA Tour wins).

The top four are probably Jones (1930), Woods (2000), Hogan (1953), and Nelson (1945). How you rank them depends on what vintage you are, which tournaments you regard as the most important, how important the size of the winning margin is to you, and what the obstacles to victory might have been: strength of field, amount of press/public pressure and expectation, injury, amount of travel, tournament draw, and so on.

Byron Nelson

1946 U.S. Women's Open

Patty Berg wins the inaugural championship.

DATE
Aug. 26-Sept. 1, 1946

LOCATION
Spokane CC
Spokane, WA
USA

PRIZE
$5,600
in war bonds

IN THE FIELD
Patty Berg
Betty Jameson
Betty Hicks
Babe Zaharias

The U.S. Women's Amateur Championship was first played in 1895, two years after the Ladies' Golf Union had held the inaugural Ladies' British Open Amateur Championship (now the Women's Amateur Championship organized by the R&A). Over their formative years, and even after World War II, both events were considered prestigious and created a number of star players, including Beatrix Hoyt, Margaret Curtis, Alexa Stirling, Virginia Van Wie, Glenna Collett, Babe Didrickson Zaharias, Betty Jameson, and Patty Berg in the U.S.; and Margaret Scott, Cecil Leitch, Dorothy Campbell, Enid Wilson, and the great Joyce Wethered in the U.K.

By the mid-1940s in the U.S., there was sufficient interest and momentum to form a professional golfers' association for women. The first such organization that sought to create and finance professional tournaments was the Women's Professional Golf Association (WPGA), founded in late 1944 by Hope Seignious, Betty Hicks, and Ellen Griffin.

The spark that had incited these women to create their own enterprise came in August of that year, when Hicks won $500 in the women's event at the All American Open played at Tam O'Shanter CC, just north of Chicago—28 times less than what Byron Nelson had earned for winning the men's competition.

Despite receiving some financial assistance from Wilson Sporting Goods, the WPGA struggled to attract sufficient revenue to survive for very long, and the association officially closed shop in 1949.

Though its life was short, the WPGA accomplished two very important goals. First, it laid the ground work for the formation of the Ladies Professional

Golf Association (LPGA) founded by 13 women—Alice Bauer, Patty Berg, Bettye Danoff, Helen Dettweiler, Marlene Bauer Hagge, Helen Hicks, Opal Hill, Betty Jameson, Sally Sessions, Marilynn Smith, Shirley Spork, Louise Suggs, and Babe Didrickson Zaharias—and initiated with the help of golf promoter, tournament director, and player agent, Fred Corcoran. Its first season (1950) consisted of 14 tournaments worth a total of $50,000. And second, it organized the first ever U.S. Women's Open Championship in 1946, retaining control the first three years before the LPGA took over.

TOP: Betty Jameson. BOTTOM LEFT: Louise Suggs. BOTTOM RIGHT: Bettye Danoff.

The fledgling professional tour then ran it until 1953 when the USGA assumed control, in an effort to promote the event more widely and give it a firmer financial footing.

The inaugural U.S. Women's Open was played at 6,387-yard Spokane CC in Washington state. The course's original nine holes were likely designed by Jim Barnes,who served as the club's head pro from 1908 to 1910. Spokane Country Club had hosted a few prestigious Pacific Northwest events in its early years before being chosen as the venue for the first U.S. Women's Open.

TOP: Marilynn Smith. BOTTOM LEFT: Helen Dettweiller. BOTTOM RIGHT: Marlene Bauer Hagge

For the only time in its history, the tournament was a matchplay event in 1946. Thirty-nine players registered, including six professionals, and seven were cut after a 36-hole strokeplay qualifier that Patty Berg from Minneapolis won by seven shots with a score of 3-under-par.

The remaining 32 players then entered a bracket with matches in the first three rounds being played over 18 holes and the semi-finals and final over 36 holes.

Not surprisingly, given how well she had played in qualifying for match play, Berg made light work of her first four opponents, winning 7&6, 5&3, 6&5, and 3&2. In the final, she met Oklahoma's Betty Jameson, who had coasted through her first three matches 9&8, 5&4, 8&6, before edging Dot Kielty 1-up in the semi-final.

After seven holes of the final, Jameson was 3-up with Berg in pain—the result of a car crash a few years before. However, Berg erased the deficit by the time they completed the morning 18 and, after lunch, she won five of the first six holes. Berg eventually took the match 5&4.

The 28-year-old redhead, a former second lieutenant in the U.S. Marine Corps Women's Reserve called "Little Miss Golfer" by the *Spokane Daily Chronicle*, gave her 14-year-old caddie $100 and a set of Berg-branded woods and irons. Berg won 63 professional events, including 15 major championships, during her career and was inducted into the World Golf Hall of Fame in 1951.

Patty Berg

The U.S. Women's Open has grown significantly in stature through the years and is universally regarded as the most prestigious event in the women's game. But it's doubtful Patty Berg, Babe Zaharias, Betty Jameson, Louise Suggs, Betsy Rawls, Hope Seignious, Ellen Griffin, Betty Hicks, and other early pioneers of women's golf could have anticipated what it has become.

1947 Ryder Cup

US vs. GB/Ireland team match returns after World War II.

DATE
Nov. 1-2, 1947

LOCATION
Portland GC
Portland, OR
USA

PRIZE
The Ryder Cup

IN THE FIELD
Ben Hogan
Sam Snead
Lloyd Mangrum
Jimmy Demaret
Byron Nelson
Henry Cotton
Max Faulkner
Fred Daly

Because of World War II, it had been 10 years since the U.S. and Great Britain had met in the Ryder Cup, and both sides were eager to resume what had been a well-received and popular event throughout the 1930s. Golf, in Britain especially, wasn't a huge priority so soon after the war, however, as more important endeavors were necessary to rebuild the country. Sending a team of golfers to America had therefore been seen as something of an avoidable expense. Samuel Ryder's commitment and generosity had been essential in financing many of the previous meetings; but Ryder died in 1936, meaning someone else would need to bear the costs if the match was to resume.

Thirty-five-year-old Ben Hogan, a 41-time winner on the PGA Tour (including the 1946 PGA Championship), was chosen as the U.S.'s playing captain, and Henry Cotton, the 40-year-old, two-time Open Championship winner led the British side. The match didn't feature any 20-something players: the U.S. team averaging 34.4 years, the British 36.7.

And, as it had in each of the six previous encounters, the format comprised four 36-hole foursomes on Day 1 and eight 36-hole singles matches on Day 2. Before the matches started, Cotton predicted a British victory, but he was gravely mistaken.

Day 1

After a week of rain and continued precipitation during the event (certainly not atypical for the Pacific Northwest in November), the Portland Country Club course was playing very soft and long, so much so one British team member described it as "a slop."

The home side adapted to the conditions best. The American pairing of Ed "Porky" Oliver and Lew Worsham hammered the significantly older British pairing of Cotton and Arthur Lees 10&9 in the opening match. And it didn't get much better for the visiting side thereafter.

Sam Snead and Lloyd Mangrum beat Charlie Ward and reigning Open winner Fred Daly 6&5, the all-Texan team of Hogan and Jimmy Demaret beat Jimmy Adams and Max Faulkner 2-up, and, in the final match, 35-year-old Byron Nelson and Herman Barron defeated Dai Rees and Sam King 2&1.

The U.S. would, therefore, go into Day 2 with a 4-0 lead, looking a very likely winner.

Hudson Puts His Hands in His Pockets

The 1947 Ryder Cup only happened because of Robert Hudson's contributions. A wholesale grocer who brought the famous Piggly Wiggly chain of self-service supermarkets to the Portland area, Hudson was described by *The Oregonian* newspaper as "batty" about sports, especially golf.

Robert Hudson

He had founded the $10,000 Portland Open in 1944, and in '47 he basically bankrolled the whole Ryder Cup, paying the U.S. team's expenses and underwriting the British team's ocean voyage on the Queen Mary to New York, where he joined the visitors for the four-day rail journey west to the Pacific coast. Hudson's home club, Portland GC, was the venue.

Day 2

If the British thought things could only improve, they were in for a shock, as the Americans continued the onslaught, winning the first seven matches. Despite the one-sidedness, the event was played in good spirits throughout, although the Snead vs. Cotton tie did become decidedly icy at times, the *Oregon Daily Journal* saying the two superstars of each team barely said a word to each other. "The crowd sensed the tension between the players," it added, "and grew deathly still as the two rivals walked across the greens."

King, who had played in the 1937 Ryder Cup, was the only British player to win a point, beating 1946 Masters champion Herman Keiser 4&3 in the very last match. Even though Leonard Crawley in London's *Daily Telegraph* named King the "hero of the match," the Englishman's victory barely prevented the visitors' blushes as the U.S. team had won the Ryder Cup by the margin of 11 points to 1.

Left to Right: Hogan, Hudson, & Oliver Jr. at Portland GC the previous year

Afterward, Cotton tried explaining the loss by saying the train had arrived late, and his team hadn't had long enough to prepare. He did, however, concede the Americans had rebuilt their games following the war far quicker than the British had.

Cotton might have had a point about the lack of practice time, but he did take some criticism for benching both Reg Horne and Eric Green, neither of whom played on either day. Horne had finished tied for 2nd at the Open Championship in July; and Green was another popular and respected player.

Given the weather and the rather uneven scoreline, the 1947 tournament may not have been the most memorable of Ryder Cups. But golfers should be grateful it was played at all, returning a now hugely popular event to the calendar. Robert Hudson, the man who made it happen, is revered in the Pacific Northwest and a very important part of the Ryder Cup's history. Max Faulkner, part of the GB team, certainly recognized Hudson's sizable contribution. "What he did was marvelous," Faulkner said. "He did everything and would not accept a penny back. We wouldn't be talking about the Ryder Cup today if it wasn't for him."

Format Changes

After five more U.S. victories and one defeat (in 1957 at Lindrick GC, England), it was agreed the format should change for the 1961 event. Instead of 12 matches of 36 holes, there would be 24 18-hole matches: four foursomes on the first morning, four foursomes in the afternoon, eight singles on the second morning, and eight singles on the second afternoon.

The format changed again in 1963, when the event was played over three days for the first time, and fourballs were introduced. There would be other minor changes up to 1981, when the format still used today—four foursomes and four fourballs on each of the first two days, and 12 singles involving every player on each team on the third—was adopted.

1950 U.S. Open

Hogan wins fourth title 16 months after horrific car accident.

DATE
June 8-11, 1950

LOCATION
Merion GC
Ardmore, PA
USA

PRIZE
$4,000

IN THE FIELD
Ben Hogan
Sam Snead
Jimmy Demaret
Julius Boros
Cary Middlecoff

In 1948, Ben Hogan won 10 tournaments, including the U.S. Open at Riviera CC in California and the PGA Championship at Norwood Hills CC in Missouri. One month into 1949, he had already added two more titles to his growing collection, winning the Bing Crosby Pro-Am at Pebble Beach and the Long Beach Open at Lakewood CC in suburban Los Angeles. The odds were pretty good the 36-year-old Texan was going to have another stellar year, add to his major count, and cement his position as the best player in the world.

On the morning of February 2 (the day after he had lost to Jimmy Demaret in a playoff for the Phoenix Open), however, the man referred to as the "Little Mr. Boom of Golf" was involved in a horrific car crash which put him out for the rest of the season.

Driving home from Arizona with his wife, Valerie, Hogan was carefully cruising along a somewhat icy stretch of Highway 80 outside Van Horn, Texas, when a Greyhound bus, traveling in the opposite direction, pulled out into the eastbound lane and ploughed head-on into Hogan's black sedan. Alvin Logan, the driver of the bus, had attempted to overtake a truck at 50 mph—a reckless maneuver given how foggy it was. In an attempt to avoid the bus, Hogan turned his steering wheel as hard to the right as he could, but it was too late. He instinctively flung himself across Valerie who fortunately escaped the wreckage with minor cuts and bruises. And although Hogan himself suffered a broken collar bone, broken left ankle, contusions to his left leg, a cracked rib, a double fracture of his pelvis, and a head abrasion, by saving Valerie he had almost certainly saved himself, too, as the car's steering column was shunted clean through the driver's seat.

Hogan spent 59 days in the hospital at El Paso, and—at one point—phlebitis caused blood clots in his leg and one in his lung that required attention from a specialist vascular surgeon from New Orleans by the name of Dr. Alton Ochsner. Ochsner tied off Hogan's vena cava vein—a procedure that might have saved the golfer again, but which did cause terrible pain for the rest of his life. Hogan would take daily Epsom salt baths and wrap his legs in ice bandages to alleviate some of the discomfort.

As his fellow-competitors had learned by now, Hogan was a grimly determined individual, and even though his doctors said there was a chance he might never walk again, let alone play golf, Hogan showed up at the Texas PGA Championship in May—three months after the crash and a few weeks after returning home—to watch Byron Nelson and other friends compete, and speak to reporters. In an interview with the *Fort Worth Star-Telegram* in March, Hogan had vowed to come back to the game despite his injuries.

Hogan revisiting his crashed car

"You work for perfection all your life, and then something like this happens," he said. "But you can bet I'll be back there swinging."

By September, he had improved sufficiently to travel to England and captain the U.S. Ryder Cup team. And he played his first 18 holes since the accident in December: a round at Colonial CC with the head professional, after which Hogan said he hadn't hit the ball terribly well. Ninety-nine per cent of golfers would surely have been pleased with Hogan's level of ball-striking but—even with fragile, painful legs—he held himself to uncommonly high standards.

Amazingly, Hogan was back competing in top-class events just a month later, returning to Riviera CC, where he had won the 1947 and 1948 Los Angeles Opens and '48 U.S. Open, and which was now being referred to as "Hogan's Alley." During a first-round 73, he asked photographers not to take pictures, saying "no pictures or no play"—a stipulation to which the photographers reluctantly agreed.

Even more unlikely than being able to play in the first place was the fact Hogan held the clubhouse lead after 72 holes—completing them on 4-under, 280. He would have won the event on Sunday evening had Sam Snead not birdied the final two holes to tie him, the final birdie coming after holing a 12-foot putt that was delayed a moment after a spectator fell out of a tree.

Though few people were expecting much from Hogan that week, Snead knew better. "A lot of people didn't think he would be able to play very well," Snead said later, "but I knew he would. Knowing Ben the way I did, I knew he would never be unprepared to play in a tournament. If he said he was ready to play, I knew he was ready to play great."

Due to heavy rain, the playoff would have to wait a week, as the players had to move on to the Bing Crosby Pro-Am at Pebble Beach, which Snead won. Back at Riviera for the 18-hole playoff, Snead won again, beating Hogan 72 to 76. Snead might have claimed the trophy and the $2,600 winner's check, but Hogan won the admiration of the gallery who learned never to underestimate him. Sportswriter Grantland Rice summed it up nicely, writing, "His legs weren't strong enough to carry his heart around."

At the Masters in April, Hogan finished tied for 4th, completing the 72 holes on level-par 288, five shots behind Jimmy Demaret who won his third Green Jacket. And though there was some doubt as to whether Hogan would be able to complete four rounds at a 6,694-yard U.S. Open venue, with 36 holes on the Saturday, Snead knew what to expect at Merion in June. "Hogan is the man who might make some trouble," he said. "He's the man I've got to beat."

After a first-round 72, Hogan led Snead by a shot, but was eight strokes behind the leader—Lee Mackey, an unknown 26-year-old from Birmingham, Alabama, described as a "medium-sized chap with a crew haircut and sun-burned face." Mackey was a late entrant, having qualified with scores of 75 and 74, and his 64 at Merion broke the U.S. Open's single-round record and gave him a three-shot lead.

The surprise early leader bombed out with an 81 the following day, while Hogan, who had removed the 7-iron from his bag for the tournament saying the course had no 7-iron shots, climbed from T18 to 5th with a fine 1-under 69 that put him just two behind the new leader, Dutch Harrison. Hogan then led after 11 holes of Round 3, but a disappointing finish saw him fall back into a tie for 3rd, a shot behind Harrison and two behind 54-hole leader, Lloyd Mangrum.

In the final round on Saturday afternoon, Mangrum struggled to the turn in 41 but settled down on the back nine, shooting a 76 for a four-round total of 7-over-par. George Fazio, who started the round in a tie for 8th, shot a closing level-par 70, joining Mangrum on 287. And Hogan, with a two-shot lead with four holes to go, bogeyed the 15th and 17th and needed to par the tough 458-yard closing hole to make it a three-way tie at the top.

After a perfect drive, Hogan was left with about 215 yards uphill and into a slight headwind. He hit a beautiful 1-iron to the front-left of the green, leaving a 40-footer for birdie and the win. His first putt was long and left, and the four-foot knee-knocker he left himself crept in the right edge of the hole for a tying par.

Hogan, Lloyd Mangrum, and George Fazio would reconvene on Sunday for an 18-hole playoff, which Hogan led by one playing the 16th hole. On the green, Mangrum marked so Fazio could finish. After replacing his ball, a bug landed on it, so

Peskin's Picture

The beautifully struck shot Hogan hit at the 18th in the fourth round that helped him get into the playoff was bettered for timing only by photographer Hy Peskin's shutter finger, which he deployed at the perfect moment to capture one of golf's (all of sports'?) greatest-ever photographs.

An intense, abrasive character, and something of a loner who did whatever was necessary to get the shot he wanted, Peskin reportedly hadn't taken a single shot before the 18th hole. And while every other photographer went ahead of Hogan to get the shot of his face after impact, Peskin remained behind him, looking down the shot line with the green and rough ringed by spectators ten-deep in places. The enormous American flag swaying in the background is a nice addition.

The photograph Peskin took is so good because it captures a history-making shot. The fact so many spectators are there, finding whatever space they can, suggests this is a moment of great significance. And there—front and center, all by himself—is a perfectly balanced Hogan, at the end of what we know was another flawless swing. Had Hogan gone on to three-putt or lose in the following day's playoff, the image wouldn't have become nearly so famous. As it is, it's the perfect portrait of a great golfer's temperament, confidence, poise, and skill.

Mangrum picked the ball up, blew away the bug, then replaced the ball. But he shouldn't have: in most professional events in 1950, players were permitted to mark their ball anywhere on the green, but in USGA strokeplay events such as the U.S. Open, players were only allowed to mark their ball if it interfered with another player's line. By picking his ball up and replacing it after Fazio had already putted out, he incurred a two-stroke penalty, putting Hogan three clear. It became a four-shot lead after Hogan made a 50-foot birdie putt on the next, and 20 minutes later he claimed his second U.S. Open title, beating Mangrum by four and Fazio by six.

Given what had happened to him just 16 months prior, the pain he played with, and the stress of five U.S. Open rounds against top-level competition—what Hogan accomplished at Merion in 1950 is truly remarkable. Plenty of other athletes have suffered injuries and later returned to professional sport, but it's unlikely any climbed as high and steep a mountain as Hogan.

LEFT: Mrs. and Mr. Hogan with the trophy. RIGHT: The plaque marks the spot on Merion's 18th fairway

1-iron or 2-iron?

A debate over whether it was a 1-iron or 2-iron that Hogan hit to the 18th green in the final round has continued for decades with many credible voices on either side of it. In his seminal instruction book, *Five Lessons: The Modern Fundamentals of Golf* (published in 1957, and co-written with Herbert Warren Wind with illustrations by Anthony Ravielli), Hogan stated it was 2-iron, but he later said it was a mistake.

The club Hogan is said to have hit is now displayed in the USGA Museum, although a certain amount of uncertainty surrounds that too, as the club was stolen from Hogan's bag sometime during or immediately after the U.S. Open and wasn't discovered for 30+ years. A club-collector from North Carolina purchased a Hogan 1-iron in 1983, and because of the wear-pattern on its face, suspected it was the club. He sent it to the Hogan club company, where Hogan confirmed it was indeed the club he had used to hit his famous approach to Merion's 18th. Hogan then sent it to the USGA.

A handful of Hogan devotees and noted golf historians have undertaken extensive research to prove one way or the other and, to anyone with even a modicum of interest in the subject, it all makes compelling reading. On the surface, it seems strange that someone as meticulous, obsessive, and detail-oriented as Hogan could possibly have made a mistake over which club he used. But his last word on the subject before he died in July 1997 was that it was a 1-iron.

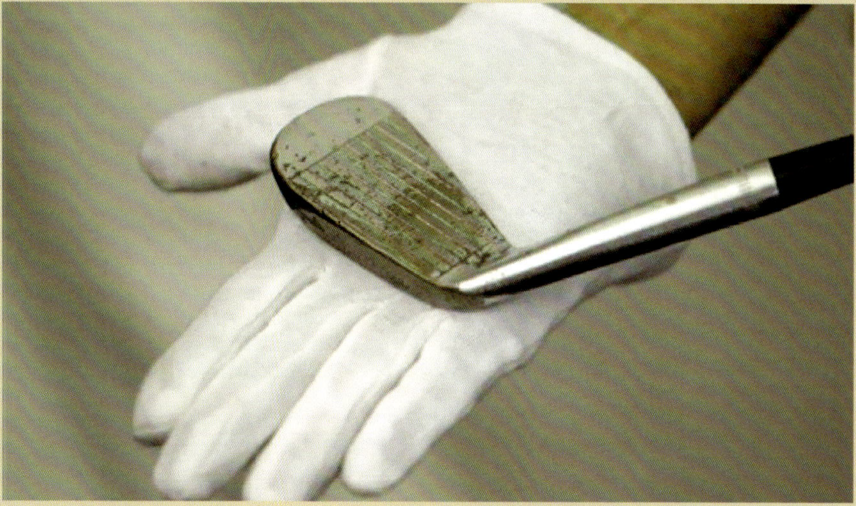

Hogan's 1-iron, displayed for the 2013 U.S. Open at Merion

1953 Open Championship

Hogan wins his first and only Claret Jug.

DATE
July 8-10, 1953

LOCATION
Carnoustie GL
Carnoustie, Angus
Scotland

PRIZE
£500

IN THE FIELD
Ben Hogan
Bobby Locke
Peter Thomson
Roberto De Vicenzo
Peter Alliss
Lloyd Mangrum

On April 13, 1953, the 40-year-old Ben Hogan won the Masters with a 14-under score of 274, beating the tournament-scoring record by five strokes and finishing five ahead of Ed Oliver in 2nd. It was Hogan's second Masters title, and he told reporters afterward, "That was as good as I can play." Two months later, he beat runner-up Sam Snead by six to win the U.S. Open at Oakmont—his fourth victory in the event.

A couple of weeks after that, Hogan was on his way to Scotland and Carnoustie to play in the Open Championship for the first time. Because of the lengthy journey, inferior prize money, unpredictable weather, and numerous other issues, not many Americans played in the Open Championship at the time—Snead had won the Claret Jug in 1946 but had never gone back saying that any time you weren't in the USA, you were "camping out"—but Hogan wanted to meet the challenge.

Over the years, he had been encouraged to play in the championship by a number of the game's elder statesmen—both American and British. The R&A's rules had changed meaning he could now use his center-shafted putter. And, because it was contested in July, there was a chance it might actually be warm. What surely appealed to Hogan the most, though, was achieving something he never had, and confirming his place among the all-time greats of the game.

He didn't go to "see" Great Britain or make a tour of the country's best golf courses. Nor did he go to sample the food or experience a different culture. This wasn't a vacation. He went to win an important golf tournament that would help complete his legacy.

Hogan arrived in Scotland with his wife Valerie two weeks before the championship in order to get acclimatized. Not only would he have to get used to a treeless, waterless, and very firm golf course where the wind blew, the caddies spoke some barely decipherable dialect (34-year-old local Cecil Timms caddied for Hogan), and where course conditions were far from manicured, Hogan would also have to become comfortable with a smaller golf ball. The 1.62-inch-diameter ball, used in Britain, behaved very differently to the 1.68" ball that had been played in the U.S. since 1932. Because the wind affected it less, the smaller ball flew appreciably farther; and because of its size, it sat down in the grass a little more, making shots from the rough a little harder.

The Hogans stayed in a private residence in Dundee, 12 miles west of Carnoustie, and Ben practiced every day at Panmure GC, a couple of miles from Carnoustie's much-feared Championship links. When not with Valerie, he spent what little spare time he had with CBS Radio's John Derr.

Despite having won the Masters and U.S. Open, Hogan still had to qualify for the championship itself, on July 6-7. Pre-qualifying was another reason so few Americans made the trip, but—with a 70 on Carnoustie's Burnside Course and a 75 on the Championship Course—Hogan progressed easily.

Ben Hogan at Carnoustie

He got off to a reasonable start in the championship proper, shooting a 1-over-par 73 in Wednesday's first round, finishing the day tied for 7th. Given the strong wind, it wasn't a bad score, and he was only three shots behind the leader—Frank Stranahan, an amateur from Ohio who had won the (British) Amateur in 1948 and 1950, and finished 2nd in the 1947 Open at Hoylake.

Hogan's only slight concern—besides the somewhat shaggy greens (the one inappropriate remark he made all week—according to reports, was to "jokingly" offer the greenkeeper use of his lawn-mower), was the quality of the players above him. A strong, young Scot named Eric Brown was a shot behind Stranahan in 2nd, and tied for 3rd was a quartet of formidable golfers: the young, talented Australian Peter Thomson, who had won the Australian Open in 1947 and finished 2nd in the Open Championship at Royal Lytham & St Anne's the previous year; Dai Rees, a gritty Welshman who'd played in four Ryder Cups (he'd go on to captain the GB & Ireland team five times), and had won the British PGA Matchplay Championship four times plus an Irish Open at the venerable Portmarnock GC; Argentina's Roberto De Vicenzo, who'd won dozens of professional events in South America, had two 3rds and a 2nd in his first three Open Championship appearances, and who had won golf's World Cup alongside Antonio Cerdá just five weeks before; and the defending champion—South Africa's Bobby Locke—who had also won the Championship in 1949 and 1950.

A second-round 71—marked by typically strong ball-striking but marred by indifferent putting—gave Hogan a 36-hole total of even-par 144 and saw him climb into a tie for 4th, just one shot behind De Vicenzo in 3rd and two behind the co-leaders, Rees and Brown.

Before Friday's closing two rounds, Hogan came down with the flu, which only a shot of penicillin could control. The previous day's mix of rain and sun, and chill and warmth, would endure, which didn't make playing any easier for Hogan, but a morning round of 70 saw him move into a tie for the lead with De Vicenzo. Cerdá,

Hogan with the Claret Jug

Rees, and Thomson were just a shot back, though Brown, Locke, and Stranahan had begun to fade.

Hogan teed off in the final round at 3:27 p.m., an hour and a half after De Vicenzo. The Argentinian shot a 73 to drop into 6th place, but with more immaculate ball-striking and slightly improved putting, Hogan shot a course record 68 to complete four rounds on 6-under 282. Four back in 2nd were Rees, Thomson, Cerdá, and Stranahan.

The "Wee Ice Mon"—the name the Scottish galleries and press had given Hogan because of his steely nerve—had now won three majors in succession. He didn't play in that year's PGA Championship because its dates overlapped with those of the Open Championship, plus he hadn't played in it since winning in 1948 anyway. His near-fatal car crash in February 1949 left Hogan with terrible injuries, and despite his rigorous effort to recover, he wasn't physically able to play 36 holes of strokeplay qualifying plus, a potential six 36-hole matches in just seven days (or 252 competitive holes in a week).

When asked who they would most like to have seen play and when, a lot of golfers will say Ben Hogan at Carnoustie in 1953. Watching 'the Hawk' anywhere would have been something, but observing him dissect a tough golf course that must have felt very alien to him and beating such a strong field while playing a strangely unfamiliar golf ball, must have been utterly mesmerizing.

A New Hogan's Alley

Following his wins at the 1947 and '48 Los Angeles Opens and the '48 U.S. Open, all of which took place at the George Thomas-designed Riviera CC, the course was dubbed "Hogan's Alley." And the 6th hole at Carnoustie became another of Hogan's alleys during the 1953 Open, for the way in which the Texan attacked it.

A par-five measuring 565 yards, the 6th was a three-shot hole for most golfers in 1953. A long iron off the tee to a safe spot short and right of the two fairway bunkers would be followed by another long iron and a wedge to the green. Hogan, however, hit a driver to a narrow stretch of fairway between the bunkers and the out-of-bounds fence on the left, in all four rounds—an extremely brave play that enabled him to go for the green in two. The hole was officially renamed "Hogan's Alley" in September 2003.

1954 U.S. Women's Open

Babe Didrickson Zaharias wins by 12 after undergoing cancer surgery the year before.

DATE
July 1-3, 1954

LOCATION
Salem CC
Peabody, MA
USA

PRIZE
$2,000

IN THE FIELD
Patty Berg
Betty Jameson
Betty Hicks
Mickey Wright
Betsy Rawls
Louise Suggs
Fay Crocker
Babe Zaharias
Glenna Collett-Vare

Born Mildred Didrickson in 1911, Didrickson was nicknamed "Babe" during her childhood (possibly after Babe Ruth, as she was something of a baseball prodigy). At the 1932 Summer Olympics in Los Angeles, she had won two golds in track and field (hurdles and javelin) and a silver (high jump). In 1935, she took up golf, and in 1938 she married pro wrestler George Zaharias, taking his name.

On April 11, 1953, after she had won 34 LPGA Tour events including two U.S. Women's Opens and three Titleholders Championships, an Associated Press report announced Zaharias would undergo major surgery following the discovery of a "malignant condition, obviously cancer." The greatest woman athlete of all time had finally met her match, the report said, adding that the cancer probably meant the end of an incredible career that took her from basketball champion to Olympic gold medalist to golfing great.

The surgery took place a few days later at Hotel Dieu (now St. Elizabeth Hospital) in Beaumont, Texas. Doctors said the condition could be corrected, but that there were no guarantees the cancer wouldn't re-appear. Despite being told by her physicians it was unlikely she'd ever be able to play golf again, Zaharias was determined to return. Perhaps not surprisingly, given her athleticism, she did make it back to the LPGA Tour in early 1954, winning the Serbin Open in Florida in February, the Sarasota Open two weeks later, and the Damon Runyon Cancer Fund Tournament in Maryland in May. And in the first week of July, 14 months after her surgery, she teed it up in the U.S. Women's Open at Salem CC, about 45 minutes' drive north of Boston.

The 1954 event was the ninth U.S. Women's Open, and the second conducted by the USGA. Zaharias had first won it in 1948 at Atlantic City CC, where she beat runner-up Betty Hicks by eight shots. Her second victory had come at Rolling Hills Country Club in Wichita, Kansas, where 2nd-placed Betsy Rawls finished nine strokes adrift.

Zaharias planned to rest before the 1954 event, hitting a few balls but avoiding full practice rounds. Two days before the championship began, however, she played the back-nine after being persuaded by her adoring gallery, which apparently was in the habit of calling her shots—challenging shots she was able to pull off more often than not.

Zaharias shot a new women's course record 72 (even-par) on the 6,393-yard layout in Round 1, tying her for the lead with Cleveland's Claire Doran. By the end of the second day, however, she was seven clear having shot another course record: a 1-under 71.

Zaharias competing professionally in golf, boxing, track, and tennis

Ahead of Saturday's final two rounds, there was obviously much excitement over Zaharias' likely victory, but also a question mark over how well she'd cope physically with 36 holes on the same day over a long and testing course. A morning 73 extended her lead to 10 shots, and a front-nine 36 in the afternoon—with the exceptionally talented 19-year-old Mickey Wright as her playing partner—made the final nine something of a procession.

Fatigue clearly set in over the closing stretch, causing Zaharias to walk significantly slower than she had been, but three straight bogeys to finish were never going to be enough to alter the result. Wearing a colostomy bag, Babe Zaharias had won the U.S. Women's Open by 12 shots. After the final putt dropped, the gallery cheered for two full minutes, knowing they had witnessed something very special.

At the prize-giving ceremony, Zaharias said that being able to play at all had been an answer to prayer. "I said, please make me able to play again. I'll take care of the winning. Today we sealed the bargain."

There were some who said Zaharias' bravery and courage had never been equaled in all of sports, which seems odd considering how close Ben Hogan had come to dying and the difficulties he'd subsequently endured just a few years before. But there's no denying Zaharias had shown remarkable resolve.

She won once more in 1954 to finish the season with five wins, and her 75.48 scoring average won her the prestigious Vare Trophy.

In 1955, Zaharias captured the last two of her 41 LPGA victories, but her cancer returned making further participation increasingly difficult. She died on September 27, 1956, in a Galveston hospital, aged just 45.

There's nothing like a great comeback story, and Zaharias' is one of the best.

Zaharias with the U.S. Women's trophy

1962 U.S. Open

Nicklaus wins his first major, beating Palmer in a playoff.

DATE
June 14-17, 1962

LOCATION
Oakmont CC
Oakmont, PA
USA

PRIZE
$17,500

IN THE FIELD
Jack Nicklaus
Arnold Palmer
Gary Player
Gene Littler
Sam Snead

Jack Nicklaus was 22 years old when he arrived at Oakmont CC for the 62nd U.S. Open. Most professionals would be learning how to perform on the world's biggest stages at that age, gaining valuable experience that could pay off later (the average age of major winners is around 32 but was slightly higher in the 1960s). But Nicklaus, of course, was an entirely different competitor.

He won the Ohio State Junior Championship for the first time at the age of 12 and took the next four titles, too. In 1953, aged 13, he broke 70 at Scioto Country Club and qualified for his first U.S. Junior Championship. He played his first U.S. Amateur in 1955, and a year later, won the Ohio Open against the state's best professionals shooting a third-round 64 (he also played an exhibition match with Sam Snead that week).

In 1957, he played in the first of 44 straight U.S. Opens, and he won the U.S. Amateur in 1959 and 1961 while attending Ohio State University. At his first ever PGA Tour event, the 1958 Rubber City Open in Akron, Ohio, he finished tied for 12th having been one off the lead after 36 holes.

His first of 45 Masters appearances came in 1959; and at Denver's Cherry Hills Country Club the following year, he finished 2nd at the U.S. Open, two back of Arnold Palmer who closed with a 65 after driving the green at the 346-yard 1st hole (an exceptional shot in 1960).

Then, after recording the first of 22 top-10 finishes at the Masters in 1961, Nicklaus tied for 4th at the U.S. Open. So, although he hadn't actually won a major yet (nor, indeed, a tournament on the PGA Tour), Nicklaus was clearly on the brink of doing so.

After initially planning to become a pharmacist like his father, and then briefly selling insurance, Nicklaus decided to turn professional in November 1961. In the first five months of the 1962 season, he played 17 PGA Tour events, finishing in the top 10 seven times. The seventh of those top 10s came the week before the U.S. Open, when he finished 2nd at the Thunderbird Classic Invitational in New Jersey.

At Oakmont, Nicklaus played with Palmer for the first two rounds along with the 1959 PGA Champion, Bob Rosburg. All three finished inside the top 10 on the first-round leaderboard. Nicklaus struggled a little on the notoriously fast greens but still signed for a 72 that put him in a tie for 9th. Palmer was a shot better, but it was Rosburg who scored the best, carding a 70 that put him a shot behind the defending champion, Gene Littler (who, in his first ever round at Oakmont—a practice round on Tuesday—had shot an 82). Palmer and Rosburg excelled on Day 2 shooting 68 and 69, respectively. They shared the lead at 139 with Billy Maxwell in 3rd, two back, and Nicklaus in a tie for 4th with Bobby Nichols and Gary Player on level-par, 142.

Poor Putting Denies Palmer

In 1962, the final two rounds were still played on Saturday (the first time the four rounds finished on a Sunday was 1965), and Palmer certainly started the day as the man to beat. Indeed, his play through the green was excellent, enabling him to build a three-shot lead at one point on Saturday morning. Ultimately, though, his putting let him down. He shot 73-71 in rounds three and four, while Nicklaus had a 72 in the morning, and followed it with a gutsy 69. He made up the two shots Palmer led by, and they both finished at 1-under, 283, for 72 holes—two ahead of Nichols and Phil Rodgers. Eighteen more holes on Sunday would be needed to break the tie.

A crowd of 10,000 showed up to watch a contest that the press termed, "The King vs. the Kid." The vast majority were there to cheer on Palmer, a Pennsylvania-native born in the blue-collar town of Latrobe, just 35 miles southeast of Oakmont.

Nicklaus didn't appear perturbed by the gallery's obvious bias (the less polite spectators focused on the younger player's weight, calling him "Ohio Fats"), though Palmer—ever the sportsman—was visibly embarrassed by it.

Nicklaus got off to the better start, making five straight fours, then a two at the 6th, giving him a four-stroke lead. The following day, the *Pittsburgh Press* said the crowd hadn't seemed overly concerned at this point, joking that their man was simply spotting Nicklaus a few strokes and liked to come from behind. Sure enough, after a Nicklaus bogey at the 9th, and Palmer birdies at the 11th and 12th, the gap was down to one with six holes left to play.

The short 13th stopped Palmer's comeback in its tracks, however, as he three-putted for the 10th time that week. "I wanted to win so badly, I think it affected me on the greens," he said afterward. "I wanted every putt to drop, and when I missed the first try, I was in a daze. That's the only way I can explain those short ones I missed."

In the end, Nicklaus shot an even-par 71, while Palmer finished with a 74. Nicklaus had won his first major—also his first PGA Tour event—and was now the reigning U.S. Open and U.S. Amateur champion.

Winning your first professional major by beating Arnold Palmer in front of his home crowd on so difficult a course would have required a lot of guts, confidence, poise, and talent. Over the next 35-40 years, Nicklaus showed us just how much of each he had.

Nicklaus & Palmer shake hands after Nicklaus' win

The U.S. Open at Oakmont

In the lead-up to the 2025 U.S. Open, the consensus among golf writers was that Oakmont was the quintessential U.S. Open venue. It had long had a reputation for being extremely difficult, with stories cropping up from time to time of the USGA actually having to slow the greens down for the championship, but there now seemed to be solid agreement among pundits, analysts, and columnists that it was only right the game's toughest tournament should be played on its toughest course. In the 2017 edition of the club's history written by Pittsburgh golf writer Marino Parascenzo, the USGA's executive director, Mike Davis, paid Oakmont the ultimate compliment saying it was the "true gold standard in championship golf."

It was designed by its owner: iron and steel magnate Henry Fownes, an accomplished golfer who wanted to build a course considerably more demanding than what the area had to offer at the time. It opened in 1903 on 191 acres of farmland, 14 miles northeast of Pittsburgh, and it hosted a couple of U.S. Amateurs and a PGA Championship (won by Gene Sarazen) before it staged its first U.S. Open in 1927.

Since then, the course has gone through two transformations. Following the 1953 U.S. Open, golf writer Herbert Warren Wind described it as an "ugly brute," prompting the club to start planting trees in an effort to make it a beautiful brute. It went from being fairly austere to a tree-lined course.

Beginning in the early 1990s, however, the club's superintendents—first Larry Napora then Mark Kuhns (supported by club greens chairman Banks Smith)—began removing trees under the cover of darkness, so as not to alert the members, most of whom took a while to gather what was happening. In the mid-late 1990s, the course lost something like 15,000 trees becoming the open, exposed layout it had been originally. The shade may have been lost, but the turf could once again benefit from air movement and exposure to the sun.

The winning scores at its first 10 U.S. Opens show just how difficult Oakmont can be—trees or no trees.

WINNING U.S. OPEN SCORES AT OAKMONT

Year	Score	Winner
1927	+13	Tommy Armour
1935	+11	Sam Parks
1953	-5	Ben Hogan
1962	-1	Jack Nicklaus
1973	-5	Johnny Miller
1980	-4	Larry Nelson
1992	-4	Patty Sheehan
1994	-5	Ernie Els
2007	+5	Angel Cabrera
2010	-5	Paula Creamer
2016	-5	Dustin Johnson
2025	-1	J.J. Spaun

The Big Three Is Established

In late 1958, a Cleveland attorney named Mark McCormack began courting professional golfers, saying he could earn them more than they were making in prize-money by setting up exhibitions and corporate appearances. Within a few months, a number of the PGA Tour's top players had signed contracts with McCormack's National Sports Management, including Arnold Palmer, who had won the 1958 Masters and was clearly the game's hottest prospect.

Within a year of signing his contract, however, Palmer had become disillusioned with the agreement. Palmer said that his wife, Winnie, was doing most of the behind-the-scenes accounts and scheduling, and that being part of the group of players McCormack was representing was actually hurting his earning potential.

If he was to stay with McCormack, Palmer said, he was going to have to be his only client. McCormack agreed, and the two shook hands. Recognizing the perfect marketing opportunity—young, star golfer from a largely working-class city having his business affairs handled by a hotshot lawyer in a sharp suit—McCormack ensured the legend of the handshake grew (even though there would eventually be a lot of legal paperwork).

He began International Management Group (IMG) in 1960, and despite Palmer's wish to be his sole client, McCormack and IMG signed Gary Player later in 1960, and Jack Nicklaus after turning professional in November 1961. Player had won 20 or so tournaments in Australia and his native South Africa, plus the Kentucky Derby Open in 1958 and Open Championship in 1959, and bought an international flavor to McCormack's stable, while Nicklaus was obviously a star in the making, even if he lacked Palmer's charisma.

Palmer's wins at the 1960 U.S. Open and Masters (plus the 1962 and 1964 Masters); Nicklaus' at the '62 U.S. Open, and '63 Masters and PGA Championship; and Player's at the 1961 Masters and '62 PGA Championship, helped establish the notion of a "Big Three" (it had been half a century since golf's Great Triumvirate of Harry Vardon, J.H. Taylor, and James Braid had dominated the Open Championship), and McCormack took every opportunity he could to make the most of it.

The 1962 U.S. Open was a good tournament for the Big Three, as they finished 1st, 2nd, and T6. The best major championship for the trio was the 1965 Masters, when all three finished on the podium—Nicklaus won, and Palmer and Player tied for 2nd nine shots behind. At the 1963 Phoenix Open, Palmer finished first, while Player was 2nd and Nicklaus 3rd; and at the 1964 Whitemarsh Open in Philadelphia, the order was reversed, with Nicklaus winning and Palmer coming 3rd.

LEFT TO RIGHT: Player, Nicklaus, Palmer

1969 Ryder Cup

The first tied match in Ryder Cup history.

DATE
Sept. 18-20, 1969

LOCATION
Royal Birkdale
Southport, England

PRIZE
The Ryder Cup

IN THE FIELD
Jack Nicklaus
Billy Casper
Lee Trevino
Peter Alliss
Bernard Gallacher
Tony Jacklin

With four contests having been cancelled due to World War II (1939-45), the 1969 Ryder Cup was the 18th meeting of the two sides. It was the first year each team had 12 players instead of nine or 10. It was the first Ryder Cup in which it was compulsory for both sides to use the larger "American" ball. The Great Britain team still flew the Union Flag (Union Jack), though Irish golfers had played since 1947. Four golfers from the Republic of Ireland played before the GB team officially became Great Britain and Ireland, in 1973: Harry Bradshaw ('53, '55, and '57) Christy O'Connor (10 straight appearances, 1955-73), Jimmy Martin ('65), and Hugh Boyle ('67).

Arnold Palmer was missing from the U.S. team for the first time since 1959. He had won four points from six matches at Royal Birkdale in 1965, and won all five of his matches in 1967 at Champions Golf Club in Texas, but he hadn't played well enough to be selected for the team in 1969. This year did, however, mark 29-year-old Jack Nicklaus' debut in the event. Even though he had turned professional eight years earlier and had won seven major championships by 1968, Nicklaus had been ineligible to play in the Ryder Cup due to the PGA of America's rule that stated players had to be a full member of its organization for at least five years before becoming eligible.

Nicklaus was one of 10 rookies on the U.S. team—the only players with Ryder Cup experience being Gene Littler and Billy Casper. Fifty-seven-year-old Sam Snead was the non-playing captain, and the average age of the team was 33.3.

For the home side, 25-year-old Tony Jacklin was making his second appearance, and had won the Open Championship just two months before. The first British golfer to win the Open since 1951, Jacklin was in excellent form and riding a wave of popularity. Scotland's Eric Brown was the non-playing captain, and the team featured five rookies, including 20-year-old Bernard Gallacher. The average age of GB's 12 players was 30.8.

Of the 17 Ryder Cups played before 1969, the GB team had won only three—its last victory coming at Lindrick Golf Club in England, in 1957. And, with another strong team crossing the Atlantic, the U.S. began the 1969 event as overwhelming favorites.

Format (used from 1963 to 1971)

Day 1—Eight foursomes (four in a.m., four in p.m.)
Day 2—Eight fourballs (four in a.m., four in p.m.)
Day 3—16 singles (eight in a.m., eight in p.m.)

Contentious Contest

For decades, the 1969 Ryder Cup has been remembered for a courageous moment of sportsmanship that occurred on the final green on the final afternoon (more on that later). Until then, however, the event had not exactly lived up to the Friends-Across-the-Ocean ideal that Samuel Ryder and the two PGAs had envisaged.

Eric Brown, captain of the GB team, had been a fine player who finished in the top 10 at the Open Championship six times. He played on four Ryder Cup teams, winning all four of his singles matches, and he won the prestigious British PGA Matchplay Championship twice. As his matchplay record suggests, Brown was a tough character, and he wasn't known for an easy-going agreeableness (his *Glasgow Herald* obituary—he died in 1986 aged 61—said he had been "one of golf's most controversial figures in his time.")

At Lindrick in 1957, Brown played Tommy Bolt in the singles and became so frustrated by Bolt's slow play that he asked his caddie to return to the clubhouse and bring back a folding chair, which he sat on every time Bolt prepared to play a shot. Upon leaving the 15th green at the end of the match, which Brown won 4&3, Bolt is said to have remarked that he hadn't enjoyed the game, to which Brown apparently replied with words to the effect of "No, I don't suppose you did. When the draw was made, you would have known you had no chance of beating me."

So it's no great surprise that, prior to the start of the first day's play, Brown instructed his players not to help the Americans find their ball if it went into the rough. He later said that was a misunderstanding, as he didn't want his players to possibly incur a penalty, but not many people bought that, and the tone for the match was set.

Brown certainly wasn't alone in risking relations, however: American team-member Ken Still did his reputation for being a feisty character no harm at all. First, he stood far too close to opponent Maurice Bembridge at times during their opening foursomes match, and on the 13th tee, when asked by Bembridge to move his shadow, sarcastically asked if the gallery should move, too. Next, he hit into a bunker on the same hole and watched as the ball rebounded off the face and hit him. The rules have since changed but, in 1969, that meant automatic loss of the hole. Still remained silent, however, meaning his playing partner, Lee Trevino, had to point it out and concede the hole. In Friday's afternoon fourball, Still was playing with David Hill against Bernard Gallacher and Brian Huggett. On the 7th green, Hill putted out of turn and Gallacher pointed it out, whereupon Still strode over to Gallacher's ballmarker, picked it up, and threw it at the young Scot, saying, "You can have the hole and the goddammed cup."

The British side ended Day 1 with a one-point lead but, by the end of Friday's matches, the U.S. had drawn level at eight points each. And the Americans would go two points clear on Saturday morning, when Trevino beat Peter Alliss, and Hill beat Peter Townsend. By lunchtime, however, the British had established a two-point lead of their own after winning each of the last four morning singles—a sequence that included Bembridge's 1-up victory over Still, and Jacklin's impressive 4&3 win over Nicklaus.

The entire match, therefore, came down to the afternoon singles. The first four matches were halved/shared, and then in the afternoon, the U.S. went two points clear with wins by Dan Sikes and Gene Littler. Brian Hugget and Billy Casper halved the 31st match of the week, meaning the last game—Jacklin vs. Nicklaus—would be the decider, and Nicklaus was 1-up on the 17th tee. Both drove well on the twisty par five, but while Nicklaus' approach finished no more than 10 feet from the hole, Jacklin's bounced off a greenside mound and wound up 40 feet short and left.

Despite starting in bright sunshine, the day had become cold and gloomy by mid-afternoon. Nobody was going anywhere, though, and the silent, 15,000-strong gallery erupted when Jacklin holed his putt for a three. Nicklaus missed, which meant they walked to the 18th—another par five—all-square. En route, Nicklaus turned to Jacklin and said, "I am not liking this any more than you."

Again, both drove well, then Jacklin hit his second shot 35 feet past the hole. Nicklaus' approach finished 25 feet right of it, and Jacklin's first putt came up about 3 feet short. Nicklaus ran his putt for the match, and the Cup, a good five feet past. Having missed four similar-length putts in the morning, Nicklaus did well to hole the comebacker for a four. Then, as Raymond Jacobs put it in the *Glasgow Herald*, Nicklaus "instinctively bowed to the proprietaries of the occasion by conceding Jacklin his putt." Nicklaus picked up Jacklin's ball marker and handed it to him, saying that he didn't think Jacklin would have missed but didn't want to give him the chance.

The match was tied at 16 points apiece, though the Americans retained the Cup, having won it in 1967.

Apart from Jacobs' line, surprisingly little was made of Nicklaus' sporting gesture in the press the following day, and the golfing world seemingly took many years to recognize its significance.

Snead, who graciously admitted the British team had played the better golf, said it was the "greatest golf match ever seen in England," but seemed frustrated at Nicklaus' decision to concede Jacklin's putt, saying later "We came here to win."

Samuel Ryder may have seen the tournament that bears his name as something of a friendly exhibition, but in truth the Ryder Cup has always been at its best when the competition comes with some good-natured needle. That needle came a little close to getting too sharp in 1969, but Nicklaus's magnanimous gesture saved the day.

Nicklaus concedes Jacklin's putt

1974 U.S. Open

The "Massacre at Winged Foot."

DATE
June 13-16, 1974

LOCATION
Winged Foot GC
Mamaroneck, NY
USA

PRIZE
$35,000

IN THE FIELD
Jack Nicklaus
Arnold Palmer
Gary Player
Tom Watson
Lee Trevino
Johnny Miller
Hale Irwin

At the 1973 U.S. Open, Johnny Miller shot a final round 8-under-par 63 to win by a stroke, having begun the day six back. To record the first ever 63 in a major championship was one thing, to do it in the U.S. Open at Oakmont was quite another. Usually regarded as the most formidable of U.S. Open venues with thick rough, lightning quick greens, and—at the time of Miller's victory—a lot of trees, Oakmont had seen some high scoring through the years (see page 143), and the club had long enjoyed its course's reputation for being extremely challenging.

Likewise, the USGA clearly relishes putting on the most demanding tournament of the year. Though it has never stated explicitly that it endeavors to make the winning score level-par or thereabouts, consistently setting up courses with 20- to 25-yard-wide fairways; thick, 3- to 5-inch-long rough, and rock-hard greens that measure 13-15 on the Stimpmeter suggest the organization has a hard time tolerating low scores and that it believes mistakes need to be punished, resulting in the loss of a stroke, or two, to par.

So you can imagine the conversations that might have occurred prior to the 1974 U.S. Open between USGA president Richard S. Tufts and championship committee member, Sandy Tatum, a San Francisco attorney who had attended both Oxford in England and Stanford in the U.S., and was the man who would be responsible for Winged Foot's set-up. Tatum later insisted Miller's 63 the previous year had not crossed his mind when setting up the West Course at Winged Foot, but the connection was an easy one to make.

The fact the 1974 U.S. Open was called "The Massacre at Winged Foot" by sportswriter Dick Schaap shortly after it concluded—a name that has stuck ever since—tells you everything you need to know about how difficult it was. The course took all the U.S. Open's usual characteristics to the extreme: fairways were only 18-22 yards wide; the rough was four-six inches long and extremely thick; and the greens were concrete firm—cut to 9/64 of an inch and measuring 12 on the Stimpmeter—not excessively quick by modern standards, perhaps, but exceptionally fast for the 1970s.

Not a single player broke par (70) in Round 1. Gary Player, a seven-time major champion (he won a total of nine in his career) and winner of the Masters a couple of months before, was the only man in the 150-man field to match it, in fact, and it gave him a one-stroke lead over Lou Graham and Mike Reasor. The average score returned on Day 1 was 77.39, with Jack Nicklaus shooting a 79 and Lee Trevino a 78. A total of 44 players failed to break 80.

The scoring average on Day 2 was a little better with four players—Hubert Green (67), Larry Ziegler (68), Frank Beard (69), and Bert Yancey (69)—managing to break 70. Green's magnificent score was the best of the week but, unfortunately, he had started with an 81 and shot two 76s over the weekend so could finish no higher than T26. The cut fell at 13-over, 153—the highest for 20 years. Trevino shot another 78, and at 16-over-par, exited quickly saying Winged Foot was the hardest course he'd even seen. Miller, the man who many said was responsible for provoking the USGA into action, shot 76-75—151 (+11) for the first 36 holes.

In a four-way tie for the lead at 3-over 143 were Player, Hale Irwin, Ray Floyd, and a 44-year-old Arnold Palmer who—despite a handful of top-five finishes—hadn't won a major for 10 years. The Associated Press called him "the aging king of another era of golfing glory," adding that, in his round of 70, he had "called on the half-remembered magic that was once his alone."

The field was cut to the top 66 players for Round 3, but scoring remained high. Tom Watson, 24 and still looking for his first PGA Tour win, went to the top of the leaderboard after a Saturday round of 69 that put him on 3-over, 213. Irwin, who had played football for the University of Colorado in his college days, was a shot back, and Palmer was still in it on 216.

Before the final round, Watson said every hole had at least one place from which you couldn't make a par, but he assured the press he expected to win. The confident talk was all for naught though, as he stumbled to a 79 on Sunday pushing him down into a tie for 5th.

With a final round 73, it was the 29-year-old Irwin who came out on top, striping a superb 2-iron approach on the 18th from about 210 yards to within 20 feet of the hole. Two putts gave him a four-round total of 287 (+7) and victory (his first of three at the U.S. Open—1974, 1979, 1990) by two strokes over Forrest Fezler. Palmer finished in the tie for 5th with Watson at 12-over, 282; Player was tied for 8th on 293; and with a

Hale Irwin lifting the trophy

final round of 69, Nicklaus climbed into a tie for 10th on 294.

Sandy Tatum

Irwin was naturally excited, but also philosophical about the win. "Winning this tournament does a lot for my ego," he said. "But I'm not going to change. There will be a reckoning, a re-evaluation. Now that I've won one, I want to do something bigger, like two major championships. Nicklaus has won 14, that's not a bad goal is it?"

The gap between Irwin's major count and Nicklaus' grew (he finished his career with three while Nicklaus amassed 18), but Irwin did collect a very impressive 83 professional titles, 45 of them on the PGA Tour Champions. He was inducted into the World Golf Hall of Fame in 1992.

Not surprisingly, Tatum and the USGA took some flak for the set-up of the course, to which Tatum famously replied "We're not trying to humiliate the best players in the world. We're simply trying to identify who they are."

U.S. Open courses are so severe at times, they tend to minimize the need for cunningly and skillfully played recovery shots. Get out of position, even slightly, and it seems the USGA would rather penalize the imprecision that put you there than give you a chance of redeeming yourself. That doesn't make for the most entertaining golf, perhaps, but the USGA has stuck to this philosophy for decades and players/viewers know what's coming. It's a grueling test and never was it so grueling as in 1974.

1975 Masters

Lee Elder becomes the first Black man to play in the Masters.

DATE
April 10-13, 1975

LOCATION
Augusta National
Augusta, GA
USA

PRIZE
$40,000

IN THE FIELD
Jack Nicklaus
Arnold Palmer
Gary Player
Tom Watson
Lee Trevino
Johnny Miller
Sam Snead
Tom Weiskopf
Lee Elder

Rightly or wrongly, golf has long been regarded as a rich man's game—old paintings of obviously wealthy gentlemen dressed in their finery and swinging a long-nosed club with their humble caddie stood close by; the price of feathery balls in the early 19th century and before; the size and opulence of some of the game's grandest clubhouses; the cost of joining its most prestigious clubs; the cost of the green fee at the world's best courses; the price tag attached to modern drivers, all contributing to the notion. Unfortunately, it's also seen by many as a predominantly white man's game. And while that is absolutely not the reality at the vast majority of clubs in the U.S.—and in most countries and cities around the world—it's an ugly stereotype that endures.

The PGA of America has a regrettably racist history, as it explicitly excluded Black players from competing in its tournaments for decades, finally removing the "Caucasian-only" clause from its Constitution in September 1961 (California Attorney General, Stanley Mosk, had barred the PGA from staging events at California's public courses, and he encouraged other states to do likewise. The PGA eventually bowed to pressure.)

Thankfully, the organization introduced several initiatives in the early 2020s to heal long-standing wounds—including the 2022 Inclusion Statement, the LEAD Program, PGA WORKS, PGA JobMatch, FairWays to Leadership, etc.—and granted posthumous memberships to Black golfing pioneers such as Bill Spiller, Ted Rhodes, John Shippen, and Joe Louis (the boxer was also a very good golfer).

And while the Masters and Augusta National Golf Club have likewise largely succeeded in losing their reputation for discrimination—the club admitted its first Black member (TV executive Ron Townsend) in September 1990 and is now thought to have several Black members—it took decades to lose the tag following a dreadful comment attributed to Clifford Roberts. According to a 2012 *New York Times* article, he once allegedly said that "As long as I'm alive, golfers will be white, and caddies will be black." (No one appears certain when he is supposed to have said this or even if he said it.) Roberts was, however, chairman of the club while it maintained its almost all-white membership, required Masters competitors to use the club's Black caddies, and maintained the Masters invitation criteria for American golfers that, prior to 1968, made it highly unlikely a Black player could qualify for the tournament.

Pete Brown was the first Black player to win on the PGA Tour—at the 1964 Waco Turner Open in Oklahoma—and he also won the Andy Williams-San Diego Invitational in 1970. Charlie Sifford won six United Golf Associations (UGA) National Negro Opens, captured two titles on the PGA Tour, and finished in the top 60 on the money list in his first nine years as a PGA Tour player. Using today's criteria, it's likely both Brown and Sifford would have earned an invitation to the Masters, but at the time the tournament didn't necessarily invite all PGA Tour winners to the following year's event (there were 26 qualifying categories for the 2026 tournament of which winning a PGA Tour event with full FedEx Cup point allocation was one) and their victories and general play apparently weren't considered worthy. The play of other Black golfers—specifically Ted Rhodes and Bill Spiller—might also have warranted invitations in previous decades.

In March 1973, a group of Congressmen appealed to the club, urging it to invite an African American to the Masters to which Roberts replied "We are a little surprised, as well as being flattered, that 18 Congressmen should be able to take time out to help us operate a golf tournament. We feel certain someone has misinformed the distinguished lawmakers, because there is not and never has been player discrimination, subtle or otherwise."

It wasn't until 1975, however, that a Black player finally received an invitation. Dallas, Texas-native Lee Elder beat England's Peter Oosterhuis in a playoff to win the Monsanto Open in Pensacola, Florida in 1974, by which time the Masters had begun inviting all PGA Tour winners (the policy was introduced in 1972 and remained in place until 1999. Now, PGA Tour winners who receive full FedEx Cup points for their victory qualify for the Masters).

Two months before the tournament, Elder received an invitation to the club for a practice round, and on the day he arrived for the tournament, he was met in front of the clubhouse by Roberts.

TOP AND BOTTOM: Elder playing the 1975 Masters

His playing partner for the first round would be the sweet-swinging, future hall-of-famer Gene Littler who had won the U.S. Open in 1961. The pair teed off on Thursday morning at 11 a.m., Elder striping one down the middle of the first fairway. He shot a 2-over 74—pretty good when you consider the distractions and pressure he must have felt, but tied for 37th, seven shots behind leader Bobby Nichols. On the second day, Elder struggled to a 78 and, at +8, he missed the cut by four strokes.

The tournament was won by Jack Nicklaus who famously holed a 40-foot putt on the 16th hole in the final round and beat Johnny Miller and Tom Weiskopf by one, finishing at 12-under, 276.

Elder would play in a total of six Masters and make the cut three times with a high finish of T17 in 1979. He won four PGA Tour events and a total of 16 professional titles.

In 2021, he was invited back to the Masters to be an honorary starter alongside Nicklaus and Gary Player. He died in November of that year, aged 87.

Elder, Player, and Nicklaus—honorary starters at the 2021 Masters

1977 Open Championship

Nicklaus vs. Watson. The famous "Duel in the Sun."

DATE
July 6-9, 1977

LOCATION
Turnberry (Ailsa)
Ayrshire, Scotland

PRIZE
£10,000

IN THE FIELD
Jack Nicklaus
Tom Watson
Arnold Palmer
Gary Player
Lee Trevino
Johnny Miller
Seve Ballesteros
Peter Thomson
Tom Weiskopf
Hale Irwin
Hubert Green
Tony Jacklin
Nick Faldo

Many older golf fans can tell you that the 1977 Open Championship is known as the "Duel in the Sun." But even now, there is disagreement over when exactly the duel began.

One half of the divide will tell you it started at about 3 p.m. on Friday, when Jack Nicklaus and Tom Watson—the duelers—went out for their third round (the championship had begun on Wednesday) while others insist it didn't properly begin until Saturday's fourth and final round, as Nicklaus and Watson had been the penultimate pairing on Friday with Roger Maltbie and Hubert Green going out last. Green had his own theory: "By the time Roger and me got to the 5th hole (in the third round), there was no gallery following us at all," he said. "I mean nobody. I think even our wives went off and watched Jack and Tom play." Whenever it started, Nicklaus and Watson's head-to-head was an epic encounter that no one lucky enough to have seen it will ever forget, no matter what age they live to.

Turnberry, located on Scotland's west coast about 20 miles south of Prestwick, was making its open debut. Its first holes had appeared in 1901, when landowner Archibald Kennedy, the Third Marquess of Ailsa, decided he should build a course on 175 of his unfertile acres to coincide with the opening of the nearby Maidens and Dunure Light Railway line. The Ailsa Course was designed by 1883 Open champion Willie Fernie, and originally had 13 holes. A second course—the nine-hole Arran—opened a few years later, but in World War I, both courses were taken over by the Royal Flying Corps, which built a base with a landing strip on them, and used the huge 1906 Turnberry Hotel on top of the hill as a hospital.

The golf courses reopened after the war, but were requisitioned again by the Royal Air Force in World War II and weren't decommissioned and returned to the golfing world until the late 1940s. Designer MacKenzie Ross then rebuilt the Ailsa course, which re-opened in 1951 and was redesigned by Martin Ebert in 2016.

The Ailsa has hosted the Open Championship on four occasions—1977, 1986, 1994, and 2009—and while all of them were notable for one reason or another, the 1977 edition may well be the most notable Open Championship ever.

Though the field was highlighted by numerous big names, little-known John Schroeder led after the first-round. With birdies at the final two holes, the one-time PGA Tour winner shot a 4-under-par, 66. More recognizable players weren't far behind, though: Nicklaus, Watson, and Lee Trevino were tied for 3rd, while defending champion Johnny Miller and Seve Ballesteros—the young Spanish star who had pushed Miller so close at Royal Birkdale the previous year—were a shot further back.

The weather, as it had been for several weeks, was hot and sunny, leaving the rough thin and wispy and the 6,875-yard course playing firm, fast, and short. Johnny Miller said that, had it not been for 18 pins located on knobs ("the 18 toughest pin placements I've ever seen") there would have been rounds in the 50s.

The sun shone again for Round 2, when Maltbie, a three-time winner on the PGA Tour and making his Open Championship debut, fired a 66 and took the outright lead at 3-under. One shot back were Nicklaus, Watson, Trevino, and Green who had won the U.S. Open at Southern Hills a couple of weeks before despite receiving a death threat. Green said he had been hoping to shoot a 60 (he made a hole-in-one at the 4th then five birdies in a row from the 8th) before becoming derailed over the final few holes.

While Green's 66 was certainly impressive, it paled against Mark Hayes' magnificent 7-under 63—only the third 63 in major championship history after Johnny Miller's outstanding final round to win the 1973 U.S. Open, and Bruce Crampton's in the second round of the 1975 PGA Championship.

While Maltbie and Green were Friday's final pairing, all the attention soon settled on the group in front. Nicklaus birdied the 1st, 4th, 6th, and 7th holes, before heavy rain and thunder stopped play for half-an-hour. Nicklaus eventually turned in 31, while Watson—who had beaten Nicklaus by two shots at the Masters in April and won the Western Open in June—was two shots behind. Both players ended up shooting 65—their third successive matching score (68, 70, 65), and at 7-under, they would begin the final Round 3 shots clear of Ben Crenshaw in 3rd, with Maltbie and Green fading a bit further behind.

"It was a good exhibition," Nicklaus told the press after the round. "We both played well. I tried to make it a one-man tournament and so did Tom. I like being involved in a challenge like that."

"It was nip and tuck," Watson said. "I hope the outcome tomorrow is like it was in the Masters. It is going to be fun as we will be paired together again. It will make me try a little harder. It's going to be interesting." Interesting would be about the 18th word you'd use to describe what ultimately happened the following day, the first 17 being synonyms of incredible.

It's unlikely the nearest challenger, Crenshaw, believed he still had a chance at the start of the day, with both Nicklaus and Watson playing some of their best golf ever. But his hopes might have improved slightly after Watson made a bogey at the 2nd. Nicklaus was still piling it on, though, going three clear after four holes.

Suddenly though, Watson came to life birdieing the 5th, 7th, and 8th. A Nicklaus birdie at the 9th put him one-up at the turn, and he went two clear with a birdie at the 12th. Watson responded magnificently, though, birdieing the 13th, and then holing a 60-foot putt from off the green for another birdie, at the par-three 15th.

On the 16th tee, Watson turned to Nicklaus and said, "This is what it's all about, isn't it?," to which Nicklaus replied, "You bet it is."

Two pars at 16 meant they were tied as they teed off at the par-five 17th. Watson hit the green in two and two-putted for a birdie, while Nicklaus hit a poor second short and right of the green. After a good chip, he had about four feet for a matching birdie.

Almost everyone watching would have said Nicklaus was going to hole the putt. But he didn't. He missed left, the ball not even touching the hole. The gallery and everyone watching on TV were stunned. BBC TV's Peter Alliss seemed less surprised than others, though, pointing out that Nicklaus had missed a few similar-length putts during the week. After the ball slid by, Alliss lamented, "If

Nicklaus does have a chink in his armor, it's just that."

Watson therefore led by one as they stood on the 18th tee. He hit a safe long-iron down the left side of the fairway, and Nicklaus—thinking he had to make a birdie—took a driver but pushed it right, his ball finishing in thick rough beneath the spines of a gorse bush. Despite the lie, Nicklaus muscled an 8-iron on to the front-right of the green about 35 feet from the hole. It was an excellent shot, but after Watson hit a 7-iron from 178 yards to about three feet, it was surely over.

Watson's caddie Alfie Fyles looked at his boss and said, "Well Sir, you've got him now." Watson knew better than to call it before the final putt had dropped, though, especially if Nicklaus was involved. "Alf, no I don't," he said. "We have to expect him to make this putt."

Of course, after missing the four-footer on the previous green, Nicklaus sank the long putt, causing the massive galleries around the 18th green to create a sound no British golf crowd had come close to making. As the ball neared the hole, Alliss said, "It can't be, can it?" And, as it dropped, "Ha, what about that, then?" He just laughed. "Well, if there are any knighthoods or honorary degrees flying about, this fellow must be due for one. I don't think

Watson approaches the 10th green, as Nicklaus and caddie look on

I've ever seen anything like it in my life. We were just thinking now wouldn't it be nice to have two putts from about three feet for the Open Championship, and suddenly, young Master Watson has to pull himself together and pop his in to be champion. What a putt, what a putt."

And then, Watson holed his three-foot putt for birdie to shoot another 65 and finish one clear of Nicklaus at 12-under 268. "Well, well, well, it was absolute drama to the end," remarked Alliss. "I don't think I've seen anything better than that in my life...and neither have you."

A few tournaments have since come close to matching this genuine edge-of-your-seat shootout drama—1986 Masters, 1991 Ryder Cup, 2016 Open Championship, and the 2025 Masters are the quartet that probably came the closest—but at Turnberry in 1977, the two best players in the world separated themselves from the rest of the competition (Hubert Green, who finished 3rd after a final round 67, said, "I won the tournament this week. I don't know what game those other two guys were playing") and conducted their own high-class competition, with it all coming down to the very last putt.

How many tournaments still make you shake your head in disbelief 50 years after they happened?

LEFT: Nicklaus and Watson arm-in-arm afterward

RIGHT: Watson with the Claret Jug

Nicklaus' Rivalries

While Jack Nicklaus is obviously one of the two best golfers to ever play the game, it must be said Tom Watson fared pretty well in head-to-head encounters against the Golden Bear, and not just at Turnberry.

Watson and Nicklaus finished 1st and 2nd (or tied 2nd) four times. All four were major championships, and Watson won all four!

- 1977 Masters (Watson by two)
- 1977 Open Championship (Watson by one)
- 1981 Masters (Watson by two over Nicklaus and Miller)
- 1982 U.S. Open (Watson by two)

Of course, Nicklaus had other great rivalries, the closest of them all surely against **Arnold Palmer**. These two finished 1st and 2nd in the same tournament five times. Again, all five were majors, with Nicklaus winning three and Palmer two.

- 1960 U.S. Open (Palmer by two over amateur Nicklaus)
- 1962 U.S. Open playoff (Nicklaus in a playoff)
- 1964 Masters (Palmer by six over Nicklaus and Marr)
- 1965 Masters (Nicklaus by nine over Palmer and Player)
- 1967 U.S. Open (Nicklaus by four)

Nicklaus and Gary Player did not finish 1st and 2nd at the same tournament except in the 1965 Masters, which Nicklaus won and where Player finished tied for 2nd with Palmer.

Nicklaus' encounters with Lee Trevino were similar to those he'd have with Watson. He and Trevino finished 1st and 2nd at the same tournament four times. Again, all four were majors, and again, Nicklaus came out second best in all four.

- 1968 U.S. Open (Trevino by four)
- 1971 U.S. Open (Trevino in a playoff)
- 1972 Open Championship (Trevino by one)
- 1974 PGA Championship (Trevino by one)

Nicklaus and Johnny Miller finished 1st and 2nd at the same tournament six times (between 1972 and 1983), of which two were majors.

- 1975 Masters (Nicklaus by one over Miller)
- 1976 Open Championship (Miller by six over Nicklaus)

While the numbers above suggest Nicklaus might not have had the best of records against his closest rivals, don't forget he won 14 majors between 1960 and 1976, and that by end of his career, he'd have 18—9 more than Player, 10 more than Watson, 11 more than Palmer, 12 more than Trevino, and 16 more than Miller.

1982 Players Championship

First Players at TPC Sawgrass.

DATE
March 18-21, 1982

LOCATION
TPC Sawgrass
Ponte Vedra Beach, FL
USA

PRIZE
$90,000

IN THE FIELD
Jack Nicklaus
Arnold Palmer
Gary Player
Lee Trevino
Johnny Miller
Seve Ballesteros
Tom Watson
Hale Irwin

It's hard to remember sometimes that the Players Championship existed before TPC Sawgrass and its (in)famous Stadium Course were built. First played at the Atlanta Athletic Club in 1974, the Players was conceived by then PGA Tour Commissioner, Deane Beman, who said he and the golfers in the Tournament Players Association (touring professionals whose number included Jack Nicklaus, Arnold Palmer, Gary Player, Lee Trevino, etc. who had broken away from the PGA of America in 1968) fully expected it to quickly be regarded as equal in status to the Masters, U.S. Open, PGA Championship, and (British) Open. "The players are resolved to make this the fifth major," Beman told the press. "It is their championship, and they are extremely proud of it."

Initially intended to be played at a rotation of select courses around the U.S., the tournament offered its winner more than what the winners of each of the majors earned—$50,000, compared to $45,000 at the PGA Championship, $35,000 at the Masters and U.S. Open, and almost three times what the 1974 Open Championship paid out. The tournament was lavishly promoted by the TPA Tour (the name didn't stick and had become the PGA Tour by early 1982) and it didn't hurt that Nicklaus won three of the first five.

After Atlantic Athletic Club, the event traveled to Colonial CC in Fort Worth, Texas (1975), Inverrary CC in Lauderhill, Florida (1976), and Sawgrass CC in Ponte Vedra Beach, Florida (1977-81), before moving to TPC Sawgrass, where the tournament has been played every year since 1982.

Despite his original intention of taking the tournament around the country, Beman ultimately decided to give it a permanent home at PGA Tour headquarters which moved from Washington D.C. to Ponte Vedra Beach, Florida in the late 1970s (when it had a staff of three and operated out of a house in the Sawgrass development.)

Beman tried to buy Sawgrass CC, but when the offer was refused he turned instead to creating the Tour's own course.

The property Beman had earmarked was 415 acres of forest, wetlands, and swampland about 25 miles southeast of Jacksonville, and a mile inland from the Atlantic Ocean. The property was owned by brothers Paul and Jerome Fletcher, two local real estate developers who had the foresight to sell it to Beman for $1, believing the new course would raise the prestige and value of the surrounding Fletcher-owner property significantly.

Beman's plan was to incorporate 30-foot-high slopes/mounds around some of the greens and teeing areas to accommodate thousands of spectators, removing the need for some grandstands. This "stadium" concept would be common to almost every course in the Tournament Players Course (TPC) network that subsequently grew around the country following the success of TPC Sawgrass.

Beman selected Pete Dye to design the course. Then in his mid-50s, Dye had forged a reputation for creating quirky, eye-catching, thought-provoking layouts at places such as Harbour Town and Long Cove in South Carolina, Crooked Stick in Indiana, Oak Tree National in Oklahoma, the Golf Club in Ohio, and Casa de Campo (Teeth of the Dog) in the Dominican Republic.

Dye broke ground at Sawgrass in February 1979, and the course opened on March 24, 1980. Though a good deal of work was required to fill the swampy areas and create the golf holes, Dye and his crew worked quickly and were aided by a fast grow-in phase.

The design was full of magazine-cover/TV-screen-friendly holes, the most notable of which was the short 17th. Dye's green was initially to be defended by a pond, but it was surrounded by quality sand that Dye used in various other areas of the course. Removing so much sand left a gaping hole and broken ground surrounding the 17th green, which Pete's wife, Alice—an accomplished golfer and talented course designer herself—suggested they fill entirely with water to create an island green (actually, it's a peninsula as there is a narrow walkway connecting the green with the "mainland") bordered by railroad ties. Pete is said not to have liked the idea initially, but he relented and now the hole, just 137 yards long with a small bunker short of the putting surface, is one of the most famous in the world.

After two years' of continued grow-in and maturing, TPC Sawgrass was ready to host its first Players Championship in March 1982. With all due respect, the first-round leaderboard was full of little-known names—George Burns, Lyn Lott, Vance Heafner, Skeeter Heath, Pat Lindsay, Bruce Fleischer, Gibby Gilbert—that made the tournament sound more like a sequel to the movie Caddyshack that had been released 18 months before.

Friday's leaderboard wasn't much more newsworthy, though at least two-time U.S. Open champion Hale Irwin moved into contention with a 68. Nicklaus, Palmer, Player, and Trevino all missed the cut, however.

The exciting Spaniard Seve Ballesteros shot a Saturday 69 to move into a tie for 10th, four shots behind the leaders Brad Bryant and Bruce Lietzke, while Irwin was tied for 6th. Also tied for 6th after the third round was 1976 U.S. Open champion

The famed island 17th green at TPC Sawgrass' Stadium Course

Jerry Pate, and it was the Georgia native that excelled in the final round, shooting a superb 5-under 67 to win by two. Dye and the course he'd designed took a lot of criticism throughout the week. Ben Crenshaw cited another recent movie saying the TPC was "Star Wars Golf, designed by Darth Vader." So it was no surprise, perhaps, when Pate pushed Dye and Beman into the lake left of the 18th hole during the prize ceremony (to show it was all light-hearted, Pate dove in himself).

The Fifth Major?

The PGA Tour has continued to promote the Players heavily over the decades, piling money into its purse and ensuring as strong a field as possible. Indeed, it has had a better field than the majors for most of its life as the lowest-ranked 50 or so golfers at the Players are considerably higher in the world rankings than qualifiers at the Open Championship and U.S. Open. The Masters has a much smaller field meanwhile, and the PGA Championship continues to include 20 club professionals.

By 2025, the event stood at a crossroads—the PGA Championship had appeared to be losing status for a few years while the Players had gained momentum. The PGA Championship may never not be a major, but talk of the Players becoming a fifth had certainly increased, and there were those who said it already had.

Others (the author included) said that, if there ever is to be a fifth major, it needs to be played somewhere other than the USA, which is already home to three of the Grand Slam events.

The most likely candidate from a handful of historic events (Canadian, French, Spanish, South African, Japan Opens) is surely the Australian Open, which was established in 1904. In addition to its longevity, the Australian Open has been played at some of the world's finest courses, has an impressive list of winners (including Gary Player with seven wins, Jack Nicklaus with six, Greg Norman with five, Peter Thomson with three, Jordan Spieth with two, plus Gene Sarazen, Bobby Locke, Arnold Palmer, Tom Watson, Adam Scott and Rory McIlroy), and is in an entirely different part of the world to where the game's four biggest events are currently played.

1984 Open Championship

Ballesteros wins his second Claret Jug.

DATE
July 19-22, 1984

LOCATION
Old Course
St. Andrews
Fife, Scotland

PRIZE
£55,000

IN THE FIELD
Tom Watson
Bernhard Langer
Greg Norman
Lee Trevino
Fred Couples
Nick Faldo

Iconic celebrations are a big part of professional sport on the largest stages. Soccer fans may recall Bebeto's baby-rocking antics after scoring for Brazil against The Netherlands at the 1994 World Cup; Marco Tardelli's impassioned scream after putting Italy 2-0 up in the 1982 final against West Germany; or Brandi Chastain's sports-bra moment at the 1999 Women's World Cup. In boxing, the pickture of Muhammad Ali looking down on a beaten Sonny Liston in 1965 is indelible; and in track, Usain Bolt's "Lightning Bolt" gesture at the 2016 Olympics in Rio de Janeiro comes easily to mind.

For many golf fans, though, the most memorable celebration might be Seve Ballesteros' right-arm thrusts toward the crowd after he holed his birdie putt on the Old Course's 18th green to win the 1984 Open Championship.

The putt never really looked like it was going in. Ballesteros had clearly played a little too much break, and it was going to miss right. The ball slowed, however, and began curling left; it decelerated a little more, curled left some more, and finally toppled into the right edge of the cup. You can watch it over and over and swear this is going to be the time the ball slides by on the high side. But it always goes in, and the thought crosses your mind it was simply acquiescing to the brooding Spaniard's unshakeable will.

The 1984 edition was the 113th Open Championship, and the Old Course at St Andrews was staging the event for the 23rd time. It measured 6,933 yards, and the pre-tournament favorite was Tom Watson, the two-time defending champion who had won a total of five Claret Jugs, three of them coming in the previous four years. And not only was his form in the Open beyond impressive, he had just defeated Greg Norman in a playoff to win the PGA Tour's Western Open before leaving for Scotland.

Ballesteros, on the other hand, had been enduring a fairly miserable year, having finished tied for 48th at the Masters (where he was the defending champion), and T30 at the U.S. Open. He'd missed multiple cuts in 12 PGA Tour events and hadn't won in Europe for nine months.

Watson shot an opening 1-under 71 in relatively benign conditions, a round he described afterward as "adequate." Leading at 5-under 67 were Greg Norman, the U.S.'s Peter Jacobsen, and Scotland's Bill Longmuir. Norman's fellow Aussie, 23-year-old Ian Baker-Finch, who was playing in his first major championship—was one back, while Ballesteros was two back.

Baker-Finch, who had turned pro at the age of 15, rose to the top of the leaderboard on Day 2, carding a superb 66 that included a par on the 17th, where he holed out from the treacherous Road Hole Bunker. Three back were Ballesteros, Nick Faldo, and Lee Trevino who joked with reporters that his game plan was failing, as he had intended being 20-under-par at this stage.

Watson was 6th, but he would surge to the top of the leaderboard after Saturday's third round, shooting a 66 to join Baker-Finch at 11-under. Bernhard Langer shot 68, moving into a tie for 3rd alongside Ballesteros.

"Touch of Class"

Ballesteros' third round 70 was fairly unspectacular, except for one exceptional moment on the par-five 5th. In the middle of the fairway after a good drive, he got a little unlucky when his ball came to rest in an awkward spot from which he'd need something special if he was to get on or near the green in two. With the ball slightly above his feet and sitting on a tricky, sidehill slope with a rise in the ground directly behind it, Ballesteros needed to grip down on the club a little (the BBC's Alex Hay speculated he was hitting "what appears to be a number 3- or 4-iron"), pick it up quite sharply, and impart a hint of fade spin to counteract the slope. The shot was incredibly complicated, but Ballesteros pulled it off as perhaps only he could, the ball pitching just short of the green and rolling up to within about 10 feet of the hole. Hay called the shot "pure magic" while on-course microphones clearly picked up Lee Trevino's (Ballesteros' playing partner) reaction: "Touch of class, baby," the American said, "touch of class."

Seve's Greatest Shot?

Ballesteros' approach to the Old Course's 5th now has hundreds of thousands of views on YouTube, with each new visitor getting a glimpse of the sort of thing Ballesteros was capable of in his prime. We're fortunate that TV cameras were present on that occasion as, nine months previously, they had missed another of his most astonishing shots. All-square with Fuzzy Zoeller playing the 18th in their important Sunday singles at the 1983 Ryder Cup, Ballesteros drove into heavy rough left of the fairway and could only hack his second into a fairway bunker, 245 yards from the hole. Knowing his opponent was more than likely to make a par or better, Ballesteros felt he needed to go for the green—an extremely difficult shot given he was in sand, the match situation, and the fact he still had so far to go.

He risked a 3-wood and hit it so cleanly he barely disturbed the sand, the ball clearing the lip with ease and flying all the way to the front of the putting surface where it came to rest about 50 feet short of the hole. Ballesteros would get up and down for a tying five.

Seve's fist pump on the 72nd

We only know this from eyewitness accounts, of course. Jack Nicklaus, the U.S. captain, did see it and called it the greatest shot he'd ever seen. CBS's Peter Kostis said it was "singularly the best shot I've seen in over 35 years of broadcasting golf."

It's probable if footage of the shot did exist, it would have even more YouTube views than the long iron to the 5th hole at the 1984 Open.

On Sunday, Baker-Finch got off to a rotten start, his approach to the 1st carrying the Swilcan Burn, but spinning back into the water. He made a bogey five and faded to a 79, finishing in a tie for 9th. Watson didn't fare well over the opening nine either, shooting 37 to drop a shot behind Ballesteros who was playing in the group in front of Watson. The Spaniard was out in 34, but Watson drew level with a birdie at the 10th, and they were still level when Ballesteros reached the tough 17th hole. Seve's drive found the left rough, leaving a difficult shot to the shallow green, but he struck a beautiful 6-iron from 200 yards, and his ball avoided both the bunker and the road, stopping about 35 feet right of the flag. Having bogeyed the Road Hole in each of the first three rounds, his two-putt par on the final day was very timely.

A few minutes later, Watson's drive at the same hole hung right, and for a moment, looked like it might fail to clear the wall in front of the Old Course Hotel. Watson held out his arms, unsure as to where his ball might have finished, so he was noticeably relieved to learn it was in perfect position on the right side of the fairway. His exact yardage to the hole wasn't given, but we do know he hit a 2-iron which seems an awful lot of club given Ballesteros had hit a 6, and that the adrenalin pumping through Watson's arms would have added a few yards to whichever club he took. Not surprisingly, perhaps, Watson's ball flew the green and finished a few feet from the stone wall that marks the course's perimeter. Meanwhile, 400 yards to the east, Ballesteros was holing his birdie putt at the 18th, putting him one ahead. And when Watson's chip from behind the 17th green ran well past the cup, leading to a bogey, Ballesteros was two clear. Watson now had to hole his second at the last hole to force a playoff, but he could do no better than four.

At 27, Ballesteros had overcome what the *Glasgow Herald* called "an ancient links with a puzzling and frustrating box of tricks," winning his second Open Championship and fourth major. Four years later, he would add a fifth and final major, winning the 1988 Open Championship at Royal Lytham and St Anne's—where he had won his first.

Ballesteros died on May 7, 2011, at the age of 54, due to complications related to a brain tumor. Those lucky enough to have watched him up close know they'll likely never see another with his touch, creativity, and genius. He was a force of nature who made hellaciously difficult shots look incredibly simple and who drew more gasps from the gallery during a single round than most pros do in a hundred.

1986 Masters

Nicklaus wins his sixth Green Jacket.

DATE
April 10-13, 1986

LOCATION
Augusta National
Augusta, GA
USA

PRIZE
$144,000

IN THE FIELD
Tom Watson
Seve Ballesteros
Greg Norman
Nick Price
Bernhard Langer
Jack Nicklaus

Jack Nicklaus had practically been written off prior to the start of the 1986 Masters—no surprise, really, as he'd not won a major championship since 1980 and had missed two cuts in the previous year's majors. He didn't win anything, anywhere, in 1985, and in the seven PGA Tour events he'd played in the first three months of 1986, he'd missed three cuts, withdrawn once, and managed a top finish of T39. Once known for his prodigious length off the tee, he was now averaging just 266 yards—20 yards fewer than the Tour's biggest hitter, Davis Love III. And he was a cumulative +15 for the season. The most concerning number of all, though, was probably the fact he was now 46 years old—about 14 years past the average age of Masters winners.

It had certainly been a frustrating few seasons for the Golden Bear, who now seemed unable to recreate anything approaching his best golf even at the tournaments in which he'd excelled for so many years. The one decent finish he'd had at a major in 1985 was a T6 at the Masters, which showed his experience at Augusta National still counted for something. Combining that local knowledge with the sort of kick in the pants he received from the *Atlanta Journal-Constitution*'s Tom McCollister prior to the 1986 tournament obviously proved very productive.

In a column published on the Sunday before Masters week, McCollister wrote that Nicklaus was "gone, done," adding that "He just doesn't have the game anymore. It's rusted from lack of use. He's 46, and nobody that old wins the Masters." A friend of Nicklaus, staying at the Augusta house Nicklaus rented that week—cut the column from the paper and stuck it to the refrigerator so that every time Nicklaus opened the door, he would see it. "If anything would motivate him, that would," fellow competitor Nick Price said later.

It didn't seem to take effect immediately, however. An uninspiring 2-over-par 74 in Thursday's opening round saw Nicklaus finish the day in a tie for 25th, six back of the lead held by the relatively obscure Ken Green and Bill Kratzert.

A second-round 71 was a marked improvement, but at +1, he was now tied for 17th and still six behind the leader—Seve Ballesteros. The Spanish star was making headlines for more than his play at the Masters, though. "Seve on the Rampage" said one headline, alluding to his ongoing feud with PGA Tour commissioner Deane Beman. Beman had instituted a new, 15-tournament minimum if players were to retain their Tour cards—a minimum Seve did not meet in 1985. Ballesteros had labeled Beman "a little man who wants to be big," and even though the two-time Masters champion was at the top of the leaderboard and looking primed for a third title in six years, the back-and-forth with Beman was hard to ignore.

This non-Masters story had taken up its share of column space up to now, but it would disappear over a weekend that no-one could have seen coming, especially Tom McCollister.

Price-less

Bruce Lietzke and Nick Price were playing in one of the earlier groups on Saturday morning. Tied for 38th, having made the cut by one stroke, they each stood at 4-over-par. Price had opened with a 79, and then improved by 10 shots on Friday. The 29-year-old from Zimbabwe had played on the South Africa and European Tours in his early-to-mid 20s, and he had one win on the PGA Tour, which he had joined in 1983. He finished 2nd at the 1983 PGA Championship at Riviera CC, and tied for 2nd at the 1985 Open Championship at Royal Troon GC, so he was far from being an unknown. And four hours after teeing off in the third round of the 1986 Masters, Price would be the most talked about golfer on the planet.

Despite making a bogey at the 1st, where he was given a bad yardage by his caddie (who had over-celebrated Price's making the cut the night before), he reached the turn in an excellent 3-

under-par 33, rising steadily up the leaderboard.

After birdies at the 10th, 11th, 12th and 13th, Price reached 7-under for the day and 3-under for the tournament, and the patrons following him were beginning to make a lot of noise. Even though he got another shockingly bad yardage at the 15th, Price made another birdie, and after hitting his tee shot at the 16th to a few feet from the hole, he was 9-under for the round and on pace to beat the course record.

Two pars on the final two holes would give Price a 63, while a birdie at either would make him the first man in history to shoot 62 at a major championship.

He parred the 17th and hit his drive at the 18th into the first of two bunkers on the left. Dave McNeilly, the caddie who hadn't exactly excelled himself so far that day, suggested Price splash out safely, but Price thought he could get a 4-iron to the green. Another excellent iron shot put him 25 feet from the hole, and the putt looked good all the way ... until it horseshoed around the cup to give him a par-four and a 63. Price's new course record beat the 64s shot by Lloyd Mangrum in 1940, Jack Nicklaus in 1965, and Gary Player in 1978.

Price's incredible 63 put him at 5-under-par for 54 holes and in a tie for 2nd with Donnie Hammond, defending champion Bernhard Langer, and Ballesteros.

The leader at 6-under was Greg Norman, whose Saturday 68 included seven birdies. Nicklaus shot 69, and for the first time that week appeared on the leaderboard. Even so, he was still four shots out of the lead, and with Ballesteros, Langer, Price, Watson, and Tom Kite, plus three others, between him and Norman, he was given little chance of winning another Green Jacket.

Nicklaus wasn't counting himself out, though. Asked if he could still win, he replied "If the putts start to drop, I'll be awfully close. This is the best I've hit the ball for years. I'm very happy with my game." He would play the final round with Scotland's Sandy Lyle, winner of the previous year's Open Championship, in the fifth-to-last group.

After a par at the 1st, Nicklaus birdied the 2nd, parred the 3rd, bogeyed the 4th, and then made four straight pars. At the 9th, he holed a slick 12-footer down the hill for a birdie to turn in 1-under 35. Now 3-under for the tournament, he was still three back of Norman, with Price, Langer, and Watson still very much in the picture. Ballesteros and Kite were there, too, each having holed for eagle from off the green at the 8th.

Moving to the back nine, Nicklaus' putter stayed hot. At the downhill, par-four 10th—often ranked the toughest hole at the Masters—he holed a right-to-left-breaking putt from 30-35 feet to go to 4-under, and at the similarly difficult 11th, he holed from 25 feet for another birdie.

Masters patrons are typically orderly, respectful, and disciplined, of course, but it would not be inaccurate to say they were pretty excited at this point. Players behind and in front knew very well that Nicklaus was doing something special, and -5, he was now tied for 3rd, two shots behind Norman and Ballesteros.

At the short 12th, Nicklaus pulled a 6-iron badly and made a bogey, but he got right back on the birdie train at the par-five 13th, following a superb drive and 4-iron to the green.

On 14, Nicklaus went through the back of the green but chipped to tap-in range for a safe 4. Moments later, however, Ballesteros hit a superb approach to the 13th green and rolled in a 10-foot putt for his second eagle of the round. At 9-

Nicklaus holing another putt on 16

under, he had a two-shot lead and was four clear of Nicklaus.

On the CBS telecast, Ken Venturi said you wouldn't want to give Seve a two-shot lead over the final five holes.

The back-and-forth rollercoaster final round continued at the 15th where Nicklaus hit another magnificent 4-iron and holed the eagle putt to go to 7-under. And if that wasn't enough, he then knocked a 5-iron to about three feet at the par-three 16th and holed that. It was exhilarating stuff, but Ballesteros, pondering his second shot at the 15th, was surely still in control.

After a 302-yard drive, he had just 198 yards down the hill and over the pond to the hole and settled on a 4-iron. At some point in his swing, however, he must have subconsciously felt he had too much club, as he eased into the strike and wound up hitting an ugly smother-hook short and left into the water. It was a dreadful shot that seemed to suck all the air out of the atmosphere for a moment.

After a drop, pitch, and two putts, the resulting bogey put Ballesteros level with Nicklaus at 8-under-par. Nicklaus' drive on the 17th flew well past Eisenhower's Tree on the left (the famous loblolly pine was removed in 2014 after sustaining storm damage), and his approach finished about 11 feet left of the hole. From there, he coaxed a delicate, left to-right-breaking putt down the slope and into the hole for his seventh birdie of the round (he'd also had an eagle and two bogies), giving him a precious one-shot lead.

At the last, Nicklaus' approach shot came up well short, finishing on the green's lower tier with the hole cut toward the back. He judged his lag putt almost to perfection, though, the ball coming up a few inches shy of the hole. He tapped in for a back-nine of 30 and a memorable round of 65 that saw him finish at 9-under-par.

Ballesteros bogeyed the 17th and was now two back with just the last to play, and neither Kite nor Price could quite find the necessary birdies to catch Nicklaus; Kite narrowly missed a putt on the last that would have put him in a tie. That left Norman, who went quiet for a spell before charging back with birdies at 14, 15, 16, and 17. At the 18th, he needed a par to tie Nicklaus and a birdie to win. He hit a good drive, but pushed his approach right of the green and was unable to get down in two. With a closing bogey, he fell back into a tie for 2nd with Kite on 280. Alone on 279, Nicklaus had won the Masters again.

With his son Jackie on the bag, it was obviously a sentimental victory for Nicklaus. Afterward, he admitted how the competition in the final round had been his motivation. "Anytime I am playing guys like that," he said, "I have more incentive; I get more excited. I'd rather play them than guys I haven't met yet."

Newspapers from Augusta to Australia reported that the Golden Bear had come out of hibernation. The Associated Press wrote, "In perhaps the finest hour of a career unmatched in golf history," Nicklaus had "barged out of an international pack to score his sixth Masters victory in the 50th playing of the revered tournament."

The week before the Masters, Nicklaus had attended a USGA event in Atlanta where he told those present that he wasn't going to retire from golf playing the way he had been lately. "If I'm going to quit," he added, "I'm going to go out playing a heck of a lot better, and I'm going to go out winning some golf tournaments."

A few days later, after Nicklaus had won his sixth Masters, there were plenty who thought he should go out on a high note and walk away from the game. Nicklaus chose not to, however, and didn't win on the PGA Tour again. But he did claim 10 Senior Tour victories, including eight senior majors, plus a handful of non-official events. He certainly didn't need those post-Masters wins to enhance or complete his record; he just loved competing in golf tournaments too much to stop.

FINAL LEADERBOARD			
1.	Nicklaus	-9	279
T2.	Kite	-8	280
T2.	Norman	-8	280
4.	Ballesteros	-7	281
5.	Price	-6	282
T6.	Haas	-5	283
T6.	Watson	-5	283
T8.	Nakajima	-4	284
T8.	Tway	-4	284
T8.	Stewart	-4	284

1990 Solheim Cup

First playing of the Solheim Cup.

DATE
Nov. 16-18, 1990

LOCATION
Lake Nona G&CC
Orlando, FL
USA

PRIZE
The Solheim Cup

IN THE FIELD
Laura Davies
Helen Alfredsson
Liselotte Neumann
Pat Bradley
Beth Daniel
Nancy Lopez
Dottie Mochrie
Patty Sheehan

Professional male golfers from the U.S. and Great Britain/Ireland/Europe (Ryder Cup), male amateurs (Walker Cup), and female amateurs (Curtis Cup) each had a biennial, trans-Atlantic team competition in place by the mid-1930s, but a team event involving professional women golfers didn't exist until 1990.

The LPGA Tour had been producing phenomenal talents for decades, but it was only in the 1980s that women's professional golf in Europe began to make some news. The British PGA organized a women's tour in 1979, staging 18 tournaments in its first year, and featuring players from five countries. Nine years later, the women formed their own organization—the Women Professional Golfers' European Tour (WPGET) with its own headquarters.

The best and most recognizable female player in Europe at the time was England's Laura Davies who won the Women's British Open in 1986 and the U.S. Women's Open in 1987. Some others were beginning to earn column space in newspapers and magazines as well, including Davies' countrywomen Alison Nicholas and Trish Johnson, Sweden's Helen Alfredsson and Liselotte Neumann (who won the U.S. Women's Open in 1988), and France's Marie-Laure de Lorenzi. And with their success, the notion that professional women's golf should have its own Ryder Cup-style competition began to gain momentum.

The energy behind—and funding for—the event was provided by Karsten Solheim, who had founded Karsten Manufacturing in 1959, and his wife Louise. The Solheims were major supporters of women's golf, sponsoring LPGA Tour events in Arizona and Massachusetts. They convinced the LPGA and WPGET that women's golf needed its own team event.

For the inaugural event, each team had eight players and a non-playing captain. Lake Nona G&CC in Florida was chosen as the venue, and the tournament would span three days with four foursomes on Day 1, four fourballs on Day 2, and eight singles on Day 3. Sixteen points were therefore available, meaning whichever team won at least 8½ would be declared the winner.

UNITED STATES	EUROPE
Kathy Whitworth (Capt.)	Mickey Walker (Capt.)
Pat Bradley	Helen Alfredsson
Beth Daniel	Laura Davies
Cathy Gerring	Marie-Laure de Lorenzi
Rosie Jones	Trish Johnson
Betsy King	Liselotte Neumann
Nancy Lopez	Alison Nicholas
Dottie Mochrie	Dale Reid
Patty Sheehan	Pam Wright

Though both teams were full of accomplished players, the star-studded American side was much stronger on paper and far more experienced. Many commentators thought the match would be hopelessly one-sided—former LPGA Tour Commissioner, John Laupheimer, remarked that, though the event could potentially blossom into something credible, 1990 was too soon for the first match.

With only the highlights shown on TV, precious little coverage in newspapers, and only a thousand or so people in attendance (restricted to family and friends of the players, Lake Nona members, and Ping's invited guests), the 1990 event was very low-key and treated as something of a trial run.

Day 1

Laura Davies and Alison Nicholas made a statement by beating Pat Bradley and Nancy Lopez 2&1 in the first match out, but the rest of the foursomes went as expected with the U.S. pairs winning convincingly. **U.S. 3—Europe 1.**

Day 2

Betsy King and Beth Daniel beat Davies and Nicholas 4&3 in the first match, before Lotte Neumann and Pam Wright beat Cathy Gerring and Dottie Mochrie. The U.S. won the two remaining matches, taking the day/session 3-1. **U.S. 6—Europe 2.**

Day 3

The Americans won the first five matches by large margins; the first match was over on the 11th hole, where Bradley closed out Johnson, 8&7. The home side had

The Man Behind PING

Born in Bergen, Norway in 1911, Karsten Solheim came to the USA when he was two, the family settling in Seattle. Since his mother died young and his father went to Alaska to pan for gold, Solheim grew up as a foster child, eventually beginning school at the age of seven. He attended the University of Washington for a year before leaving to help his father (who had returned from Alaska) run his shoe shop. In the early 1940s, Solheim continued with his engineering studies via extension courses with the University of California, and soon after began working in the defense industry.

A General Electric (GE) employee in the 1950s, Karsten lived and worked in New York, and after being invited for a game of golf with colleagues, began tinkering with putter design. He established Karsten Manufacturing while still with GE, and after being transferred to Redwood City, California he created an odd-looking putter with most of the weight pushed to the heel and the toe. He called it the Ping 1-A, because of the "ping" sound it made at impact.

Solheim touted the instrument at professional events, and though players took a lot of convincing because of its unconventional appearance, the putter slowly earned a reputation for correcting poor strikes. Solheim left GE, and by 1966, believed there was sufficient interest in his putters for him to move the company to Phoenix, Arizona. He soon designed the Anser putter (Louise had suggested the name "Answer," which they shortened by removing the "w"), and in 1969, the company introduced its first iron: the K1.

therefore already won the tournament and its beautiful Waterford Cystal trophy by the time the Europeans won two late victories—Davies beating Rosie Jones, and Dale Reid getting the better of Patty Sheehan. Wright halved with King in the final match to make the final score. **U.S. 11½—Europe 4½.**

The first Solheim Cup may not have been terribly close but it was mostly successful, and lit a fire under the European team which won the event two years later—at Dalmahoy in Scotland—11½—6½ (each team had 10 players meaning there were two more singles matches).

In winning the 2024 event at Robert Trent Jones GC in Gainesville, Virginia, the U.S. extended its lead in the matches to 11-8 (defending champion Europe retained the Cup in 2023 following a tie at Finca Cortesin in Spain).

All such competitions take time to build momentum. The Ryder Cup went ahead without much fanfare for nearly 50 years before its popularity and the amount of attention/revenue it generated suddenly exploded in the mid-1980s. From humble beginnings, the Solheim Cup has grown into one of golf's most exciting competitions, receiving a great deal more press and TV coverage than it once did.

The victorious U.S. team, with members of the Solheim family

1991 Ryder Cup

An incredibly tense—and at times acrimonious—"War on the Shore."

DATE
Sept. 27-29, 1991

LOCATION
Kiawah Ocean Course
Kiawah Island, SC
USA

PRIZE
The Ryder Cup

IN THE FIELD
Seve Ballesteros
José María Olazábal
Bernhard Langer
Colin Montgomerie
Ian Woosnam
Paul Azinger
Hale Irwin
Payne Stewart
Corey Pavin
Steve Pate

The 1991 edition was the 29th playing of the Ryder Cup and the seventh since Continental European players had been added to the Great Britain and Ireland team in an effort to bolster an event that had become stale and predictable, thanks to repeated U.S. victories.

Despite having Spain's Seve Ballesteros and Antonio Garrido on its team, Europe lost quite badly in 1979, and it did so again in 1981 (see Honorable Mentions).

The 1983 encounter was much closer, however, the U.S. winning by a single point at PGA National in Florida, and it demonstrated the addition of superstars such as Ballesteros and West Germany's Bernhard Langer was beginning to have the desired effect.

The Europeans finally broke through in 1985, winning 16½ to 11½ at The Belfry in England, and two years later, it won at Muirfield Village in Ohio—its first victory in the U.S. Back at The Belfry in 1989, the Ryder Cup's second tie (see 1969 Ryder Cup) added fuel to a fast-growing fire.

By the time the 1991 matches rolled around, the U.S. and Europe had played each other six times with the U.S. winning the first three matches and Europe the next two, then retaining the cup as defending champion in 1989. Jack Nicklaus' hope that the addition of Continental players might resurrect the competition had certainly borne fruit. With the leveling of the playing field, however, came a sharp rise in competitiveness that would frequently become unseemly.

Poor Relations

Though still extremely hard-fought and competitive, the Ryder Cup today is essentially a match between friends, and even neighbors. Since several of the Europeans now live (or have homes) in the U.S. and play on the PGA Tour, members of recent Ryder Cup teams know each other well.

In 1991, however, Europeans were still having a hard time getting into the U.S. majors and played almost entirely on the European Tour. So they and the Americans didn't hang out like they might now, and there was still a large discrepancy between the teams in terms of status and wealth. Ballesteros, Europe's talisman, hadn't exactly endeared himself to U.S. players and the PGA Tour over the years, either. There was a genuine animosity that had grown over the years, thanks to a perfect storm of inequality, unfamiliarity, and probably a little envy.

And, speaking of storms, the U.S. military had been engaged in Operation Desert Storm in the Middle East that year, fueling a sense of nationalism among the U.S. team that was evident on the golf course. The antagonism and hostility that transpired weren't entirely unexpected, therefore.

Relations soured before Friday's first shot following a disastrous gala event on Wednesday evening, where attendees watched a somewhat one-sided film detailing the history of the Ryder Cup. Strangely, the film didn't include mention of any British, Irish, or European players, which was obviously seen as something of a slight by the visiting team. Staff at the European's hotel had also given some of the players' room numbers to a local radio DJ who phoned them at 5 a.m. in a prank he called "Waking the Enemy." And to finish off the pre-tournament un-pleasantries, President George W. Bush said during the opening ceremony that he hoped the U.S. won. Some might say that's an okay thing for a U.S. president to say, while others might think the opening ceremony is neither the time nor the place for a show of partisan support. Either way, it just added to the tension. If the Europeans had been looking for some pre-game motivation, they didn't have to search too hard.

UNITED STATES	EUROPE
Dave Stockton (Capt.)	Bernard Gallacher (Capt.)
Paul Azinger	Seve Ballesteros
Chip Beck	Paul Broadhurst
Mark Calcavecchia	Nick Faldo
Fred Couples	David Feherty
Ray Floyd	David Gilford
Hale Irwin	Mark James
Wayne Levi	Bernhard Langer
Mark O'Meara	Colin Montgomerie
Steve Pate	José María Olazábal
Corey Pavin	Steven Richardson
Payne Stewart	Sam Torrance
Lanny Wadkins	Ian Woosnam

Kia-what now?

The Ocean Course at Kiawah Island hadn't even been designed when, in May 1989, it was announced it had been awarded the 1991 Ryder Cup. PGA West in California had been the PGA of America's original choice of venue, but to ensure greater coverage on the East Coast of the U.S. and in Europe, the organization decided to move the event to Kiawah Island in South Carolina, where the 10,000-acre Kiawah Island Golf and Tennis Club had recently been purchased by the Landmark Land Company for $265 million.

Pete Dye was hired for the job of creating the course (his wife Alice would provide a significant assist). Already beset by tight deadlines, the Dyes needed a lot of things to go in their favor, but only a few months into construction, Hurricane Hugo hit. Pete and his crew had to work incredibly quickly to redesign and rebuild the course on a site that had changed dramatically. Getting the Ocean Course ready in time would be touch and go, so a plan was in place to move the event to nearby Osprey Point, if necessary.

Construction was complete by late 1990, meaning the course had only nine months or so to grow in before staging the game's most prestigious team event. Work was actually still being carried out just weeks before the Ryder Cup began.

Given the hurricane's terrible timing, there's no doubt Dye and his team did an incredible job getting the course ready, and it was also clear they built an excellent course. Invariably ranked in the top 30 courses in the U.S., it would later host the PGA Championship in 2012 and 2021, and it was selected to host the PGA again in 2031.

Day 1

The ill-feeling resulting from the numerous pre-tournament snafus spilled over into the very first match of the event—a Friday morning foursome between Paul Azinger/Chip Beck and Seve Ballesteros/José María Olazábal.

On the 9th hole, the Spaniards discovered the American pair had violated the rules by changing its ball (in alternate-shot, each team has to declare which ball they will be playing for the entirety of the match). Azinger and Beck played different compression balls and had swapped the team ball depending on who was teeing off.

The first violation might have happened on the 7th, and the Europeans just didn't notice what was happening until the 9th, by which time it was too late to claim holes that had already been played.

It was a confusing situation, and Olazábal wasn't happy with how it all played out. And, as Azinger and Ballesteros were the two most fiery players on either side and had shared words over a ruling at the 1989 match, the situation grew unpleasant. It was eventually resolved after about half an hour, but the damage had been done and the confrontational tone never abated. Clearly angered, the Spanish duo played like men possessed, winning the match 2&1. Later, Ballesteros said the American team was made up of "11 nice guys and Paul Azinger."

In the afternoon, Corey Pavin arrived for his match wearing a battle-fatigue cap, something the Europeans felt unnecessarily contributed to the swirling jingoism. Pavin explained that, since Desert Storm had been an Allied operation, he didn't feel it was insensitive to the Europeans and that he was merely showing respect and gratitude to the troops. One is inclined to give Pavin the benefit of any doubt, though his room-reading skills might have been better.

The Americans won the last three morning foursomes, and in the afternoon fourballs, Europe won two, the U.S. one, and one match was halved. At the end of the day, therefore, the U.S. led 4½ to 3½.

Day 2

On Friday morning, the U.S. won three of the foursomes matches, with Azinger and Mark O'Meara beating Nick Faldo and David Gilford 7&6. During the match, 34-year-old Faldo, a veteran of seven Ryder Cups, is said not to have spoken with his 26-year-old partner, a Ryder Cup rookie—a story that stuck and is still used today. Like a lot of the anecdotes and "memories" from that week, however, you take it with a pinch of salt, as Gilford later said Faldo was friendly enough and had spoken to him, just not much because neither of them were particularly big talkers. (This was well before Faldo began his TV-commentating career.)

The Americans came into 1991 well aware of Ballesteros' reputation for gamesmanship, especially in match play. And though they were certainly to blame for the rules infraction on Day 1, they were on the lookout for the Spaniard's jiggery-pokery during his morning foursomes match with Olazábal against Ray Floyd and Fred Couples. To keep the healthy flow of ill-feeling going, an unimpressed Ray Floyd confronted Ballesteros after he'd heard him coughing during a swing. Floyd reportedly said something to the effect of, "Seve, I'm much better at that sort of thing than you," adding that he might be forced to reciprocate. The Spaniards ultimately won the match 3&2, and their partnership had now reaped 8½ points from a possible 10 dating back to the 1987 contest (they would go on to become one of the Ryder Cup's greatest ever partnerships winning 12 points from 15 matches—11 wins and two halves).

Seve & Jose Maria read a putt

In the afternoon, Europe won three of the four fourballs, setting up an exciting final day, when the outcome would remain in the balance right to the final green of the final match.

Day 3

The day began with some additional controversy (because, of course it did), when U.S. captain Dave Stockton announced that Steve Pate would not be playing his singles match because of an injury he had sustained on Wednesday evening (while en route to the gala dinner, his limousine was involved in a collision with another team limousine that resulted in a hip injury and bruised ribs). Pate had played through the pain on Saturday afternoon (partnering Corey Pavin in a 2&1 loss to Langer and Colin Montgomerie), but on Sunday morning he couldn't hit a wedge more than 40 yards on the range.

Conspiracy Theory

The Europeans suspected Pate had been withdrawn because he was scheduled to play Ballesteros who was in such scintillating form that week he would most likely have won the match (the rules stipulated that each player would get half a point in the case of an injury.)

But was Pate really lined up to play Ballesteros, or had his name come out of the blind draw next to Gilford's? Whatever happened, Europe's captain, Bernard Gallacher, had to bench a player for the singles and chose Gilford who was absolutely gutted he couldn't play (the controversial "envelope rule" would be used again in 2025 when Europe's Viktor Hovland sat out the singles because of a slipped disc in his neck—an ailment some Americans doubted.)

Ballesteros ended up playing, and beating, the out-of-form Wayne Levi. Perhaps only Stockton, the U.S team and a few others close to the situation will ever know the absolute truth of what transpired, but it just added to an already fragile atmosphere.

Europe won the first two singles matches, with Faldo defeating Floyd and David Feherty beating Payne Stewart. In the third match, however, Mark Calcavecchia built a commanding lead over Montgomerie and looked sure to earn the U.S.'s first point of the day. But as his nerves grew ever-more unpredictable over the final few holes, his game unraveled and he lost the last four, coming out with only a half point.

It could have spelled disaster for the U.S., but Stockton insisted Calcavecchia's early play had inspired his teammates, which could well have been the case as Azinger beat Olazábal, Pavin beat Steven Richardson, and Chip Beck beat Ian Woosnam. With Ballesteros beating Levi, and Paul Broadhurst defeating O'Meara, the overall match score remained incredibly tight.

Couples then beat Sam Torrance and Lanny Wadkins beat Mark James giving the U.S. a 14-13 lead, which meant it all came down to the final match—Hale Irwin for the U.S. against Bernhard Langer for Europe. A halved match would make the final score 14½—13½ to the U.S. But, if Langer could win a full point, the score would be 14-14 and Europe would retain the Cup again (they had retained it in 1989 after the tie at The Belfry which followed their victory at Muirfield Village in 1987).

Despite struggling with his swing, Irwin was 2-up after 14 holes. Langer then won the 15th, made a six-footer for a half at the 16th, and holed a now-or-never four-footer to win the 17th. It meant the match was all-square (tied) heading to the final tee.

Somehow, there hadn't been any genuine controversy for a few hours which seemed odd, but there was time for one last unfortunate, though never-to-be-confirmed, incident. After hooking his drive toward what looked like a troublesome area, Irwin's ball suddenly appeared in a perfectly playable lie on the edge of the fairway. Accounts later said how the ball had struck someone in the gallery, preventing it from reaching the rough, but the video is totally inconclusive.

Langer after the decisive missed putt

Irwin hit his second right of the green and then a poor chip that grabbed too soon and came up about 25 feet short. Langer, meanwhile, had hit a good drive but his long-iron approach also missed the green to the right. From there, he hit his first putt a little strong, the ball coming to rest about six feet past the hole. Irwin missed his putt for a four, meaning Langer had a putt for the hole, the match, and the Cup.

Thinking the spike mark just in front of his ball was large enough to deflect it off-course (you couldn't repair spike marks until 2019), Langer elected to hit the putt straight, and watched in horror as the ball curved right, braising the edge of the hole, but failing to drop.

The U.S. had won by a point, and decades of nitpicking could now begin. Depending on which side of the Atlantic you lived, and which country's newspapers you read, you either felt the U.S. had taken an unsporting, win-at-all-costs attitude into the event, manifesting itself in some questionable activity, or the Europeans were being a little dramatic and over-sensitive. As is usually the case with this sort of thing, both perspectives were probably somewhat valid, and neither entirely false.

Regardless, the rivalry became something of a feud in 1991, and in less than a decade, the Ryder Cup had morphed from an intense competition only golfers might enjoy, or even understand, into what felt like charged, confrontational combat where sports fans who might not even play the game could show their colors.

The victorious U.S. team, celebrating on the beach on Kiawah Island

The Battle of Brookline in '99

While the undercurrent of bitterness and antipathy never seemed far below the surface, the subsequent matches—1993, '95, and '97—did go off relatively peacefully. In 1999, however, it turned ugly again. Thanks to more inspired team/pairs play, especially from Sweden's Jesper Parnevik and Spain's Sergio Garcia, who together won three and a half points from four matches, the Europeans led 10-6 by the end of the second day. They would need just four points from Sunday's 12 singles matches to retain the cup they had won at Valderrama in Spain two years before.

Traditionally strong in the singles, the U.S. players hadn't given up all hope, though, and captain Ben Crenshaw certainly wasn't beaten yet. At the end of his Saturday evening press conference, the two-time Masters champion remarked, "I'm going to leave you with this thought, and then I'm going to leave. I'm a big believer in fate. I have a good feeling about this. That's all I'm going to tell you."

The next morning, Crenshaw sent his strongest players out first, hoping to get some red on the board early, and Tom Lehman, Hal Sutton, Phil Mickelson, Davis Love III, Tiger Woods and David Duval all won their matches convincingly, turning the four-point deficit into a two-point lead.

The victorious Team USA

The crowd was growing berserk, and when Justin Leonard miraculously holed a 40-foot putt on the 17th green in his match against José María Olazábal, a stream of U.S. players, caddies, and wives ran across the green to celebrate. Olazábal still had a 20 to 25-foot putt of his own to match Leonard's birdie and keep the match all-square—and Europe's fading hopes alive—but it took a few minutes for order to be restored.

Eventually, the Spaniard was able to putt but missed, and because Jim Furyk had soundly beaten Garcia to make the match score 14-12, Leonard's assured half-point would enable the U.S. to reach the 14½ points it needed to win back the cup. Olazábal birdied the 18th to square the match, and Payne Stewart sportingly conceded his match to Colin Montgomerie to make the final match score 14½—13½.

Later, a handful of European team members said how poorly they thought the American team had behaved when Leonard holed his putt, as neither the hole nor the match was over at that point. And European Captain Mark James wrote a stinging account of the event—*Into the Bear Pit*—that was published in June 2000. It's a shame many golfers still remember the 1999 Ryder Cup for the unfortunate scene toward the end, because even devoted European supporters have to concede that, on that memorable final day, the Americans were outstanding.

Leonard as the famous putt goes in

1994 Curtis Cup

An exciting tie in women's amateur team competition.

DATE
July 30-31, 1994

LOCATION
The Honors Course
Chattanooga, TN
USA

PRIZE
The Curtis Cup

IN THE FIELD
Catriona Matthew
Janice Moodie
Carole Semple Thompson
Jill McGill
Stephanie Sparks
Emilee Klein

Just as the Ryder and Walker Cups evolved into official events following informal matches between British golfers and their American counterparts who crossed the Atlantic to play in the Open or Amateur Championships, so the Curits Cup had its beginnings in a light-hearted, unceremonious encounter.

The first of them happened in 1905 (several years before either of the male team contests) at Royal Cromer on the north Norfolk coast—150 miles northeast of London—five days before the British Ladies Amateur Championship began. On that occasion, seven singles matches were played with the British ladies beating the visitors 6-1.

The next informal gathering took place at Sunningdale GC—25 miles southwest of London—in May 1930. Five foursomes and 10 singles were played and the British won again 8½-6½.

It's not entirely clear why it had taken 25 years for a second match to be organized, but a number of factors were likely to blame—trans-Atlantic voyages were long and expensive so not enough players made the trip; the advent and aftermath of World War I; and women's golf lacked strong institutional and financial support.

Talk of a more regular formal event had begun in the mid-1920s, however, much of it fueled by the Curtis sisters—Harriot and Margaret—who had played at Royal Cromer in 1905. They envisioned an international team competition involving several other nations, but for whatever reason (likely finances), the only organizations that committed to such an event were the USGA in America and LGU (Ladies Golf Union) in Britain.

The Curtises had donated a trophy in 1927, inscribed with the words "To stimulate friendly rivalry among the women golfers of many lands," but it wasn't until 1931 that the USGA and LGU agreed to co-sponsor a competition.

The cup wasn't actually awarded, but the first official match is recognized as the 1932 meeting at Wentworth GC, just a few miles from Sunningdale. Three foursomes and six singles matches were played and, though Joyce Wethered beat Glenna Collett 6&4 in their singles match, the U.S. team ran out 5½-3½ winners overall.

Up to the end of 2024, there have been three ties, the last of those three ties happened in 1994 at the Honors Course in Chattanooga, Tennessee, and is widely regarded as the most exciting match in the Cup's history as no more than one point separated the sides at the end of any of the four sessions.

Three of the U.S's eight players (Emilee Klein, Jill McGill, and Stephanie Sparks) would play on the LPGA Tour, and the team also featured the highly decorated amateur Carol Semple Thompson, who was making her eighth appearance (she'd eventually play in 12 Curtis Cups and captain the team twice more).

The Great Britain & Ireland team also had three future LPGA players, including Catriona Matthew, who would win the Women's Open in 2009 and captain the European Solheim Cup team.

The Curtis Cup

The U.S. led after the first morning's singles 3½ to 2½, and after the three afternoon foursomes were all halved, the home team took a 5-4 lead at the end of the first day.

On Day 2, GB & Ireland won the morning foursomes session 2-1 to level the score at 6-6. The afternoon singles then produced a thrilling climax to the event with each team winning three of the six matches to make the final score 9-9. GB & Ireland retained the cup, having won it at Royal Liverpool in England two years previously.

That win at Hoylake was one of just nine the GB & Ireland team recorded in the event's first 92 years. The U.S., meanwhile, racked up an impressive 31 victories, and there had been three ties. Just like the U.S. Ryder and Walker Cup teams, the U.S. Curtis Cup team has clearly held the upper hand through the years, though it was GB & Ireland that won the most recent match, at Sunningdale in Surrey, England, in 2024.

Alumnae of the event include Nancy Lopez, Laura Davies, Beth Daniel, JoAnne Gunderson (Carner), Patty Sheehan, Michelle Wie, Stacy Lewis, Juli Inkster, Paula Creamer, Georgia Hall, Lexi Thompson, Jessica Korda, Charley Hull, Cristie Kerr, Carol Semple Thompson, and Anne Quast.

The victorious GB & Ireland team

The Curtis Sisters

Harriot (1891) and Margaret (1893) Curtis were born into a wealthy Massachusetts family and were encouraged to take up golf in their early teens by their cousin, Laurence Curtis (who served as the USGA's second president in the late 1890s.)

Harriot won the U.S. Women's Amateur Championship in 1906 while Margaret, despite not being able to play for a few years because of ill health, won the following year at Midlothian Country Club in suburban Chicago, beating Harriot 7&6 in the final. Margaret won her second title in 1911, and a third the following year at the Curtis sisters' home course, Essex County Club north of Boston.

The sisters were busy off the course, too. They founded Boston's Maverick Dispensary, a health clinic for Italian Americans that would treat 40,000 patients a year by the 1930s. Opening the clinic was only the first sign of what exceptional humans the Curtis sisters were. Harriot was the director of the Associated Charities in Boston and worked at the Red Cross' Home Service Division during World War I. She later became Dean of Women at Hampton Institute, a college for African American students in Richmond, Virginia.

As for Margaret, she began volunteering for the Red Cross in Paris the year before the U.S. entered World War I and was awarded the Medaille de Guerre from the French Red Cross in 1919, and the Medaille de la Reconnaissance Francaise from the French government the following year. She continued her volunteer work in Europe after the War, eventually returning to the U.S. in 1923. During World War II, she served as a member of the War Production Board, and headed the agency that placed war-affected children from Europe (mainly Britain) into Massachusetts homes.

Harriot Curtis (left) and Margaret Curtis (right)

They both lived into the mid-1960s—long enough to see the team competition they had founded grow into a popular and highly anticipated event.

1997 Masters

Tiger Woods wins his first Green Jacket.

DATE
April 10-13, 1997

LOCATION
Augusta National
Augusta, GA
USA

PRIZE
$486,000

IN THE FIELD
Nick Faldo
Greg Norman
Fred Couples
Colin Montgomerie
Bernhard Langer
Phil Mickelson
Ernie Els
Jack Nicklaus

The previous year's edition of the Masters had seen England's Nick Faldo turn a six-shot deficit after 54 holes into a five shot win, as he out-maneuvered his great Australian rival, Greg Norman, in the final round with a superb 67 that won him a third Masters title. Despite the somewhat humiliating defeat, Norman began the 1997 tournament as a 6-1 favorite, with Faldo—the man who had crushed him 12 months prior—starting at an apparently generous 10-1. Third in the betting (most often at 12-1) was a 21-year-old who had finished T41 in his Augusta debut two years before and then missed the cut in 1996. So young a player with that sort of record wouldn't normally attract the attention of serious bettors, but this kid was different. People felt his game was well-suited to Augusta National.

Prodigy

Tiger Woods was born in December 1975 in Cypress, California, 28 miles southeast of downtown Los Angeles. He hit golf shots on TV on the Mike Douglas Showat the age of two, and he attended Western High School in Anaheim, where his schoolmates voted him most likely to succeed (you think?).

By the time he graduated from high school, Woods had already won three straight US Junior Amateur titles, and in 1994, a few months after receiving his high-school diploma, he claimed the first of three straight U.S. Amateurs. In the last of those wins, Woods was 5-down to Steve Scott in the final after the morning 18. A lesson from Butch Harmon during the break proved timely, however. Woods turned it on in the afternoon and eventually won on the 38th hole to capture his sixth consecutive USGA title.

Given his high school and Junior Amateur records, Woods was obviously a target for college recruiters, and after choosing to play for Stanford (the reigning NCAA champions), he won his first collegiate event. He'd win 10 more, including the individual title at the 1996 NCAA Championship, before deciding to turn professional. He took the plunge (not that difficult a decision really with $40 million and $20 million deals with Nike and Titleist respectively waiting for him) on August 27, 1996, two days after defeating Scott at the U.S. Amateur, and two days before teeing it up at the PGA Tour's Greater Milwaukee Open—his 14th PGA Tour event, but first as a professional. At Brown Deer Park GC, he shot three rounds in the 60s and had a hole-in-one in the final round, but would eventually tie for 60th, 12 shots out of the playoff.

Woods finished 11th, T5, and T3 in his next three tournaments, then won his first PGA Tour title on October 6, when he beat Davis Love III in a playoff to win the five-round Las Vegas Invitational. He'd win again two weeks later in Florida, and at the first event in the 1997 season, he won his third event in nine PGA Tour starts as a pro. After a 2nd at Pebble Beach and another top 10 at Bay Hill, Woods was firing on all cylinders ahead of the Masters, his first major championship in the paid ranks. Perhaps the bookies who positioned him so high in the betting for the '97 Masters weren't crazy, after all. The course measured 6,925 yards—not terribly long for someone averaging 302.8 yards off the tee on the PGA Tour.

He had earned his invitation to Augusta National by winning the U.S. Amateur, but had forfeited that method of qualification by turning professional. No matter, his Las Vegas victory on the PGA Tour got him in. As the reigning U.S. Amateur champion, Woods would be paired in the first round with the defending Masters champion—Nick Faldo. Before the round, Faldo was asked about Woods' chances, and while he didn't dismiss them entirely, Faldo did suggest winning on his pro debut would be a tall order. "It took me about half a dozen years before I got the gist of the place," Faldo told the press. "I think there's a learning curve of playing Augusta and the discipline of playing the golf course—where to hit the ball and where not to. It's not impossible for Woods to win, but I think that experience does help here."

Only three players had won the Masters on their pro debut—Horton Smith in 1934, Gene Sarazen in 1935, and Fuzzy Zoeller in 1979—

(technically, this wasn't Woods' debut, as he had played twice as an amateur), and Faldo's words regarding Woods seemed even more justified as he struggled to an outward 4-over-par 40.

Something strange and wonderful happened to Woods on the second nine, however. Later he would say it was simply case of improved mechanics: "Once you find your position at the top of the golf swing," he said, "all you have to do is come down and hit it solidly. I wasn't able to do that on the front nine." There was probably a little rage in there too. But whatever it was, Woods came home in a brilliant 6-under-par 30, highlighted by an eagle at the par-five 15th, where he hit a wedge for his second shot. Halves of 40 and 30 yielded a first-round 70 that left Woods in 4th place, just three shots off the lead.

A columnist for the *Atlanta Journal* felt the writing might already be on the wall. "The Tiger Woods warning sirens are really going off all around the Augusta National property now. It was his first sub-par showing at this tournament, giving some substance to those who have already ceded Woods this and all foreseeable golf tournaments."

If his Thursday back-nine had sent murmurs darting between Augusta National's stately pines that this Tiger Woods guy might be pretty special, a second-round 66, the best score of the day, confirmed he was the real deal and that it would take some very special golf to beat him. Standing at 8-under-par through two rounds, he opened up a three-shot lead over Scotland's Colin Montgomerie, who made the error—much more pointedly than Faldo had—of underestimating Woods' ability. The Scot spoke of how much more experience he had, and how much pressure Woods would be under.

Woods with the trophy

Out in 39 to Woods' 32, the more-experienced Montgomerie fell 10 shots behind Woods after 45 holes, and despite a creditable 35 from the Scot on the second nine, the gap grew even wider, as Tiger came home in 33 for a round of 65.

While Montgomerie fell into a tie for 6th, Woods' lead at the top had increased to nine, with Italy's Costantino Rocca earning the right to accompany Woods on Day 4. Probably feeling a mix of astonishment, shock, fear, and even a little embarrassment, Montgomerie let reporters know exactly how he felt after the round: "There is no chance that Tiger Woods is going to lose this tournament," he said. "No way. This is different to last year. Faldo is not lying 2nd, and Tiger Woods is not Greg Norman. I appreciated how far he hit his driver, and how he hit his irons, but I did not appreciate how he can putt. He is nine clear now, and I am sure it will be higher tomorrow."

Maybe for the first time that day, Montgomerie was spot on, as Woods' lead would increase in the final round. Though Woods was careful not to get ahead of himself and start celebrating his first major win prematurely ("It's a big lead," he said, "but I still need to go out tomorrow and shoot a good number,") really the only thing that held people's attention on the Sunday was how many records Woods could break. With a final round 69—and a final putt fist-pump that would become one of the most iconic and recognizable in the sport's history—Woods became the tournament's youngest ever winner at the age of 21 years, three months, and 14 days. In winning by 12, he beat Jack Nicklaus' 1965 nine-shot margin of victory, and with a 72-hole total of 18-under 270, he beat the 271 Ray Floyd had shot in 1976.

What Now?

Golf commentators had long been speculating on how good Woods might become, but it felt like his dominating win at the '97 Masters got everyone, inside and outside the game, talking. Back pages around the world tended to go with some variation of "Woods Roars to Victory," though the most telling headline might have come from the Associated Press, which led with "It's Tiger's Game Now."

A couple of golf greats made bold statements. Jack Nicklaus, whose 18 major wins Woods would spend the next 20-25 years pursuing, said, "He hits so many short irons to par fives, it just makes the course melt away. I don't think there's much hope for the field." And Gary Player, never one to pass up the opportunity for a little hyperbole, offered this: "Tiger Woods has an opportunity to do something for the human race that no other golfer has ever done."

2000 U.S. Open

Woods wins his first U.S. Open by an inconceivable margin.

DATE
June 15-18, 2000

LOCATION
Pebble Beach
Pebble Beach, CA
USA

PRIZE
$800,000

IN THE FIELD
Tiger Woods
Ernie Els
Vijay Singh
Padraig Harrington
Lee Westwood
David Duval
Phil Mickelson
Colin Montgomerie

It's likely the group of men who established the USGA in 1894 hoped the organization would be staging a major national tournament for centuries to come, but they couldn't have expected it. As it happens, two world wars have so far been the only reason preventing it from being played every year (it survived the Great Depression), and in 2000, the U.S. Open would be played for the 100th time.

The venue was Pebble Beach, the beautiful oceanside course on California's Monterey Peninsula developed by Samuel Morse and the Del Monte Properties Company, and designed by amateur course architects Douglas Grant and Jack Neville.

It opened in 1919 and, 10 years later, staged its first national championship—the U.S. Amateur won by Jimmy Johnston (Bobby Jones won the strokeplay medal but shockingly went out in the first round of matchplay). It would host the U.S. Amateur four more times over the next 90 years (most recently in 2018 when Viktor Hovland won) as well as two U.S. Women's Amateurs, the 1977 PGA Championship (won by Lanny Wadkins) and three U.S. Opens—1972 (Jack Nicklaus), 1982 (Tom Watson), and 1992 (Tom Kite).

For the 2000 U.S. Open, the course would play as a par 71 of 6,846-yards. As per U.S. Open tradition, the course was set up to be extremely difficult, with fairways averaging 27 yards in width, the primary cut of rough set at 3.5 to 4 inches-long, and the greens—some of the smallest in championship golf, averaging approximately 3,500 square feet—rolling at about 12 on the Stimpmeter. It would prove to be a stern test—for 155 of the 156 competitors anyway.

Woods started the championship a strong favorite, having won 24 times (19 PGA Tour events including two majors, and five overseas tournaments) over the previous four seasons. Significantly, the 17th of those victories had come four months before the U.S. Open in the AT&T National Pro-Am at Pebble

A Big Hole in the Field

The field for the 2000 U.S. Open certainly had its share of star names, but it was missing that of the defending champion: Payne Stewart, the three-time major champion who had died tragically four months after his win at the 1999 U.S. Open at Pinehurst No. 2.

Stewart was flying in a private jet from his home city of Orlando, Florida to Houston, Texas for the season-ending Tour Championship when the plane lost cabin pressure, and all its occupants—pilots Michael Kling and Stephanie Bellegarrigue, and passengers Robert Fraley (Stewart's agent), Van Arden (president of the Leader Enterprises sports management agency), Bruce Borland (golf architect), and Stewart—were disabled by hypoxia (a lack of oxygen in the brain and body's tissues). Instead of turning west toward Texas, the plane continued on autopilot until it ran out of fuel and crashed into a field in South Dakota.

Payne Stewart

The day before Thursday's first round, a special ceremony honoring Stewart took place on the 18th hole, where his widow Tracy, close friend Paul Azinger, and the PGA Tour's chaplain Larry Moody (Stewart was a member of the Tour's Bible study group) addressed the 2,000 or so attendees. After they had spoken, 42 players (two groups of 21) hit drives into Stillwater Cove, and the following morning, Jack Nicklaus called for a moment's silence just prior to hitting his opening tee shot to honor both Stewart and Borland who worked for his design company.

Beach. Woods had surprisingly finished 5th (six shots behind winner Vijay Singh) at the Masters in April, but won the Memorial by five a couple of weeks before returning to Pebble Beach.

The bookmakers were so confident in Woods' abilities that many of them offered him at even-money—unheard of at a golf tournament with 156 of the world's best players making up the field. His closest contenders, in the betting at least, were Phil Mickelson at 5-1, Ernie Els at 10-1, and Singh at 12-1.

The first round was affected by dense fog that saw 75 players unable to complete all 18 holes. One player who did get them all in was Woods, who took advantage of an early tee-time and a two-hour putting session with his coach Butch Harmon the day before to shoot a 6-under-par 65 that gave him a one shot-lead over six-time European Tour winner Miguel Ángel Jiménez of Spain.

On Day 2, the wind got up, resulting in a scoring average of 75.3. Fortunately for Woods, the wind had died down by the time he teed off in the afternoon, though he was able to finish only 12 holes before darkness halted play. His round was highlighted by a miraculous shot out of deep rough to the right of the 6th fairway. With a tree and steep hill in front of him, he muscled a 7-iron 202 yards out of the thick grass, the ball managing to find the front of the green. Astonished by Woods' power, NBC commentator Roger Maltbie joked, "It's just not a fair fight."

Woods returned to complete his round early Saturday morning, eventually signing for a 69 that gave him a 36-hole total of 8-under 134—six better than Jiménez and Denmark's Thomas Bjørn.

Scoring conditions for the third round were similarly as difficult as they has been for the second round, leading to a scoring average of 75.8 (Bjørn soared to an 82). The only player to beat par was Ernie Els, who shot a 3-under 68 to move into 2nd place. Woods found trouble early in the round, making a triple bogey at the 3rd hole, but he managed to make enough birdies to shoot even-par for the day and extend his lead to 10. After 54 holes, Woods stood at 8-under-par and was the only player in red figures.

Woods could have been forgiven for treating the final round as something of a procession, but that was never his style. Indeed, on a day when only six other players broke 70 and the average score was 75.6, Woods shot the best round of the day: a 67 that gave him a 72-hole total of 12-under, 272. Els and Jiménez, who tied for 2nd, were a distant 15 shots behind.

Not surprisingly, Woods broke a number of records that week. He became the first player to complete four rounds at the U.S. Open double digits under par. And he secured the widest margin of victory in major championship history, beating the 13 shots Old Tom Morris had beaten the field by in the 1862 Open Championship at Prestwick.

Woods didn't three-putt once all week, nor did he suffer a single double bogey. The data point of "strokes gained" didn't exist at the time, but it's estimated Woods gained around 21 strokes on the field. The 15-shot gap between him and the joint runners-up was still the widest gap in the majors at the time of writing (end of 2025), and it's likely to remain so for a very long time. A 2011 article on Grantland.com compared the best major finishes since 1960 and calculated Woods' winning total was 4.12 standard deviations better than the field (accounting for both the average result and the full range of performances from top to bottom). Incredibly, Davis Love III's win in the 1997 PGA Championship at Winged Foot was 2nd to Woods at Pebble Beach, but closer, statistically, to the 20th best major finish—Bobby Nichols' win at the 1964 PGA Championship. Most of those fortunate to have witnessed Woods' performance will tell you that golf may never

Woods with the U.S. Open trophy

2001 Masters

Tiger wins the "Tiger Slam."

DATE
April 5-8, 2001

LOCATION
Augusta National
Augusta, GA
USA

PRIZE
$1,008,000

IN THE FIELD
Tiger Woods
Phil Mickelson
Ernie Els
Vijay Singh
David Duval
José María Olazábal
Bernhard Langer
Fred Couples
Mark O'Meara
Colin Montgomerie

Because of the incredible golf he'd played the year before, Tiger Woods arrived at Augusta National in April 2001 with a chance to do what no other golfer had ever done. Actually, Woods had done what no other golfer had ever done numerous times already, but this particular feat would be beyond exceptional.

Having won the U.S. Open (by 15 shots), the Open Championship (by eight), and the PGA Championship (in a playoff with Bob May) in 2000, Woods could make it four consecutive wins at the modern majors, becoming the first ever player to hold all four titles at the same time.

As we know, Bobby Jones won the Grand Slam in 1930 (see pages 96-100), but two of the four events he won were amateur competitions that involved match play—which is absolutely not to take anything away from what was a colossal achievement, but comparing it with what Woods was about to do is apples to oranges.

In an effort to prevent competitors (Woods specifically?) from overpowering it, Augusta National GC began lengthening the course in 2002, a couple of years after it had added a few trees and introduced a 1⅜-high "second cut" of grass. The policy became known as "Tiger-proofing" in the popular press (a term not used by the club itself), but in reality, it served only to improve Woods' chances of winning; from 2002-13, he won twice more and had a total of nine finishes of T6 or better. In 2001, however, the course measured only 60 yards longer (6,985) than it had in 1997, when Woods first won the Masters.

In the last three months of 2000 and first two of the 2001 season, Woods played in eight official PGA Tour events and finished in the top five in five of them. In the other three, he was T8, and T13 twice. At the end of 2000, he was also 2nd at the Williams Challenge and partnered with his good friend David Duval to win golf's World Cup. At the beginning of March 2001, he finished 2nd at the Dubai Desert Classic on the European Tour (now DP World Tour), after double bogeying the 72nd hole to lose by two. Certainly, the final hole mistakes in Dubai were bothersome, but it was a pretty good run of tournaments that every golfer (except maybe Jack Nicklaus, Ben Hogan, and Bobby Jones) would surely have been pleased with.

And yet, sports' dreaded s-word began to circle. Including the Dubai event, Woods hadn't won in nine official, individual events, and people were saying he might be in a ... slump. Half the world thought the slump-sayers were crazy, but even the highly respected U.S. weekly golf publication *Golf World* seemed concerned. "What's wrong with Tiger?," it asked on its March 9th cover, before adding: "Woods' woes continue with final hole collapse in Dubai."

Such talk was short-lived, however, as Woods returned to the winner's circle in the third week of March, defeating Phil Mickelson by a shot to win his second Bay Hill Invitational (now the Arnold Palmer Invitational), a tournament he would win a total of eight times in 14 tries, between 2000 and 2013. The following week, Tiger holed his famous "better than most" putt in the third round at TPC Sawgrass, and the next day, he beat Singh by a shot to win the first of two Players Championships.

After a week off at the end of March, he traveled to the Masters as such a strong favorite the best odds you might have found for him were 2-1.

At the start of Thursday's first round, Woods blocked his opening tee shot to the right, the ball finishing behind three newly planted pine trees. He failed to find the green with his second shot, and wound up with a bogey which could have been worse. The rest of the round was a little up-and-down, too. Though Woods was far from happy, his 2-under-par 70 and tie for 15th certainly wasn't disastrous. Masters debutante Chris DiMarco, using his strange, new "claw" putting grip, shot 65 to finish the day with a one-shot lead.

A second-round 69 suggested that DiMarco—then a one-time winner on the PGA Tour—was not going to give up the lead easily, and at 10-under through 36 holes, he set a Masters rookie record. A quick glance at the two names in 2nd—Phil Mickelson (no wins in the majors yet, but 11 top 10s and 18 PGA Tour wins) and Tiger Woods (who shot a Friday 66)—might have given DiMarco pause, but he seemed confident enough. "Before Woods, Duval, and Mickelson were Woods, Duval, and Mickelson, they had to get there somehow, right?" he explained to the press. "Maybe this is my week to get there." When asked if he belonged at the top of the leaderboard with those players, he said simply, "I guess I do this week."

The next afternoon, DiMarco played with Woods, and though the tournament leader wasn't nearly as sharp as he'd been the previous two days, he did manage to shoot even par. He lost the lead with his 72, but it was good enough to keep him tied for 3rd with Mark Calcavecchia, one shot behind Mickelson who birdied the final two holes for a 69, and two behind Woods, whose second-nine 33 gave him a 68 and a 54-hole total of 12-under-par.

On Sunday, Woods pulled his opening tee shot into the trees on the left this time, and made another opening-hole bogey.

Woods eyeing an approach shot

Mickelson made a par to tie for the lead alongside Woods and Calcavechia who had birdied the 1st. Woods and Mickelson both birdied the par-five 2nd, and Woods birdied the 7th and 8th. Mickelson made three more birdies of his own, and the two both made it to the turn in 34, with Woods at 14-under and Mickelson a shot behind.

Woods wasn't alone at the top of the leaderboard for long, however. Calcavecchia may have started to drop back, but playing two groups ahead of Woods, David Duval—who had 12 PGA Tour wins, had been world number one for 13 weeks in 1999, had become the first man to shoot 59 in the final round of a PGA Tour event, was the player who'd won the World Cup alongside Woods in Argentina five months before the Masters, and who would win the Open Championship three months later—made six first-nine birdies to reach the turn in 32. And then he birdied the 10th to join Woods at 14-under.

Following a 306-yard drive at the 11th, Woods had just 149 yards downhill to the hole. Instead of taking a pitching wedge, which he could easily carry that far, however, he gripped down on an 8-iron, preventing the excessive backspin the wedge would surely have imparted. His ball pitched short and right of the hole, spun sideways, very nearly went in, and finished about a foot away. The resulting birdie put Woods one clear.

Woods then bogeyed the 12th but birdied the 13th after hitting a high draw off the tee with a 3-wood, a shot he later said he had been practicing for months. Duval birdied the 15th, but Woods three-putted the par-5 from just 15 feet for a disappointing par. They were tied again at 15-under with Mickelson a shot back. At the 16th, Duval made a bogey, and 15 minutes later, Mickelson's tee shot pitched about 25 feet right of the usual Sunday hole location, the ball sticking rather than spinning back and to the left as expected. It left a difficult putt with a huge right-to-left break, which Mickelson didn't read as well as he might. His putt missed on the low side and ran six feet past the hole from where he missed left and made bogey.

Woods' tee shot likewise flew right and almost landed on top of Mickelson's ball. Happily for Woods fans, though, his ball did

Woods tees off

spin back slowly, eventually finishing 20 feet short of the hole and leaving a relatively easy putt up the slope without nearly as much break. He missed the birdie try but made a safe par to stay one ahead of Duval and two clear of Mickelson. They all parred the 17th, then Duval missed a makeable birdie putt at the 18th that would have put him in a tie with Woods at 15-under. He hit a 327-yard drive up the hill at the last, leaving just 78 yards to the hole. Mickelson's drive flew into the trees on the right, but it ricocheted out to the edge of the fairway, 50-60 yards behind Woods. A good approach found the middle of the green, leaving Mickelson a 20-foot birdie putt he'd have to make if he was to have any hope. Woods' pitch wasn't the best, finishing slightly farther from the cup than Mickelson's ball. If Mickelson were to hole and Woods three-putt, the two of them would tie Duval at 14-under.

But it didn't work out like that. As the truly great players tend to do, Woods hit the right putt at the right moment, the ball falling into the hole at the perfect speed. With a final-round 68, he finished at 16-under-par, 272. It didn't really matter as the chance to win had gone, but Mickelson missed his putt and finished in 3rd place, three shots back.

CBS's Ken Venturi said we had witnessed a miracle, and in the Butler Cabin, Jim Nantz asked Woods how it felt to have accomplished something that Hogan, Nelson, Snead, Nicklaus, Palmer, Player, and Watson never had. "Right now, it's hard to explain," Woods replied. "It's an eerie calmness. I've succeeded in what I wanted to accomplish, and it feels great, but I don't really feel ecstatic yet because it hasn't sunk in."

A Grand Slam?

Of course, the question arose over what to call Woods' achievement. Was it a Grand Slam, or did someone have to win all four majors in the same calendar year for that? Three people close to the issue at the time it happened said it was a Grand Slam: Woods' teacher, Butch Harmon; Woods' father, Earl, and significantly (but not conclusively, perhaps), Woods himself, who said it was a Grand Slam "because I won four majors in a row."

In the years since the 2001 Masters and Woods' feat, the world seems to have come to terms with the fact it wasn't a Grand Slam in the strictest sense, and the name "Tiger Slam" has stuck. The significance of Woods' achievement has not diminished even slightly, however.

2003 Colonial

Sorenstam becomes the first woman in a PGA Tour event since 1952.

DATE
May 22-25, 2003

LOCATION
Colonial CC
Fort Worth, TX
USA

PRIZE
$900,000

IN THE FIELD
Phil Mickelson
Nick Price
Corey Pavin
Justin Leonard
Mark Calcavecchia
Tom Lehman
Steve Elkington
Annika Sorenstam

In May 2003, Sweden's Annika Sorenstam became the third woman to play in a PGA Tour event, following in the footsteps of the remarkable Babe Didrickson Zaharias, who teed it up seven times on the men's tour between 1935 and 1946, and Shirley Spork who played in the 1952 Northern California-Reno Open.

Sorenstam received her invitation to play in the Bank of America tournament at Colonial CC three months before the event, in early February, and after some back and forth between her agent and the bank's representatives, she accepted on February 12.

While a woman receiving a sponsor's exemption to play in a PGA Tour event was a very rare occurrence (and questioned in some quarters), there was a definite feeling Sorenstam, who grew up 10 miles north of Stockholm, was also a talented skier, tennis player, and footballer (soccer), and who had attended the University of Arizona, deserved hers. After winning her first LPGA tournament in 1995—the U.S. Women's Open no less—she had won a further 41 times (including three more majors), and also claimed nine titles in Europe, four in Australia/New Zealand, and three in Japan. She dominated the women's game, and though she initially had reservations, she was also very curious to see how she might fare against the best male players in the game.

Not surprisingly, Sorenstam was extremely nervous before teeing off. On the one hand, she had nothing to lose—there were no expectations of her making the cut or contending. She might even struggle to break 80 on a 7,054-yard course set up for a PGA Tour event. On the other hand, though, she had plenty to lose:

What if she failed to break 85 or even 90? What if she completed 36 holes in last place and finished a long way behind the man in second to last? That wouldn't be a good look for her, women's golf, Bank of America, or the PGA Tour.

Ron Sirak, writing for *Golf Digest*, recalled Sorenstam telling him she'd had two thoughts before teeing off, first that her cat, Nelson, would still love her whatever happened; and secondly, wherever the first drive went ("and it can go anywhere,") she was going to find it and then hit it again. Sorenstam's friend, mentor, and coach Pia Nilsson wished her the best of luck before heading out and remembers Sorenstam not being able to voice any words.

Despite being 504 yards longer than any LPGA Tour course in 2003 (the longest course was Pumpkin Ridge's Witch Hollow Course at 6,550 yards), Colonial CC was considered a good fit for Sorenstam's game, as it typically rewarded accuracy over distance.

For the opening two rounds, she would be paired with Tour rookies Dean Wilson and Aaron Barber, both of whom treated her with respect, celebrated her good shots with fist bumps and high-fives, and who were clearly very impressed with her game. After flushing her first tee shot down the middle—a 255-yard 4-wood (a club she usually hit 225-230 yards), Sorenstam hit 16 more fairways and a total of 14 greens (she putted from the fringe on the other four). She hit 36 putts, making one birdie, two bogeys, and 15 pars to shoot a 1-over-par 71.

The following day, Sorenstam shot a 74 and wound up at 5-over, missing the cut by four shots. It didn't matter: she had beaten 11 men (including Barber) and proven to herself that she could handle the occasion.

Sorenstam won a total of six LPGA events in 2003 (five after Colonial) and was inducted into the World Golf Hall of Fame in October that year. The following season, she added eight more titles, and in 2005 she won a dozen times around the world. She retired at the end of the 2008 season with 97 professional wins—a staggering total that included 10 majors.

Sorenstam in the 2003 Colonial

Women on the Men's Tour

1. Babe Didrickson Zaharias

After taking up golf in 1935, the phenomenal athlete, born Mildred Didrickson in 1911, entered the Cascades Open

in Virginia, where she shot 86-88 to miss the cut. She qualified for the 1937 Chicago Open, but withdrew after an opening 86. She then played in the 1938 Los Angeles Open, where rounds of 81 and 84 again saw her miss the weekend. In 1945 at Riviera CC, she did make the 36-hole cut, but a third-round 79 meant she didn't make it to the final 18. She played two other PGA Tour events in '45—the Tucson Open at El Rio GCC, where she qualified for the weekend and finished tied for 42nd; and Phoenix Open at Phoenix CC, where rounds of 77, 72, 75, and 80 put her in a tie for 33rd. Her last appearance on the PGA Tour came at the 1946 Los Angeles Open, where two 81s weren't enough to progress to the third round.

2. Shirley Spork

Despite not winning an LPGA event (she was more of a teacher than a player), Spork was invited to play in the 1952 Northern California-Reno Open at Washoe County Golf Club where she finished tied for 105th in the no-cut event.

3. Annika Sorenstam

The Swede received a sponsor's invitation to the 2003 Colonial tournament in Fort Worth, Texas but, despite acquitting herself well with rounds of 71 and 74, she missed the cut by four.

4. Suzy Whaley
The head pro at Blue Fox Run GC in Avon, Connecticut, and a former LPGA player, Whaley qualified for the 2003 Greater Hartford Open by winning the previous year's Connecticut PGA Championship at Ellington Ridge, where she'd been allowed to play from forward tees and shot a 54-hole total of 211 (-5). At the GHO, she shot 75 and 78 and missed the cut by 13, but she counted it as a win, since she had inspired countless young girls to try golf, raised money for the March of Dimes, and made her dad proud.

5. Michelle Wie
After playing in the 2004 Sony Open in Hawaii (for a full account, see pages 218-9), at the age of 14, Wie would go on to appear in seven more PGA Tour events, but she didn't make a cut.

6. Brittany Lincicome
Lincicome was invited to play in the 2018 Barbasol Championship at Keen Trace GC in Kentucky, where she missed the cut with rounds of 78 and 71.

7. Lexi Thompson
After receiving a sponsor's exemption to play in the 2023 Shriners Children's Open at TPC Summerlin in Las Vegas, Thompson missed the cut by three after shooting 73 and 69. She did, however, beat 33 men in the field.

2003 Presidents Cup

An exciting tie at Fancourt.

DATE
Nov. 20-23, 2003

LOCATION
Fancourt Hotel & CC
George, South Africa

PRIZE
The Presidents Cup

IN THE FIELD
Tiger Woods
Davis Love III
Jim Furyk
Phil Mickelson
Ernie Els
Vijay Singh
Mike Weir
Nick Price
Retief Goosen
Robert Allenby

Tiger Woods had just defeated Ernie Els 4&3 in their Sunday singles match, meaning that after three extraordinary days of gripping matchplay action, the 2003 Presidents Cup would boil down to the very last pair on the course: Davis Love III of the U.S. and the International team's Robert Allenby. One-up after 17, Love III only needed a half to ensure outright victory for the U.S., and he hit a fine drive down the middle of the fairway at the 563-yard 18th. His second came up short of the green, but a pitch and putt would surely be enough. Love didn't strike his third cleanly, however, and the ball failed to find the putting surface. After another unconvincing pitch, he missed his putt for a five. Love III and Allenby halved their match with each earning half a point. After 34 matches, the final score was 17-17.

The format called for 12-man teams (the International team comprising players from countries outside the U.S. and Europe) each with a non-playing captain.

Four days, 34 matches
Day 1—Six foursomes
Day 2—Five fourballs, five foursomes
Day 3—Six fourballs
Day 4—12 singles

Thursday's six foursomes matches had gone the way of the Internationals, 3½ to 2½. The two most favored pairs—Retief Goosen (ranked 7th in the world) and Vijay Singh (2nd) for the International team, and Tiger Woods (1st) and Charles Howell III (21st) for the U.S.—both won handily. Goosen and Singh were split up for Friday morning's fourballs, but the Woods-Howell pairing remained intact. They were beaten soundly (5&3), however, by Els and fellow South African Tim Clark. The Americans then took the afternoon foursomes 4-1, with Woods and Howell beating Goosen and Clark 1-up.

By the end of Friday, the U.S. team had built a 9½ to 6½ lead and were looking very strong heading into the weekend.

It's not known what Gary Player told his team on Friday night or Saturday morning, but whatever it was, it certainly had the desired effect, as the Internationals won all six matches that day with Singh and Goosen beating Woods and Howell 2&1, and Adam Scott and K.J. Choi recording the biggest win of the day: a 5&4 win over Kenny Perry and Jerry Kelly. At the end of Day 3, therefore, the Internationals led 12½ to 9½.

The U.S. put up a strong showing in the Sunday singles—as they tend to in team competitions—winning the day 7½ to 4½. It was tense and thrilling throughout, but when Woods beat Els so convincingly and Davis Love III came to the last with a slender lead, few would have expected anything other than a win for Team USA. But Love III's unfortunate finish would hand the home team a lifeline.

At the Ryder Cup, if the two teams are tied at the end, the previous winners retain the cup. In other words, the team that was beaten at the previous match has to win the next one outright to take possession of the cup. The format for the Presidents Cup was different, however. Following a tie, a player from each team, nominated by their captains before Sunday's singles matches began, would meet in a sudden death play-off to decide the winner—no draws or ties.

As expected, Nicklaus had chosen Woods, and Player had selected Els. Reportedly, neither captain particularly liked the idea of a team event being decided by two individuals playing off in sudden death, but the likelihood of there being a tie after 11 foursomes matches, 11 fourball matches, and 12 singles seemed pretty remote, so the format was agreed. (Through 2025, a tie has happened twice at the Ryder Cup, once at the Walker Cup, once at the Solheim Cup, and three times at the Curtis Cup).

In the tie-breaker, Woods and Els slugged it out, draining putts for halves that defied belief given the amount of pressure both players must have felt and the fast-disappearing light. After Woods curled in a 15-foot putt with a foot of break for a three at the third extra hole (the 216-yard 2nd), Els needed to follow him in from seven feet to keep the match alive. Though he looked incredibly calm—as befits a man known as "The Big Easy"—Els would later say his legs were shaking and he had never felt so nervous. He put a beautiful stroke on his putt, though, and the ball moved unerringly into the middle of the hole.

It was so dark by now, playing a fourth extra hole would have been ridiculous and a sad way to end so exhilarating a contest. Tim Finchem, Commissioner of the PGA Tour which owns and organizes the event, spoke about the U.S. retaining the cup, Ryder Cup-style. But Player and his International team weren't having that, and thankfully Nicklaus agreed, saying it would have been a terrible thing for golf had either team lost. So after a lot of fraught, tense deliberation, everyone agreed the Presidents Cup should be shared, with each team holding the trophy for a year. "I think the people here are very happy that both teams won," Nicklaus said afterward. "They enjoyed it. It was a very popular decision."

Following the 2003 event, the format for the competition was changed to reflect this gesture of sportsmanship. In the event of a tie, the teams now share the Presidents Cup, each taking possession for one year.

Why, Where, When, and How?

The best answer to the question, "Why is there a Presidents Cup?," should really come in the form of another question: "Why did it take so long for it to exist?"

The Ryder Cup—initially the U.S. against Great Britain, then the U.S. against Great Britain and Ireland, and from 1979, the U.S. against Europe—was first officially played in 1927. The Presidents Cup didn't arrive for another 67 years, which means players like nine-time major champion Gary Player, five-time Open Championship winner Peter Thomson, four-time Open Championship winner Bobby Locke, two-time major champion David Graham, winner of the Open Championship and 228 other professional tournaments, Roberto de Vicenzo, and Japanese legend Isao Aoki never got to play in a team matchplay competition against the United States.

Canadian greats such as Al Balding, Pat Fletcher, Jules Huot, Stan Leonard, George Knudson, and Moe Norman did play against the U.S. in the Americas Cup (amateur) or Hopkins Cup (professional) during the 1950s, but neither competition attracted significant global attention or lasted terribly long.

It's probably fair to say a 12-player International team wouldn't have put up much of a fight against the consistently strong U.S. sides prior to the 1990s (much like the Ryder Cup, then). And the event would never have succeeded, but since the early '90s, the game has grown significantly outside the U.S. and Europe, meaning an international team can hold its own against the U.S.

The other convincing factor in the potential success of a Ryder Cup-style event with players from nations outside of Europe was Greg Norman. Winner of the Open Championship in 1986 and 1993, the Players Championship in 1994, and 11 other PGA Tour events before the Presidents Cup was first played in September 1994—the Australian was a big draw around the world. (Ironically, he would have to pull out of the inaugural match because of illness.) He was certainly a popular figure in the U.S. where he was given the nickname the Great White Shark, following his play at the 1981 Masters when he finished 4th. (Norman's somewhat questionable comments and dealings in the 2020s opened him up to criticism, at least some of which seems justified. But that criticism shouldn't conceal the fact he was a brilliant golfer who won a total of 88 professional tournaments around the world, including 20 PGA Tour events).

The PGA Tour conceived, founded, and owns the Presidents Cup. They decided to play the first two editions at Robert Trent Jones GC in Gainesville, Virginia. The U.S. won by eight points in 1994, but the '96 match was much closer: a one-point victory with Fred Couples defeating Vijay Singh in the final singles match.

The competition first went overseas in 1998, when the International team trounced the visitors 20½ to 11½ at Royal Melbourne. Norman won 3½ points from a possible 5 and was narrowly beaten by Tiger Woods in the singles. But the U.S. was back on track two years later, recording an 11-point win at Robert Trent Jones GC.

The discussed, tied match then occurred in 2003, and since then, the U.S. has not lost again through 2024. The current individual match totals are 268 for the U.S. and 205 for the Internationals.

The Ryder Cup lost a significant amount of its appeal between the 1940s and late '70s—a period during which the U.S. team was utterly dominant—and it would be a shame to see the Presidents Cup become so one-sided that golfers become similarly disinterested. Thanks to the power of television, however, and exciting young players such as Tom Kim and Min Woo Lee, it seems safe for a while yet. With that said, the International team does need to win again soon.

2004 Sony Open

Fourteen-year-old Michelle Wie misses the cut by one stroke.

DATE
January 15-18, 2004

LOCATION
Waialae CC
Honolulu, HI
USA

PRIZE
$864,000

IN THE FIELD
Ernie Els
Vijay Singh
Davis Love III
Vijay Singh
Jim Furyk
Retief Goosen
Paul Azinger
Michelle Wie

After Annika Sorenstam played in the 2003 Colonial tournament, and club professional Suzy Whaley competed at the Greater Hartford Open two months later, the idea of outstanding women golfers being invited to—or qualifying for—the "men's" tour suddenly seemed almost plausible.

However, no one expected the next woman to tee it up alongside the game's best players to be just 14 years old. The idea of a similarly aged boy playing in a PGA Tour event was preposterous enough, so it was utterly surreal for a schoolgirl to receive a sponsor's exemption.

The amazing thing is, Michelle Wie being invited to the Sony Open on the Hawaiian island of Oahu actually made sense. Born in Honolulu in 1989, Wie was the only child of South Korean parents who had emigrated to the U.S. a few years before. Hailing from the host island was a nice connection certainly, but more than that, Wie was clearly a prodigious talent. Like, really, really prodigious.

Wie had begun playing at the age of four, and six years later she became the youngest ever to play in the U.S. Women's Amateur Public Links Championship. That same year, she shot a 64 on the regulation-length Olomana Golf Links in Waimanalo, Hawaii.

At 13, already a Hawaii State Women's Amateur champion and the youngest player to qualify for an LPGA event (Takefuji Classic in Hawaii), she won the 2003 Public Links, becoming the youngest player (man or woman) ever to win a USGA adult event. Also in 2003, Wie had made the cut in two women's majors: the Kraft Nabisco Championship in California, where she played in the final group on Sunday and eventually finished tied for 9th; and the U.S. Women's Open, where she tied for 39th.

Waialae Country Club in Honolulu had been the venue for the Sony Open (originally the Hawaiian Open) since 1965. In 2004, it measured 7,044 yards—considerably longer than anything Wie was used to. Paired with

Craig Bowden and Kevin Hayashi, she shot a first-round 72 (+2), and a Friday 68 to complete 36 holes at level-par 140, missing the cut by only one stroke. Despite not advancing to the weekend, Wie had beaten 47 players and tied the reigning U.S. Open champion Jim Furyk and Open Championship winner Ben Curtis.

Before the tournament had begun, Wie had played a practice round with Ernie Els who was extremely impressed. "I saw Tiger (Woods) before he turned pro," Els said. "A lot of what Michelle did reminds me a lot of what he used to do. As a woman golfer, she's going to take it to the next level."

Perhaps the best quote of the week, however, came from Tom Lehman. "She's got star power," said the 1996 Open Championship winner. "She holds her head high. She walks like Seve [Ballesteros] used to, when he was like, 'Watch this next shot. It's going to be the greatest you ever saw.'"

Remarkable & Also Disappointing

When you're undoubtedly one of the most naturally talented players to ever play the game, one major championship and four other Tour wins are, perhaps, a little underwhelming. Not forgetting the incredibly gifted Joyce Wethered, Glenna Collett-Vare, Mickey Wright, Kathy Whitworth, Patty Berg, Betsy Rawls, Louise Suggs, Sandra Haynie, Joanne Carner, Babe Didrickson Zaharias, Annika Sorenstam, and numerous other special talents, it could be argued Wie was the greatest talent of them all. She shot a 68 on a 7,000-yard PGA Tour course at the age of 14! So for her to end her career not ranked among the top 20 women players of all time is as odd as it is dissatisfying.

Only Wie, perhaps, will ever know the real reason for the less than stellar record, but it seems a number of factors were at play. Starting a career in such a spotlight at such a young age has taken a toll on numerous others who have been in that position. Wie might have felt overburdened with pressure from her parents, sponsors (Nike, with whom she signed a $20 million deal at 15), and fans. She also suffered her share of injuries to her right wrist, with an avulsion fracture, bone spurs, and a trapped nerve. It's said she was even arthritic in both wrists when she retired from competitive golf following the 2023 U.S. Open at Pebble Beach. And, it's argued, she became bogged down in excessively technical thoughts under David Leadbetter's tutelage impeding her natural skills.

Embracing opportunities after pro golf, Wie became an investor in women's sports initiatives and host of the Mizuho Americas Open on the LPGA Tour. She is married and the mother of two children.

2007 Walker Cup

Perhaps the strongest U.S. Walker Cup team ever.

DATE
September 8-9, 2007

LOCATION
Royal County Down
Newcastle,
Northern Ireland

PRIZE
The Walker Cup

IN THE FIELD
Dustin Johnson
Webb Simpson
Billy Horschel
Rickie Fowler
Chris Kirk
Rory McIlroy
Danny Willet

In the 85 years between the inaugural Walker Cup (see pages 84-7) and the 41st match—played at Royal County Down Golf Club in Northern Ireland, the U.S. had built a somewhat lopsided 32-7-1 lead, showing a similar dominance to the U.S. Ryder Cup team. A number of notable players who would go on to win major championships had represented the U.S. in the event including Bobby Jones (1922, 1924, 1926, and as playing captain in 1928 and 1930) Jack Nicklaus (1959, 1961), Tiger Woods (1995), and Phil Mickelson (1989, 1991). There was also 12-time participant—three as the non-playing captain—Francis Ouimet (who won the U.S. Open before he played in a Walker Cup); and Jay Sigel, who played in eight (two as playing captain). Though the Great Britain & Ireland team had won five of the nine previous encounters—including three in a row in 1999, 2001, and 2003—the U.S would be defending the Cup it won at Chicago Golf Club in 2005. And it named an extremely strong team ahead of the 2007 match.

Before the R&A established the World Amateur Golf Ranking (WAGR) in 2007 and, indeed, for a few years after that (the USGA didn't endorse the WAGR until 2011), both governing bodies did employ some sort of points system to make up the teams, though the selection process wasn't exactly common knowledge, and every team seemed to have one or two members whose inclusion was a surprise. Even now, though the WAGR does a good job of identifying the worthiest contenders for a spot on the team, eyebrows do occasionally rise when the two sides are announced.

The R&A's selection criteria are:

1. That year's Amateur champion (if eligible)
2. That year's U.S. Amateur champion (if eligible)

3. The top-5 highest ranked GB&I players in the WAGR a month before the event (date may vary).

4. The remaining players are selected by the captain.

The U.S. team is selected by the USGA's International Team Selection Working Group (ITS) which doesn't include the captain. Since 2018, the ITS has automatically selected the top-three ranked U.S. players in the WAGR in mid-June of Walker Cup year (two additional players may be added in late July based on current form.) The remaining players are then announced following the U.S. Amateur. An unpublished points system is kept to assist the ITS which considers a player's integrity, team skills and sportsmanship in addition to his playing ability.

Some said Michael Thompson and Drew Weaver deserved spots on the 2007 U.S. team, but choosing either of them over any of the 10 players that did go to Northern Ireland would certainly have been knotty. The USGA has a policy of including at least one mid-amateur (at least 25 years old) on the team, so even 35-year-old Trip Kuehne—who had played in four U.S. Opens—was a legitimate pick; he would win the U.S. Mid-Amateur Championship a month after this Walker Cup.

While Kuehne obviously raised the team's average age, 39-year-old Nigel Edwards did the same for the GB & Ireland team. The other nine U.S. players averaged 20.7 years, while the GB & Ireland team averaged 21.1 years without Edwards.

Fowler (l.) and McIlroy (r.)

The first morning's foursomes were shared 2-2. The biggest winners were the U.S.'s Billy Horschel and Rickie Fowler, who beat Scotland's Lloyd Saltman and Wales' Rhys Davies 4&3. Among the highlights of the afternoon's eight singles matches were Horschel beating Ireland's Rory McIlroy 1-up, Fowler beating Saltman 5&4, Davies beating Dustin Johnson 5&4, and Colt Knost defeating Danny Willett 2-up. A closely fought day ended with the teams locked on six points each.

Team USA put on an incredible display the following morning when they won all four foursomes matches to take a 10-6 lead. In the afternoon, an equally strong performance from the GB & Ireland team made the last hour or so incredibly tense.

McIlroy got revenge on Horschel 4&2, Davies beat Fowler 3&2, and the next three matches brought two wins and a half for the home team. The U.S.'s Jamie Lovemark then beat England's Jamie Moul (the No. 1 amateur in the world for much of that year). With two games left on the course, the U.S. led by a point and they clinched the victory when Jonathan Moore closed out Edwards on the last hole, after hitting a 252-yard 4-iron to three feet. England's David Horsey beat Webb Simpson in the final match to make the final score 12½ to 11½.

The victorious Team USA

Where Are They Now?

The 2007 U.S. Walker Cup team included several future PGA Tour winners and a couple of major champions-to-be, while the Great Britain & Ireland team had a couple of future major champions of its own.

Team U.S.A.

Dustin Johnson	2 majors, 24 PGA Tour wins, World #1 for a total of 139 weeks, 5 Ryder Cups, 4 Presidents Cups
Webb Simpson	1 major, 7 PGA Tour wins, 2018 Players Champion, 3 Ryder Cups, 3 Presidents Cups
Rickie Fowler	6 PGA Tour wins, 2 DP World Tour wins, 9 top 5s in majors, 2015 Players Champion, 2 Walker Cups, 5 Ryder Cups, 3 Presidents Cups
Billy Horschel	8 PGA Tour wins, including Tour Championship; 2 DP World Tour wins, 1 Presidents Cup
Chris Kirk	6 PGA tour wins, 1 Presidents Cup
Kyle Stanley	2 PGA Tour wins

Team Great Britain & Ireland

Rory McIlroy	5 majors (career Grand Slam), 29 PGA Tour wins, 2019 and 2025 Players Champion, 19 DP World Tour wins, 8 Ryder Cups
Danny Willett	1 major, 8 DP World Tour wins, 1 Ryder Cup
David Horsey	4 DP World Tour wins
John Parry	2 DP World Tour wins
Rhys Davies	1 DP World Tour win
Jonathan Caldwell	1 DP World Tour win

2016 Open Championship

Stenson and Mickelson in epic head-to-head final round.

DATE
July 14-17, 2016

LOCATION
Royal Troon GC
Ayrshire,
Scotland

PRIZE
$1,175,000

IN THE FIELD
Phil Mickelson
Rory McIlroy
Dustin Johnson
Jon Rahm
Jim Furyk
Sergio Garcia
Jordan Spieth
Padraig Harrington
Henrik Stenson

The nail-biters and knee-knockers would have had an uncomfortable afternoon on July 17, 2016 watching Sweden's Henrik Stenson and the U.S.'s Phil Mickelson slug it out for the Claret Jug over the beguiling undulations and imposing dunes of Royal Troon GC. So pulsating was the see-saw action that the outcome lay in the balance all afternoon. Only when Stenson had come up short of the right fairway bunker with his tee shot at the potentially dangerous final hole, and then hit a short iron about 20 feet from the cup, he was more of less assured of the title.

Even then though, Mickelson could have holed his 60-footer for birdie and Stenson three-putted, but the Swede actually rolled in his birdie putt, making the final three-shot margin of victory seem a little wider than the intensity of the confrontation had suggested.

Wearing a black ribbon on his hat to commemorate the recent death of a friend, Stenson shot a brilliant 63, which included 10 birdies, to complete the four rounds at 20-under-par, 264. Mickelson, who said he probably played his best golf ever without winning, shot 65, finishing on 267 (-17)—an amazing 11 shots ahead of 3rd-placed J.B. Holmes.

Inevitably, the question came up as to which final-round Open Championship duel—the Stenson/Mickelson one in 2016, or Nicklaus/Watson one in 1977 (see next page)—had been the more exciting, and the debate still engages those fortunate to have witnessed both.

Mickelson Out Ahead Early

The wind that sweeps across British links courses is very different to the gentle breezes that occasionally affect PGA Tour venues. It's strong, salty, and can be uncomfortably cold, cutting through you like a chilled knife. Mickelson, who grew up and still lives in southern California, has described it as "heavy" and having significantly more effect on his ball than the Westerlies he might encounter in San Diego.

Add unsettling winds to the difference in turf types (marram and fescue on the U.K. coastline; lusher Bermuda, zoysia, rye, Kentucky bluegrass, poa annua, bent, etc. in the U.S.), density of bunker sand, and green-speeds (10-11 on the Stimpmeter at the Open Championship; 13-14 at the Masters or at Oakmont CC in Pennsylvania), and you can see why it might take a while for an American player to adapt to links golf. (Mind you, all these factors didn't seem to bother Denny Shute, Ben Hogan, Tony Lema, Tom Watson, Ben Curtis, or Collin Morikawa, who all won the Open Championship on their debuts).

It would take 12 attempts before Mickelson was finally able to record a top 10 in the Open Championship—a surprising wait for a golfer of his talent. His 3rd-place finish at Royal Troon in 2004, when he finished a shot behind Ernie Els and surprise winner Todd Hamilton, came three months after he had beaten Els by a shot to win the Masters—the first of his six major titles. Another seven years would elapse before he secured a second top 10 (T2 at Royal St. George's). Then at Muirfield in 2013—24 years after his debut in the event—Mickelson finally captured the Claret Jug with a final round of 66, which the R&A described as a round of "immense class."

A tie for 23rd in 2014 and for 20th a year later weren't bad, but they suggested it might be a while before we saw Mickelson conquer the links again. And prior to arriving at Royal Troon for the 2016 Open Championship, he had missed the cut at the Masters, U.S. Open, and Players Championship.

It came as something of a surprise, then, when Mickelson lit up the Ayrshire course with a 63 on Day 1. Out in 4-under 32 and back in 4-under 31, he came painfully close to shooting 62, but his birdie putt at the last burned the edge and refused to drop.

Mickelson still led after a Friday 69, but what had been a three-shot cushion at the start of the day was cut to one following Stenson's 65 (he'd shot 68 in Round 1). After a third-round 68 from Stenson and a 70 by Mickelson, the two swapped places at the top of the leaderboard, and the

Swede would go into the final round leading by one on 201 (-12).

Final Day Fireworks

The lead changed again early on Sunday, when Stenson three-putted for a bogey at the 1st and Mickelson made birdie. Going behind apparently kicked Stenson into gear, as he birdied the next three holes. When Mickelson eagled the 4th, the two were tied at 14-under. "It was like prizefighters exchanging blows," said Sky Sports' Tim Barter. Both players birdied the par-five 6th, and then Stenson birdied the tiny par-three 8th ("Postage Stamp"), too.

They each turned in 32, with Stenson leading by one at -16. They then made birdies on the tough par-four 10th before Stenson bogeyed the 11th to fall back into a tie. After a couple of pars at 12 and 13, Stenson found another gear, birdieing

Stenson hits a shot while Mickelson looks on

the 14th and then holing from 50 feet for another birdie at the 15th. "I was never going to feel bad about making that 50-footer," Stenson told *Golf Digest* in 2024 ahead of Royal Troon's 10th Open Championship. "I had seen too many other guys do that to me over the previous 18 months or so."

"The putt at 15 was just shocking," said Mickelson. "For him to make that was just ... you couldn't expect that, even though you probably should." Stenson now led by two.

Both birdied the 16th, and then at the short 17th, Stenson hit the 4-iron of his life. "I don't think I even watched it finish," he said. "I just walked back to the bag and handed the club to Gareth [Lord—his caddie]." Mickelson holed a 15-footer for par, and after Stenson missed his birdie putt, the two protagonists headed to the 18th tee with two shots separating them.

The 18th at Troon is a tough par four with a bunker on the right at about 310 yards. With the adrenalin coursing through his veins, Stenson knew a driver would reach it, so he chose to hit a 3-wood. But after absolutely crushing his tee-shot, he watched as the ball rolled perilously close to the sand. It came to a stop about 18 inches short, however, leaving him with just a pitching wedge to the green. His birdie putt had a significant break from the right, the ball curling dramatically over the last few feet before toppling over the edge.

Stenson became the first Swedish man to win one of golf's major championships (Annika Sorenstam won 10 majors between 1995 and 2006). And what a way to do it!

Stenson celebrates

The Better Duel?

There are statistics that suggest the Stenson/Mickelson showdown at Royal Troon was the better of the two final-round thrill-rides, while there are plenty of people who saw both that will tell you the drama at Turnberry (see pages 158-62) was superior.

Let's look at a few numbers—Stenson shot 63 in the fourth-round at Troon, Mickelson 65 making an aggregate score of 128, or 14-under-par (Troon played to a par of 71). Stenson's 63 equaled Johnny Miller's 63 at Oakmont CC in the 1973 U.S. Open for lowest round to win a major. Stenson had 10 birdies (and two bogeys), Mickelson four and one eagle (no bogeys). Their 64 average was 9.02 shots better than the rest of the field.

Tom Watson won the 1977 Open with a final round 65. and Jack Nicklaus shot 66—an aggregate of 131, or 9-under par (Turnberry was a par 70). Watson had seven birdies, Nicklaus four, for a shared total of 11. Their 65.5 average was 9.00 shots better than the rest of the field.

According to the numbers, it appears Stenson and Mickelson played better golf. Their aggregate total was three shots better, and together, they were five shots better in relation to par. They were 0.2 of a shot better than their respective fields, and Mickelson (2nd in 2016) finished 11 shots clear of Holmes in 3rd place while Nicklaus (2nd in 1977) finished 10 ahead of Hubert Green in 3rd.

BUT—and it is an all-caps BUT—Watson and Nicklaus are two of the greatest links players of all time. Stenson came into Royal Troon ranked 6th in the world, while Mickelson was 19th. And while Mickelson will surely go down as one of the top 20 golfers in history, Stenson now shares 90th position in the list of golfers with the most major titles, tied with 143 others.

And what about last-hole drama? Watson came to the 18th tee one shot ahead of Nicklaus and hit safely down the fairway before hitting a 7-iron approach to three feet from the flag. Under the circumstances, it was a brilliant shot, and with Nicklaus in heavy rough and surrounded by gorse having leaked his drive right, it seemed to put the seal on a famous victory. Nicklaus was unlikely to reach the green even, but he muscled a short iron to a spot about 30 feet right of the flag. Two putts would give him a 67 and probably see him finish two back, but Nicklaus, being Nicklaus, sent his ball into the middle of the cup at perfect pace, causing the packed grandstands to erupt and putting all the pressure back on Watson. Doug Sanders had missed a similar-length putt (maybe a little longer) on the 72nd green at St Andrews to win the Open Championship (and subsequently lost the playoff to Nicklaus) seven years before, but Watson made no mistake, promptly holing his birdie putt for a 65 and his second Claret Jug.

So which was better; which would you have rather watched? A very sound argument can be made for each. It's interesting to hear what Watson and Nicklaus think.

"The last round that Tom and I played, it was 65, 66," Nicklaus said. "And they [Stenson and Mickelson] were 63, 65. And a par 71, and we were a par 70. So they scored better. Did that mean they played better? I don't know. When Watson and I did it, we were the one and two players in the game. Those guys sure put on one heck of a show. I thought it was one of the great events that I really had the pleasure to watch."

Watson gives it to Stenson and Mickelson, too ... sort of. "What happened at Troon was better simply because they played better. They shot lower scores. But I do think ours had more drama. Henrik sort of pulled away there toward the end. Jack and I were right there together all the way to the last hole, and the putt he made at 18 ... you always expect him to do things like that. And he forced me to make my putt. We were locked up right to the last shot."

2019 Augusta National Women's Amateur

Jennifer Kupcho impresses in new pre-Masters event.

DATE
July 14-17, 2019

LOCATION
Champions Retreat &
Augusta National
Georgia, USA

PRIZE
Sterling Cup
and invitations

IN THE FIELD
Jennifer Kupcho
Maria Fassi
Yuka Saso
Allisen Corpuz
Maja Stark
Rose Zhang
Andrea Lee
Jeeno Thitikul
Linn Grant

In October 2017, Fred Ridley became Augusta National GC's seventh chairman. At his first press conference, ahead of the 2018 Masters Tournament, the former U.S. Amateur champion made an important announcement: Beginning in 2019, the club would be sponsoring and co-hosting a 54-hole women's amateur event, with its final round played at Augusta National. It would be called the Augusta National Women's Amateur (ANWA).

For an 80-year-old club that had admitted its first women members—former U.S. Secretary of State Condoleezza Rice and businesswoman/philanthropist Darla Moore—just five years before Ridley spoke with the press, this was a very big deal.

It's hard to say exactly when the idea for the ANWA first started percolating though the clubhouse's elegant but extremely private hallways, but Ridley was obviously keen to make it happen as soon as possible.

The only Augusta National chairman to have played in the Masters, Ridley wouldn't have been appointed had he wanted to transform the club and eradicate its oldest traditions, but he did bring a considerably more progressive approach than his predecessors.

Ridley wasn't finished making significant moves. In 2021, he invited Lee Elder, the first Black man to play in the Masters (see pages 154-7), to serve as an honorary starter, and announced that the club would be funding two scholarships in Elder's name at Paine College—an historically Black college in Augusta—while also establishing a women's golf program. Together with corporate partners, the club would donate $10 million to impoverished Augusta neighborhoods. And then, in one of the handful of ways the club was seeking to grow the game among minorities and women, there was the ANWA. "I thought that this was the right time to do this," Ridley said. "It was the right time for the women's game. And I thought for us to have the greatest impact on women's golf we needed to be committed to do it here at Augusta National."

Seventy-two players are invited to participate with Champions Retreat GC, 17 miles northwest of downtown Augusta, staging the first 36 holes on the Wednesday and Thursday of tournament week. The top 30 advance to the final round at Augusta National on Saturday (with a playoff for the last spots if necessary), but all 72 get to play the Masters venue on the Friday. Champions Retreat uses the Island Nine (Palmer) and Bluffs Nine (Nicklaus) for the tournament (6,360 yards), as they are considered more championship-caliber and more spectator-friendly.

In 2019, the 36-hole cut fell at 147, and Wake Forest's Jennifer Kupcho (USA) won the tournament at 10-under-par, firing an impressive 67 in the final round at Augusta National (6,365 yards) to beat University of Arkansas' Maria Fassi (Mexico) by four. Kupcho and Fassi were the only two college players to make it through the 2018 LPGA Q-school, but both deferred their professional statuses.

The final round boiled down to a virtual matchplay contest between the two, but Fassi had no answer to Kupcho's scintillating finishing stretch—the Demon Deacon playing the final six holes in 5-under-par. Finishing 3rd was Yuka Saso, born in the Philippines but now representing Japan, who was eight shots back of Kupcho.

As professionals, Fassi has yet to win on the LPGA Tour but has played in two Olympics, Kupcho won her fourth LPGA title in June 2025, and Saso has won the U.S. Women's Open twice—in 2021 and 2024.

Kupcho hoists the ANWA trophy

ANWA Winners

2019—Jennifer Kupcho (USA)—206
2020—*Cancelled due to pandemic*
2021—Tsubasa Kajitani (Japan)—217
2022—Anna Davis (USA)—215
2023—Rose Zhang (USA)—207
2024—Lottie Woad (England)—208
2025—Carla Bernat Escuder (Spain)—204

2019 Masters

Tiger Woods claims fifth Green Jacket, 14 years after winning his fourth.

DATE
April 11-14, 2019

LOCATION
Augusta National
Augusta, GA
USA

PRIZE
$2,070,000

IN THE FIELD
Dustin Johnson
Brooks Koepka
Patrick Reed
Xander Schauffele
Francesco Molinari
Rory McIlroy
Jordan Spieth
Bryson DeChambeau
Phil Mickelson
Tiger Woods

He had last won a major championship at the 2008 U.S. Open and had just one PGA Tour victory in the previous five and a half years (the 2018 Tour Championship which may have featured the top 30 players on the Tour that season, but was a limited-field/no-cut event all the same.) Getting older had inevitably taken its toll physically on the 43-year-old Tiger Woods, but a somewhat loaded list of injuries and surgeries had been more to blame for his noticeably diminishing powers. Even a less-than-comprehensive list of his medical issues shows what Woods had had to deal with over the years.

It started in 1994 when the then 19-year-old had two benign tumors removed from his left knee. Surgery on the anterior cruciate ligament (ACL) followed in 2002, when cysts were also removed from that problematic left knee. A muscle in his left shoulder was damaged in fall 2006, and in 2007, he ruptured the ACL in his left knee but somehow managed to play through the discomfort. Two days after the 2008 Masters, Woods finally had surgery on his left knee to clear out cartilage, and a month later, doctors revealed he had two stress fractures in his left tibia. A few weeks after that, Woods overcame tremendous pain to win the U.S. Open at Torrey Pines, after which he had his left ACL repaired using a tendon from his right thigh.

He recuperated for several months but, six months into his rehabilitation, he damaged the Achilles tendon in his right leg, which meant he played the 2009 season in quite a bit of pain (not too much, obviously, as he won six times). In 2010, he had to withdraw from the Players Championship with an inflamed neck joint, and the following year was almost as uncomfortable as 2008-09 had been as the medial collateral ligament in his left knee and left Achilles tendon required attention, causing him to withdraw from the Players Championship again.

His left Achilles acted up again early in 2012, but the second half of the year and 2013 were relatively healthy. Back problems (spasms and pain) began appearing early in 2014, however, and he had his first back surgery in April. His second came in September 2015—a procedure that required a follow-up a few weeks later. He reported more back spasms in February 2017 and had a third back surgery in April.

All that to say Woods' body had seen more than its share of turmoil and pain through the years. But he still came out fighting in 2018, making the cut at the Masters (his last made cut in a major had come at the 2015 Masters), tying for 6th in the Open Championship at Carnoustie, and finishing 2nd at the PGA Championship at Bellerive in August. His win at the Tour Championship six weeks later confirmed Woods was back—not to his 2000 best, perhaps, but certainly to a level that would make him competitive at the 2019 majors ... assuming he could stay fit for them, of course.

Indeed, at Augusta National in April, Woods began the week as third or fourth favorite at 16-1, about 10 points behind a highly favored Rory McIlroy who had finished in the top 10 in all seven of his early season starts on the PGA Tour, winning the Players Championship.

The course now measured 7,475 yards, making it 185 yards longer than when Woods had last won the Masters in 2005, and 550 yards longer than it had been in 1997 when he first won. Unlike most players who had benefited from better equipment and were hitting the ball significantly farther, Woods was averaging just two yards more off the tee than he had in 1997 (his aging/damaged body apparently negating all the equipment advances), and instead of being 2nd in driving distance on the PGA Tour, he was now the equivalent (he didn't play the minimum number of rounds for many of his statistics to be official) of 71st.

In an era when the importance of distance had become paramount, Woods' driving average appeared to put him at a disadvantage. But of course, he had a pretty good record at the Masters—four wins and 13 top 10s, and experience at Augusta National seems to count for a lot more than it does elsewhere.

A first-round 2-under-par 70 put Woods four shots behind leaders Bryson DeChambeau and Brooks Koepka who had won two majors the previous season. After birdieing the 13th, Woods was just one back of the lead, but he'd finish the day in a tie for 11th.

With a second-round 68, during which an eager security guard slipped on wet ground and tumbled onto Woods' foot, causing him to limp for a while, the 14-time major champion rose steadily up the leaderboard into a tie for 6th, just a shot behind the five-way tie for the lead held by Jason Day, Adam Scott, Louis Oosthuizen, Francesco Molinari, and Koepka—all major champions.

A Saturday 67 put Woods at 11-under-par (205) for 54 holes, tied for second with Tony Finau who had shot a superb 64. Leading was Molinari whose 66 put him two clear at -13. Koepka, Johnson, and Oosthuizen were all still in the picture.

Because of the threat of thunderstorms, the final round began at 7:30 a.m., with players going off the 1st and 10th tees in groups of three. Woods, Finau, and Molinari began at 9:20 a.m., and after limited first-nine leaderboard movement, Molinari still held a two-shot lead after 11 holes. Everything was about to change, though.

After nearly holing his tee shot at the 12th the day before with the pin on the left, Molinari came up short in Round 4, the ball pitching into the bank between Rae's Creek and the green and falling back into the water. With the pin on the right, he'd taken too aggressive a line, perhaps. Having seen Molinari's ball disappear, Woods played safely to the middle of the green. It's unclear what Finau was attempting, as his aim suggested he was taking the same line as Woods, but just as Molinari's had, Finau's ball flew on line with the pin before coming up short and hopping back into the creek.

As Koepka in the group ahead had, Molinari and Finau made double bogeys. Woods, though, made a par, and at -11, was tied for the lead with Molinari.

This wasn't a two-person duel, however; there were plenty of challengers lurking just behind them. Xander Schauffele, in the fourth-to-last group, then birdied the 13th and 14th to go to 12-under, while Patrick Cantlay who'd started the round seven shots behind, eagled the 15th to join him at the top of the leaderboard.

Woods and Molinari then birdied the 13th, while Cantlay slipped back with bogeys on 16 and 17. Koepka eagled the 13th and birdied the 15th. Dustin Johnson made his third birdie in a row at the 17th, and all of a sudden there was a five-way tie at 12-under, comprised of Johnson, Schauffele, Koepka, Woods, and Molinari. At the par-five 15th, Woods made a birdie, while Molinari made another gruesome double bogey after his lay-up went astray, finishing left of the fairway, and his third caught a branch, the ball dropping into the pond short of the green.

Woods celebrates as his win sinks in

Woods then hit a superb 8-iron at the 179-yard 16th, the ball pitched about 25 feet right of the hole and curved toward the traditional Masters Sunday pin position. It passed by the cup about five inches to the left and stopped rolling a couple of feet away.

He knocked in the putt going to 14-under, parred the 17th, and arrived on the 18th tee knowing a bogey would be good enough to give him a one-shot victory. His 3-wood off the tee found the right edge of the fairway, and with an overhanging tree limb a concern, he hit a high, cutting 8-iron approach that came up well short and right of the green. A pitch and two putts was good enough, though. Woods finished the 72 holes at 13-under-par—one better than Johnson, Koepka, and Schauffele.

After his 275th shot of the tournament found the bottom of the cup, Woods gave a little fist-pump with his right hand before raising both arms to the sky and throwing his head back in delight. For the first time in his career, he had won a major after starting the final round out of the lead. It was his 5th Masters victory and 15th major. A full 10 years, 10 months, and 42 of the tournaments he covets most had passed since he'd won one. It was a monumental achievement and one of the Masters' most memorable moments.

Woods lifts the Masters trophy

The Greatest Comeback?

After all the injuries, surgeries, scandals, withdrawals, treatments, and rehabilitation he'd endured, it wasn't surprising Woods' victory at the 2019 Masters was considered perhaps the greatest sporting comeback of all time. And, if not the greatest sporting comeback, then at least the greatest golfing comeback.

There are probably too many plausible candidates for "greatest sporting comeback" to give a definite answer but, in golf, there are really only two other candidates.

The first is Ben Hogan who, in February 1949, was driving a car that was hit by a bus, causing him devastating injuries (see pages 124-7). But he fought his way back despite terrible pain to win six more majors, for a career total of nine.

Woods was asked about the potential stature of his own comeback at the 2018 Masters, but even he was in no doubt that Hogan's revival was more noteworthy. "I think that one of the greatest comebacks in all of sport is the gentleman who won here, Mr. Hogan," he said. "I mean, he got hit by a bus and came back and won major championships. The pain he had to endure, the things he had to do just to play, the wrapping of the legs, all the hot tubs and just ... how hard it was for him to walk period. ... That's one of the greatest comebacks there is, and it happens to be in our sport."

After Woods won the 2019 Masters, the question of whose comeback was greater came up again. And while most commentators acknowledged it was an impossible question to answer, it was generally felt the severity of his injuries and the magnitude of his post-accident record gave Hogan the edge.

The second candidate is Babe Zaharias, who won the 1954 U.S. Women's Open plus four LPGA tournaments just one year after major cancer surgery. While she didn't go through the same painful procedures Hogan did just to prepare for a round of golf, there's no doubt her return to the very top of the game took a mental and physical fortitude very few humans are capable of.

2022 LIV Golf London

The Saudi Arabia-funded breakaway tour's inaugural event.

DATE
June 9-11, 2022

LOCATION
Centurion Club
St Albans, Hertfordshire
England

PRIZE
$4,000,000
$3,000,000 for team

IN THE FIELD
Phil Mickelson
Sergio García
Dustin Johnson
Lee Westwood
Louis Oosthuizen
Bryson DeChambeau

Rumors surrounding the formation of a breakaway golf tour involving a few of the world's best players began to emerge in the middle of 2019—talk that became public in early 2020. A company called World Golf Group was proposing an 18-tournament series known as the Premier Golf League (PGL), in which fields would comprise 48 players, prize money would be significantly higher than what existing tours offered, there would be no cut, and players would compete both as individuals and as part of a team. World Golf Group partnered with the Raine Group, described as an "integrated merchant bank advising and investing in high growth sectors of technology, media and telecom."

Rory McIlroy, who said he had been approached as early as 2014, publicly rejected the advances and committed to the PGA Tour. Around the mid-year, the Saudi Arabia Public Investment Fund (PIF), a sovereign wealth fund whose assets are estimated at over $900 billion, joined the discussion proposing its own tour. Later in the year, however, it was suggested the PIF and PGL might join forces with a view to possibly working alongside the PGA Tour.

Talks between the PIF and PGL broke down, however, and by the middle of 2021, it seemed the PIF's economic strength would enable it to forge ahead alone, offering top players huge contracts to reject the PGA and European Tours entirely and play exclusively on what would be called LIV Golf (the Roman numeral for 54—the number of holes played in LIV events.)

In October 2021, Greg Norman was named CEO of LIV Golf Investments, and the LIV Tour's format was revealed—54 holes (expanded to 72 holes for 2026), shotgun start, no cut, with team and individual formats—to be very similar to what PGL had proposed, but with much greater prize money.

In May 2022, LIV's first signings were revealed. They included Dustin Johnson, Sergio Garcia, Lee Westwood, Ian Poulter, Louis Oosthuizen, Martin Kaymer, Charl Schwartzel, Graeme McDowell, and Kevin Na. Three days before the inaugural event—LIV London, to be played at the Centurion Club in St. Albans, 27 miles northwest of London—Norman announced Phil Mickelson would also be playing. The American's involvement had been rumored, but it still sent shockwaves through golf media.

The 48 players were divided up into 12 teams, each with their own uniform. The team names were: 4 Aces GC, Cleeks GC, Crushers GC, Fireballs GC, HyFlyers GC, Iron Heads GC, Majesticks GC, Niblicks GC, Punch GC, Smash GC, Stinger GC, and Torque GC. (Punch GC became Ripper GC ahead of the 2023 season, and early that year Niblicks GC was renamed RangeGoats GC. In January 2024, Legion XIII, captained by Spain's Jon Rahm, was added making 13 teams in total.)

The Centurion Club course opened in 2013 and proved a testing layout for LIV's first event, with Charl Schwartzel winning on 7-under-par, 203. The 2011 Masters champion beat countrymen Hennie Du Plessis (2nd at 204) and Branden Grace (T3 with the U.S.'s Peter Uihlein on 205) to become LIV's first ever tournament winner. The team event was won by the all-South African Stinger GC, made up of Schwartzel, Du Plessis, Grace, and Oosthuizen who finished 1st, 2nd, tied 3rd, and 12th, respectively.

A rebranded London taxi cab brings players to their starting hole

Ongoing Saga

In June 2023, the PGA Tour, DP World Tour (formerly the European Tour), and LIV entered into a framework agreement that would merge the commercial rights of the three entities into a new, for-profit, organization backed by significant investment from PIF. Given the ill-feeling between the PGA Tour and LIV/PIF up to this point, the announcement came as a huge shock to golf fans around the world as well as PGA Tour players who said they had not been informed of the talks ahead of time.

Negotiations over how exactly this new entity would operate stalled, however and, two years later, the operation was no closer to being confirmed. The PGA Tour remained adamant it would not enter into a deal in which LIV remained intact. Jay Monahan, commissioner of the PGA Tour, insisted it would have to be absorbed.

Some fundamental disagreements over the identity, handling, control, and leadership of the proposed organization continued to thwart progress and the lethargic nature of the discussions led to Monahan and the PGA Tour signing a deal with Strategic Sports Group (SSG) in January 2024. SSG invested $1.5 billion into a new company called PGA Tour Enterprises, of which Monahan was made CEO and which gave long-serving, high-achieving members of the

Jay Monahan (l.) and Yasir Al Rumayyan (m.) play in the Pro-am ahead of the 2024 Alfred Dunhill.

PGA Tour the opportunity to become equity holders.

John Henry, principal owner of the Fenway Sports Group and SSG's Manager consented to a future investment from PIF "subject to any necessary regulatory review and approvals."

In January 2025, LIV Golf replaced Greg Norman with a new CEO Scott O'Neill, former CEO of Merlin Entertainments. Talks between LIV Golf and the PGA Tour continued, though nothing of substance ever seemed to come of them, the in-joke being that every meeting resulted in a press release saying negotiations had been "cordial and successful" or something similar. By summer 2025, all hope (well, most of it) had been lost, and the patience of players and fans was wearing thin.

Former NFL executive, Brian Rolapp, was appointed the new CEO of the PGA Tour in June 2025 and, in his first press conference (three months after being appointed), said he had not spoken with anyone from PIF, which indicated that a deal with the Saudis was no closer to being made.

After three years with two separate tours (three if you count the DP World Tour, which formed a Strategic Alliance with the PGA Tour in 2020—extended in 2022 to run through 2035), the golf world seemed to have grown used to the situation and didn't seem terribly concerned with what happened next.

Other top players—Jon Rahm, Bryson DeChambeau, Brooks Koepka, Cameron Smith, Paul Casey, Joaquin Niemann, Bubba Watson, Patrick Reed, Tyrrell Hatton, and Marc Leishman had joined LIV by this point, and their transition could have been seen as extremely damaging to the PGA Tour. However, the refusal of McIlroy, Tiger Woods, Scottie Scheffler, Xander Schauffele, Justin Thomas, Jordan Spieth, and others to accept LIV offers and switch tours, continued coverage on major U.S. TV networks, and the relative failure of LIV players at the major championships (with one or two notable exceptions) ensured the PGA Tour remained prominent ... at least to the end of 2025.

2025 Masters

McIlroy finally wins the Masters, the career Grand Slam, and his 5th major.

DATE
April 10-13, 2025

LOCATION
Augusta National
Augusta, GA
USA

PRIZE
$4,200,000

IN THE FIELD
Rory McIlroy
Scottie Scheffler
Bryson DeChambeau
Xander Schauffele
Jon Rahm
Patrick Reed
Hideki Matsuyama
Dustin Johnson
Ludvig Åberg

Go almost 11 years without winning a major championship and we can be fairly sure your Grand-Slam tournament-winning career is over. You might pop up now again in a season-starting/ending tournament, opposite-field event, or post-season hit-and-giggle, but for the most part, your time atop the leaderboards that really matters is probably a thing of the past.

During his major-winning years, the longest period that Jack Nicklaus endured without adding to his tally was five years, and that was in his early 40s. From the time he started winning majors to the time he won his last, Ben Hogan never went more than a year without a major victory. Bobby Jones had eight straight years of major wins before retiring. Between 1914 and 1929, Walter Hagen had only two years when he didn't win a major (not counting 1915-18, during World War I).

Tiger Woods did endure a 30-major drought from the middle of 2008 to April 2019 though, to be fair, he had to tolerate a lot of injuries (some self-inflicted) during that time.

When Rory McIlroy arrived at the 2025 Masters, however, it had been 10 years, 8 months since he had last won a major. He had 20 top-10 finishes and 5 top-3s in that span, but he hadn't added to the four majors he won between June 2011 and August 2014. And the drought had become a major talking point in McIlroy's press conferences ahead of every major.

Anyone not familiar with the Northern Irishman might have assumed he was nearing the age of 50 and was no longer considered a threat at the legacy-building events. Remarkably, though, he was only 35. And at No. 2 in the world rankings, he was still very much a threat at the big tournaments.

The reasons for his inability to win a fifth major weren't entirely clear. He became a parent during the "lean" golfing years, but that hadn't stopped many other players from winning them—Nicklaus won all 18 of his Grand Slam events after he and his wife Barbara had the first of their five children. And McIlroy did claim 22 titles in the U.S. and Europe while going major-free.

Golfers—and certainly the golf press—prefer to be able to explain phenomena like this. We need to know what's going on, and why, as it gives us a sense of control over the world, no matter how fragile. It settles us mentally when we can explain (at least make a plausible attempt to explain) something that seems inexplicable.

When a golfer as young, healthy, and brilliant as Rory McIlroy goes the better part of 11 years without winning a major, it messes with our heads. It doesn't make a shred of sense, and not being able to comprehend something—on any level—is discombobulating.

At the Masters in 2011, a 21-year-old Rory McIlroy had the world at his feet. He had finished in the top three at three of the previous five major championships (missing the cut in the other two, strangely), and had won the PGA Tour's highly competitive Wells Fargo tournament at Quail Hollow with a closing 62, just a few months before.

At Augusta National, he opened with a 65, held a four-shot lead after 54 holes, and even after a shaky start to his final round, still had the lead heading into the second nine.

By the time he'd reached the 13th tee, however, he had vanished from the first page of the leaderboard. At the 10th, he hit a wild hook off the tee and his ball finished so far left of the fairway, TV cameras couldn't get to where it was. After more mishaps farther down the hole, he eventually holed out for a triple-bogey seven. At the 11th, he three-putted for a bogey, and after safely finding the green with his tee shot at the short 12th, he hit four putts, walking off with a double bogey five. He had dropped six shots to par in three holes and would eventually finish in a tie for 15th—10 shots behind eventual winner, Charl Schwartzel.

On Twitter/X, McIlroy was philosophical: "Well that wasn't the plan," he wrote. "Found it tough going today, but you have to lose before you can win. This day will make me stronger in the end. Hopefully, if I can get myself back into this position pretty soon, I will handle it a little bit better."

He *was* back in that position pretty soon (a different major, but still a major), and boy did he handle it better. Given how thoroughly shell-shocked and demoralized he must have felt after the 2011 Masters disaster, winning the U.S. Open just two months later was incredibly impressive.

And, after three more major victories over the next three years, a number of commentators shifted from saying Woods was going to be the one to overhaul Nicklaus' major total, to believing McIlroy might actually surpass them both.

As it became increasingly unlikely McIlroy would surpass either of them (at the end of 2025 and aged 36, he was still 13 majors short of Nicklaus' total and 10 behind Woods), the focus for the media, his fans, and possibly McIlroy himself became less about matching Nicklaus or Woods and more about achieving the Career Grand Slam—winning each of the four professional major championships at least once.

He'd won the Open Championship in 2014, the U.S. Open in 2011, and two PGA Championships—in 2012 and 2014, leaving just the Masters. Like every professional golfer stuck in a similar winless streak, McIlroy downplayed the importance of winning a Green Jacket. It was clear, though, the Jacket and a Masters title were what Rory coveted most.

The final sentence in his 2011 post-Masters tweet said, "I'll get over it. I'll have plenty more chances—I know that." That's true, but only partly. In the 13 Masters that McIlroy played from 2012 to 2024, he finished in the top-10 seven times, but the closest he ever got to the winner was three shots. He hadn't lost in a playoff or come to the final two or three holes with a definite chance of winning.

So what might happen when he really was a legitimate contender? Because he was still in his 30s and clearly capable of playing exceptional golf, most golf fans thought McIlroy probably would win it one day. But what if he didn't? Expecting something to happen is no guarantee that it will.

McIlroy arrived at Augusta National ahead of the 2025 tournament with all the now-familiar questions still circulating about his form, mental state, confidence level, swing, putting, caddie, home life, and so on. One more had begun to emerge, though: Could he, or anyone else for that matter, beat Scottie Scheffler?

The 28-year-old Texan (actually born in New Jersey) had won the Masters twice already—in 2022 and 2024—and had amassed 13 PGA Tour wins in the previous three seasons. Scheffler's statistics in numerous performance categories were exceptional—significantly better, in fact, than even the second-best player. Commentators, most notably Brandel Chamblee on the Golf Channel, were beginning to point out that Scheffler's statistics were similar to those of a younger Tiger Woods.

Scheffler and McIlroy were the two clear favorites according to the bookies, though Scheffler (+400) was a much clearer favorite than McIlroy (+650). To even the odds just a little, McIlroy met with Nicklaus, winner of six Masters, the week before the tournament for a frank discussion on how to play the course, reportedly going hole-by-hole and shot-by-shot.

A first-round 68 (-4) put Scheffler in a tie for 2nd place and was just the sort of solid start you'd expect of a favorite. For most of McIlroy's opening round, he too looked like he would finish the day well-satisfied. Standing on the 15th tee, he was 4-under-par having made birdies at the 3rd, 8th, 9th, and 13th holes. Disastrous double bogeys at the 15th and two holes later at the 17th dropped him to level-par, however, and instead of matching Scheffler's 68 and tying for 2nd, he wound up tied for 24th. Leading after Round 1, for the fifth time in his career, was England's Justin Rose, who shot 65.

Rose maintained his lead at the end of Day 2, adding a 71 to complete 36 holes on 8-under-par, though the news of the day was McIlroy's 66 that vaulted him into a tie for 3rd, two shots back. Scheffler shot a 71, and was three behind Rose, one back of McIlroy, and tied for 5th. In 2nd place was Bryson DeChambeau, a two-time U.S. Open winner who had been playing on the LIV Tour since June 2022.

Playing with the Canadian Corey Conners, McIlroy began his third round with six straight threes (-5) and ended up shooting another fine 66. At 12-under through 54 holes, he had a two-stroke lead over DeChambeau and four over Conners. Seven back, and seemingly out of it now, were Rose (75) and Scheffler (72).

McIlroy was striking the ball so well it seemed nothing could prevent him from winning—not Rose, Conners, Scheffler, Ludvig Åberg or Patrick Reed tied for 4th, or even DeChambeau, his playing partner for Round 4 and something of a nemesis having beaten McIlroy in a tensely fought duel at the U.S. Open less than a year before.

At the 1st, however, the Ulsterman's tee shot found the large fairway bunker to the right of the fairway, and after making a double bogey six, his lead was wiped out and he suddenly seemed a little ill-at-ease. When he found another fairway bunker at the par-five 2nd and finished the hole with a deflating par, he had the look of a man who thought it might all be unravelling again.

McIlroy steadied himself with birdies at the 3rd and 4th, however, regaining the lead after DeChambeau bogeyed both holes. And after making a birdie three at the 9th, McIlroy reached the turn in 35, four shots clear.

He then birdied the difficult 10th hole and walked to the 11th tee with a five-shot lead. At this point, Nicklaus and Woods would likely have begun aiming for the middle of each fairway and green, seeking to par in the rest of the way and run out an easy winner. But this was Rory McIlroy at the Masters; anything might happen and perhaps not even his biggest fan felt entirely comfortable.

He bogeyed the 11th—no disaster, it's a tough hole—and made a safe three at the 12th. Then at the par-five 13th, he hit a fine drive, and though his lay-up second probably finished a little farther left than he intended, he was dry and had a simple pitch to the green.

But with just 82 yards to the hole and a lot of green to the left of the flag to aim at, McIlroy hit an appalling shot, the ball hitting the bank to the right of the green and bouncing down into the creek. A drop, pitch, and two putts later, he walked off the green with a double bogey seven. With Rose surging from behind, making birdies on the 11th, 12th, and 13th, McIlroy's lead was suddenly down to one. Another bogey on the 14th followed, and birdies by Rose and the sweet-swinging Åberg at the par-five 15th meant there was now a three-way tie at the top.

Leaking oil and Rose and Åberg looking strong, McIlroy probably looked the least likely of the three to win. And he looked even less likely to come out on top when Rose birdied the par-three 16th to go one clear. McIlroy then drove left at the 15th, his path to the hole blocked by the trees on that side of the fairway. A birdie four would still be possible certainly, but earning it just got a little harder.

His approach to the shallow green was every bit as brilliant as his pitch to the 13th green had been awful, however. From 207 yards out, McIlroy hit a 20-yard hook with a 7-iron that pitched on the front-right of the green and spun left, finishing about six feet from the hole. It was an extraordinary shot that noticeably put the pep back in his step.

He missed his eagle putt, but the birdie stopped the rot. Rose then bogeyed the 17th but holed a long putt

McIlroy lets out a roar after winning the Masters

at the 18th for his 10th birdie of the round, a closing 66, and the clubhouse lead at -11. Åberg, meanwhile, three-putted the 17th then made a triple-bogey on the 18th to finish at 6-under-par.

After a less-than-ideal tee shot at the 17th, McIlroy had to call on his freakish talent to hit a towering 8-iron from 196 yards that finished three feet from the hole. The birdie took him to 12-under, one clear of Rose, meaning he just needed to par the 18th to win.

A big drive left him just 125 yards to go, but another shockingly bad wedge put him in the bunker to the right of the green. A mediocre explosion shot left him about five feet short of the hole, and he missed the putt. McIlroy ended up with a crazy, rollercoaster 73 that put him in a tie with Rose, who would be playing in his second playoff at the Masters (he had lost to Sergio Garcia in 2017).

At the first playoff hole (the 18th), both players hit the fairway and green, McIlroy redeeming himself with a superb wedge to three feet. Rose missed his birdie putt, but McIlroy holed to win a tournament he'd had in his pocket a couple of hours before, thrown away, and somehow retrieved.

"Emotional" doesn't begin to describe McIlroy's reaction. He was overwhelmed and, on the 150-yard walk to the scoring room, he looked utterly exhausted but, at the same time, intense and hyper. He was a Masters champion at last, and the relief and joy were palpable.

A relieved McIlroy with the Masters trophy

The (Professional) Career Grand Slam

Historically speaking, what has constituted a major championship is a complicated subject. The Masters wasn't played until 1934 and not considered an elite tournament immediately. The Western Open was once regarded as a major, but is now a FedEx Cup playoff event called the BMW Championship. And the North & South Open was likewise extremely prestigious in its day.

The current canon—Masters, U.S. Open, PGA Championship, Open Championship—became the accepted Grand Slam events thanks to Arnold Palmer in 1960. Only one professional golfer has held all four titles at once: Tiger Woods, who won them consecutively in 2000-01. No one has come close to that since.

Winning majors is so difficult only six golfers since 1934 have won all four of the modern majors at least once each during their career. McIlroy joined this very exclusive club when he won the Masters—25 years after Woods achieved the Career Grand Slam for the first time (he did it twice more).

Golf fans might not have to wait another quarter-century to see the seventh player join their ranks, though: Entering 2026, Scottie Scheffler Scheffler just needed to win the U.S. Open to complete the set. Two other active players one win away from the Career Grand Slam were Phil Mickelson, who had six major wins but no U.S. Open title (despite six runner-up finishes), and Jordan Spieth who just needed a PGA Championship to win all four. You had to say though, that, of the three, Scheffler was by far the most likely to become the seventh Career Grand Slammer.

	Masters	**U.S. Open**	**PGA Championship**	**(British) Open**
Gene Sarazen	1935	1922, 1932	1922, 1923, 1933	1932
Ben Hogan	1951, 1953	1948, 1950, 1951, 1953	1946, 1948	1953
Gary Player	1961, 1974, 1978	1965	1962, 1972	1959, 1968, 1974
Jack Nicklaus	1963, 1965, 1966, 1972, 1975, 1986	1962, 1967, 1972, 1980	1963, 1971, 1973, 1975, 1980	1966, 1970, 1978
Tiger Woods	1997, 2001, 2002, 2005, 2019	2000, 2002, 2008	1999, 2000, 2006, 2007	2000, 2005, 2006
Rory McIlroy	2025	2011	2012, 2014	2014

15
32 4 17
11 13
1
36
20
10
45
46
19
9
33
8
29
40
3
23
38
21
47 31
35 41
14

HONORABLE MENTIONS

HONORABLE MENTIONS

With so many tournaments in the calendar, picking 50 of the best was tricky and would inevitably mean some very significant events being left out. Here are 25 more that were considered for a long time before ending up on the cutting room floor.

1880 Tennant Cup

The little-known Tennant Cup is the oldest surviving amateur stroke-play event in the world and hosted by the Glasgow Golf Club in Scotland. It was first played in 1880—pre-dates the (British) Amateur Championship by five years—when industrialist Sir Charles Tennant donated the trophy to the club. Today it is played over 72 holes—36 on the club's Gailes Links on the Ayrshire coast and 36 on its parkland course at Killermont. Winners include internationals, Walker Cup players, and a future Ryder Cupper and Ryder Cup captain, Bernard Gallacher.

1895 U.S. Women's Amateur

A month after the first U.S. Amateur and U.S. Open at Newport CC, the USGA decided to hold a tournament for ladies. It was an 18-hole strokeplay event (it would become a matchplay competition the following year) held at the Meadow Brook Club on Long Island, N.Y., and won by Lucy Barnes Brown who shot a 132 and played under the name Mrs. Charles S. Brown representing Shinnecock Hills GC.

1932 Wallasey Stableford

Surgeon Dr. Frank B. G. Stableford was a member at Glamorganshire Golf Club in Wales and Wallasey Golf Club near Liverpool and often became frustrated when a couple of bad holes ruined his medal score. He devised a scoring system that would keep players' interest alive throughout their round, and after being tested at Glamorganshire, it was first used in competition at Wallasey in May 1932. An instant hit, it became extremely popular, especially in the U.K., and modified Stableford systems have been used in a handful of professional events, most notably the International on the PGA Tour (1986-2006). The winner of that first event in 1932 was a five-handicapper named Fred Lister, who scored 36 points.

1949 U.S. Women's Open

The fourth U.S. Women's Open was held at Prince George's Country Club in Maryland. Louise Suggs was the winner, finishing at 9-under, 291—14 shots better than Babe Zaharias in 2nd.

1960 Open Championship

Prior to 1960, only a handful of American golfers would make the costly and lengthy trip across the Atlantic to play in the Open Championship. Arnold Palmer recognized its significance and place in the game, and after winning the Masters and U.S. Open in 1960, he was determined to add the Claret Jug to his trophy case. One of only four Americans to play in the event that year at the Old Course in St Andrews, Palmer finished 2nd, a shot behind Australia's Kel Nagle. Palmer would win the Open Championship the following year and again in 1962, and his appearances helped make the event what it is today.

1964 U.S. Women's Open

One of the women's game's greatest ever players and the owner of one of golf's best ever swings, Mickey Wright won 82 LPGA titles including four U.S. Women's Opens, her last win coming at her home course of San Diego Country Club in 1964 when she beat Seattle's Ruth Jessen in an 18-hole playoff.

1965 World Match Play

The World Match Play Championship was a popular event that featured 8-24 of the world's best players every year, competing over 36-hole matches. It was conceived and organized by Mark McCormack's International Management Group (IMG), and held between 1964 and 2014. For the first 40 years, Wentworth Golf Club near London was the venue and the scene of numerous memorable matches including Gary Player's come-from-behind semi-final win over Tony Lema in 1965. One-up after 10 holes of the first round, Player lost seven holes in a row and finished the morning round 6-down. After losing the 1st in the afternoon, he went 7-down with 17 to play. He suddenly found his form and started making birdies, eventually winning the 18th/36th hole to square the match. He then won the first extra hole to advance to the following day's final, where he beat Australia's Peter Thomson 3&2.

1965 Australian Open

It doesn't appear on too many superstars' schedules these days, but the Australian Open was once a very prestigious tournament (and can be again) that attracted some of the biggest names in the game. Arnold Palmer won at Royal Queensland in 1966 and Jack Nicklaus won it six times between 1964 and 1978. Gary Player went one better than Nicklaus with seven victories between 1958 and 1974, the most notable of them coming in 1965 at Kooyonga where he completed 72 holes on 28-under, 264 and beat Nicklaus (and Frank Phillips) by six strokes after recording two rounds of 62.

1967 U.S. Women's Open

Played on the Cascades Course at the Homestead in Virginia, the 1967 U.S. Women's Open was won by a 22-year-old French amateur named Catherine Lacoste who was so far ahead after 54 holes she still won by two after a final-round 79.

1980 Atlantic City Invitational

The Senior PGA Championship was founded in 1937 but, for 40 years, that was about it for professional senior golf (there were a few other low-key events). In 1978, a tournament called the Legends of Golf, featuring famous names from the past playing in two-man teams, and conceived by TV executive Fred Raphael, was played at Onion Creek Club in Austin, Texas, co-owned by three-time Masters champion, Jimmy Demaret. Sam Snead and Gardner Dickinson won, and it was so popular, it happened again the following year. PGA Tour commissioner, Deane Beman, saw this and began thinking about establishing a tour for former Tour players over the age of 50. A four-tournament series was scheduled for 1980—the Senior PGA Championship, the inaugural U.S. Senior Open and two regular events. The first of them was the Atlantic City Invitational, played in June at the historic Atlantic City CC. Don January, the 1967 PGA Championship winner, shot 5-under 208 for the 54 holes becoming the first ever champion on the Senior PGA Tour (now the PGA Tour Champions) and earning $20,000. January, who'd won 10 times on the PGA Tour, won 22 events on the senior tour, including the Senior PGA Championship in 1982.

1981 Ryder Cup

When people talk about the greatest Ryder Cup teams ever assembled, the U.S. side in 1981 invariably gets a mention. With nine major champions (two more players would go on to win Grand Slam events), and only three players who wouldn't end up in the World Golf Hall of Fame, Team USA was a formidable outfit. The Europeans (this was only the second time that Continental players were part of the Ryder Cup) were without Seve Ballesteros who refused to play in a lot of the bigger tournaments in Britain, because he wasn't receiving an appearance fee and thus didn't earn enough to qualify automatically (and didn't get a Captain's pick because his inclusion in the team would likely have caused controversy and ill-feeling). Missing such a key player made it even more difficult for the home team to keep pace with their opponents, but they made a valiant attempt and actually led 4½-3½ at the end of the first day. The Americans were virtually unstoppable over the next two days, however, and eventually ran out comfortable winners 18½-9½.

1982 U.S. Open

Tom Watson had a surprisingly good record against Jack Nicklaus (see page 163) beating him at the 1977 Masters, 1977 Open Championship, 1981 Masters and 1982 U.S. Open where he finished 72 holes on 6-under, 282—two better than the Golden Bear—and hit one of the most memorable shots in the Championship's history. Long and left of Pebble Beach's par-three 17th green and sitting in some typically thick U.S. Open rough (the lie was actually decent), Watson chopped out as delicately as he could and watched as the ball ran into the cup at almost perfect speed.

1987 Masters

At the end of 72 regulation holes of the 1987 Masters, three were tied at the top of the leaderboard—Spain's Seve Ballesteros, Australia's Greg Norman, and Larry Mize, an Augusta native who had one win on the PGA Tour. At the first extra hole (10th), Ballesteros three-putted from just off the back edge of the green while Norman and Mize both made pars. At the second extra hole (11th), Mize hit his approach a good 20 yards right of the green. Norman missed a little right, too, but was much closer to the hole. Norman was probably the favorite to win at this point, but Mize tore his heart out by miraculously holing his 40-yard chip shot for a birdie three. Norman couldn't follow him in, leaving Mize the champion.

1988 Nabisco Dinah Shore

Amy Alcott won the 1988 Nabisco Dinah Shore at Mission Hills in Rancho Mirage, California, beating Colleen Walker by two. It was her second win at the Dinah, her 27th LPGA Tour title, and fourth major. And she was so excited, she spontaneously ran toward the water hazard right of the 18th green ... and jumped in with her caddie, Bill Kurre. She did it again in 1991 and Donna Andrews became the first to copy the leap, in 1994. When Nanci Bowen did it in 1995, it stuck, creating a lasting tradition of winners jumping into what became known, in 2006, as Poppie's Pond (Tournament Director Terry Wilcox was called "Poppie" by his grandchildren). When Chevron took over the tournament and moved it to the Woodlands near Houston, Texas, the tradition came with it. Now, players jump into the natural lake between the 9th and 18th holes, which needed to be cleaned and dredged before anyone would jump in. And netting had to be installed around the dock to guard against alligators.

1991 PGA Championship

John Daly was ninth alternate for the 1991 PGA Championship at Crooked Stick in Indiana, but he got the call to play less than 24 hours before the first tee time. Without a practice round, he shot an opening 3-under 69 on the 7,289-yard, Pete Dye-designed course, and by the end of 36 holes, he was on top of the leaderboard with a second-round 67. Daly's powerful, way-past-parallel swing was a huge hit with the galleries and reduced many of the par fives and long par fours to drive and short-iron holes giving him a significant advantage, provided he hit the fairway. A third-round 69 gave him a three-shot leading going into Sunday, and a closing 71 was good enough for a three-shot victory at 12-under, 276. Given this was his first ever major championship and that he had started the week with a very small chance of playing at all, Daly's win has to be one of the most unlikely in the game's history.

1996 Masters

After 54 holes, Greg Norman led the tournament at 13-under, 203, and with a six-stroke lead over Nick Faldo, was obviously well-positioned to finally win the Green Jacket he'd come so close to winning a number of times before. But, while he unraveled badly in the final round (78), Faldo played an exceptional closing round (67), the 11-shot swing, earning Faldo his third Green Jacket and sixth major.

1998 U.S. Women's Open

In 1998, 20-year-old Se Ri Pak was the only South Korean player on the LPGA Tour. She'd won six times over the previous couple of years in her homeland, moved to America, and by the end of July had won four times, with the first two victories being majors. In May, she won the LPGA Championship at DuPont CC in Delaware, and seven weeks later, at Blackwolf Run in Wisconsin, she won a 20-hole playoff against Jenny Chuasiriporn (after both had finished 72 holes on 6-over 290) to become the youngest ever winner of the U.S. Women's Open. Her win triggered a revolution in the women's game as 10 years later there were 45 Koreans on the LPGA Tour. *Golf World* magazine said she was a pioneer who had changed the face of golf even more than Tiger Woods. Five years after her sensational rookie year on the LPGA Tour, she played in a men's professional event in Korea and finished 10th. She retired in 2016 having won 25 times on the LPGA Tour—a total that included five majors.

1999 Open Championship

A tough course without any help from the weather or greenkeeper, Carnoustie was at its meanest during the 1999 Open Championship thanks to narrow fairways and rough made long and lush by Spring rain. France's Jean van de Velde, a one-time winner on the European Tour, was the only man to match par through 54 holes and he started Sunday's final round with a five shot-lead. He'd lost it to playing partner—Craig Parry of Australia—by the time the they reached the 12th hole, however, but Parry's triple-bogey at the 479-yard par four handed it right back to van de Velde. The Frenchman then played the next five holes in 1-under-par and arrived at the 18th with a commanding three-stroke lead over Scotland's Paul Lawrie, who'd shot a final round of 67 and the U.S.'s Justin Leonard, both of whom were in the clubhouse on 6-over, 290. A six on the 487-yard par-four closing hole would have been good enough for van de Velde to become the second Frenchman to win the Open Championship after Arnaud Massy in 1907 (see pages 56-9), but a horrific combination of poor decision-making, bad execution, and rotten luck resulted in a disastrous triple bogey 7 that put him in a four-hole playoff. With the shock of what had just transpired fresh in his mind, it was unlikely van de Velde was going to regroup, and sure enough, he had to take an unplayable lie after a poor tee shot at the first extra hole (15th), eventually winding up with a double bogey. Lawrie and Leonard each made bogeys on the first two extra holes, though, and when van de Velde holed a birdie putt on the third playoff hole (17th) there was a three-way tie for the lead, albeit momentarily. Lawrie followed him in and after another birdie three on the 18th after a superb 4-iron to four feet (van de Velde and Leonard each made a bogey), he won the playoff by three, becoming the first Scotsman to win the Open Championship since Sandy Lyle in 1985.

2007 Women's British Open

In its first 30 years, the Women's British Open (now the AIG Women's Open) had been played at a lot of great courses but had never been to St Andrews. It visited for the first time in 2007 (first ever women's professional tournament there) when Mexico's Lorena Ochoa went wire-to-wire (she shot a 6-under-par 67 in the first round to lead by two) and won by four shots over Sweden's Maria Hjorth and Korea's Lee Jee-Young.

2008 U.S. Open

After surgery on his left knee in April and after doctors had discovered two stress fractures in his left tibia, Tiger Woods played the 2008 U.S. Open at Torrey Pines in California in terrible pain. On numerous occasions, the 13-time major champion grimaced following a shot, often doubling over to find a moment's relief. Incredibly, though, he holed a 12-foot putt for birdie on the 72nd hole to get into an 18-hole playoff with Rocco Mediate who had finished at 1-under, 283. The two were still tied after 90 holes, each having shot a level-par 71 on that Monday. Woods, though, captured his third U.S. Open with a four on the first sudden-death hole (7th).

2009 Open Championship

Tom Watson didn't much like links golf after his first try, thinking it a bit flukey as seemingly good drives could take wicked bounces off firm, rippled fairways and end up in the rough. He quickly realized this was just part of the game, though, and that he'd have to deal with it. Over the next nine years, he dealt with it rather well winning five Claret Jugs (joining James Braid, J.H. Taylor, and Peter Thomson). In 2009, Watson returned to Turnberry where he'd beaten Jack Nicklaus in the "Duel in the Sun" 32 years before (see pages 158-62) but, at the age of 59, it was surely just a sentimental visit. He opened with a 5-under 65, however, and was just one shot out of the lead held by Spain's Miguel Ángel Jiménez. After a second-round 70, he was tied at the top of the leaderboard with the U.S.'s Steve Marino, and he led on his own after 54 holes. After birdieing the 17th hole in the final round, he took a one-shot lead to the final hole and the seemingly impossible dream of matching Harry Vardon on six Open Championship victories (and becoming the oldest winner of the Claret Jug, "beating" Tom Morris Sr. by 13 years) was very much on. After a perfect tee shot at the 461-yard home hole that had been renamed "Duel in the Sun," Watson hit an 8-iron approach downwind that took a hard bounce and finished through the green about 55 feet from the hole. He chose to putt through the back fringe but hit it a little hard, the ball finishing about seven feet past the hole. The putt to win wasn't his best effort, coming up short and right and leaving him tied with Stewart Cink at 2-under, 278. Watson lost all momentum and finished six shots behind Cink in the four-hole playoff. Through no fault of his own, Cink became probably the least popular Open Champion in the tournament's 149-year history.

2009 PGA Championship

Tiger Woods had gone into the final round of a major championship with the lead 14 times and won every one of them. On this occasion though, he'd finally be beaten after shooting a disappointing final round of 75. South Korea's Yang Yong-eun (Y.E. Yang) had started the final round two back, and his closing 70 was good enough for him to win by three on 8-under, 280. Not only did he break Woods' record, Yang became the first Asia-born player to win a men's major.

2012 Ryder Cup

The 2012 Match was the 39th Ryder Cup and played on the #3 Course at Medinah CC, 30 miles west of downtown Chicago. The captains were Davis Love III for the U.S. and José María Olazábal for Europe. After two days, the U.S. team had built a 10-6 lead and would need just 4½ points from Sunday's singles to win. The Europeans were determined to avenge the 1999 defeat (they had likewise led by four going into the final day but ended up losing 14½-13½—see pages 190-1). The visitors won the first five matches with England's Justin Rose winning a vital point in an exciting match against Phil Mickelson. The next seven points were shared meaning Europe won the singles 8½-3½ and the match 14½-13½. Germany's Martin Kaymer holed a six-foot putt on the 18th to beat Steve Stricker 1-up and make it five wins for Europe from the previous six Ryder Cups.

2021 Open Championship

The Open Championship was played at Royal Portrush in 1951, when England's Max Faulkner won by two shots at 3-under, 285. The Troubles (a period of violence and political unrest between Unionists/Loyalists and Catholic Republicans, and which lasted from the late 1960s to the late 1990s), prevented the Championship from coming back, but with peace restored, it returned to Northern Ireland in 2019. The fact that one of the world's great courses was again able to host the game's oldest major was worthy of celebration, but that party was somewhat limp compared to the merrymaking that happened after Ireland's own Shane Lowry won the tournament by six shots, finishing at 15-under, 269.

2021 PGA Championship

Phil Mickelson was 24 days short of his 51st birthday when he teed it up in the 2021 PGA Championship at Kiawah Island in South Carolina. His last win on the PGA Tour had come more than two years previously, and since then he had missed 20 cuts in 48 PGA Tour events with just three top 10s. So it was a huge surprise when he won the tournament by two shots, shooting a 6-under 282 for the four rounds. In winning his sixth major, Mickelson became the oldest player to win a men's major, surpassing the previous "leader," Julius Boros, by two years and seven months.

BIBLIOGRAPHY

Barrett, David. *The Story of the Masters* (2021).

Benedict, Jeff and Keteyian, Armen. *Tiger Woods* (2019).

Browning, Robert *A History of Golf: The Royal and Ancient Game* (1955).

Bubka, Bob and Clavin, Tom. *The Ryder Cup: Golf's Greatest Event* (1999).

Casper, Billy, with James Parkinson. *The Big Three and Me* (2012).

Clavin, Tom. *Sir Walter* (2012).

Cook, Kevin. *Tommy's Honor* (2008).

Cook, Kevin. *The Tiger Slam* (2024).

Dabell, Norman. *How We Won The Open* (1990).

Dodson, James. *American Triumvirate* (2013).

Feinstein, John. *A Good Walk Spoiled* (1996).

Feinstein, John. *The Majors* (2000).

Frost, Mark. *The Greatest Game Ever Played* (2004).

Gay, Timothy. *Rory Land* (2024).

Green, Robert. *Seve: Golf's Flawed Genius* (2012).

Harig, Bob. *Drive* (2024).

James, Mark. *Into the Bear Pit* (2001).

Jenkins, Dan. *Jenkins at the Majors* (2009).

Jones, Bobby, and Keller, O.B. *Down the Fairway* (1927).

Jones, Bobby. *Golf is My Game* (1960).

Joy, David, and Lowe, Iain. *St Andrews and the Open Championship* (1999).

Kirsch, George. *Golf in America* (2008).

Macpherson, Scott. *The Evolution of the Old Course* (2007).

Malcolm, David and Crabtree, Peter. *Tom Morris of St. Andrews, the Colossus of Golf 1821-1908* (2008).

Matthew, Sidney. *The Life and Times of Bobby Jones* (1995).

McDaniel, Pete. *Uneven Lies* (2000).

McStravick, Roger. *In the Footsteps of Old Tom Morris* (2015).

McStravick, Roger. *A History of Golf* (2017).

McStravick, Roger, and Williams, Bill. *Allan Robertson of St. Andrews, The King of Clubs* (2024).

Millar, Neil. *Early Golf: Royal Myths and Ancient Histories* (2022).

Morrison, Michael. *The Great English Golf Boom* (2022).

Murray, Francis. *The Open* (2000).

Nelson, Byron. *How I Played the Game* (2006).

Owen, David. *The Making of the Masters* (2003).

Price, Charles. *A Golf Story* (1986).

Proctor, Stephen, *Monarch of the Green* (2019).

Proctor, Stephen. *Long Golden Afternoon* (2022).

Reid, Kenny. *Seve Ballesteros's Touch of Class* (2024).

Sampson, Curt. *The Masters* (1999).

Sampson, Curt. *Hogan* (1997).

Schupak, Adam. *Deane Beman: Golf's Driving Force* (2011).

Shipnuck, Alan. *LIV and Let Die* (2023).

Sommers, Robert, and Brown, Cal. *Great Shots* (1989).

Wind, Herbert Warren. *The Story of American Golf* (1948).

Newspapers

Atlanta Journal-Constitution
Augusta Chronicle
Dundee Courier
Dundee Evening Telegraph and Post
Edinburgh Courant
Edinburgh Evening News
Fifeshire Journal
Fife Herald
Glasgow Herald
London Evening Telegraph
London Times
New York Sun
New York Times
New York Tribune
The Scotsman

Magazines/Journals

Golf Journal
Golf Illustrated (US)
Golf Illustrated (UK)
Sports Illustrated
The American Golfer
The New Yorker

Websites visited regularly

europeantour.com
golfcompendium.com
golfdigest.com
leith-rules-golf.co.uk
lpga.com
masters.com
muirfield.org.uk
pgachampionship.com
pgatour.com
randa.org
scottishgolfhistory.org
theopen.com
usga.org
wikipedia.com

Photography Credits

Many of the images in this book are courtesy of Alamy Images, including pages: 0, 15, 31, 36, 42, 45, 55, 67, 75, 79, 89, 115, 119, 130, 133, 134, 137, 139, 149, 157, 161, 162, 166, 170, 186, 188, 189, 191, 195, 203, 206, 208, 209, 211, 213, 226, 227, 228, 229, 231, 235, 236, 239, 240, 247, 248, 277.

p. 9: Photo of the 1744 Silver Club head, courtesy of The Honourable Company of Edinburgh Golfers.

p. 11: Photo of the John Rattray Statue, courtesy of the Leith Rules Society.

p. 11: Photo of the Prize of the Silver Golf Club, courtesy of Scotland's National Galleries.

p. 14: Photo of Painting of Major Fairlie, courtesy of Prestwick Golf Club.

p. 18: Photo of Prestwick minute book, courtesy of Prestwick Golf Club.

p. 23: Photo of Willie Park Sr., courtesy of Mungo Park.

p. 39: Map of the 1891 Muirfield Course, courtesy of The Honourable Company of Edinburgh Golfers.

p. 40: Photo of Harold Hilton's portrait by Richard Jack (1913) and Image of Hilton's 1892 Open medal, courtesy of Royal Liverpool GC.

p. 74: Photo of Harry Vardon on Prestwick's 9th hole by Popperfoto, courtesy of Getty Images.

p. 98: Photo of Bob Jones accepting the Havemeyer trophy courtesy of the Sidney L. Matthew Bobby Jones Archive at Emory University Library.

p. 104: Aerial photo of Augusta National courtesy of the Sidney L. Matthew Bobby Jones Archive at Emory University Library.

p. 105: Map of Augusta National GC, courtesy of Frederick Law Olmsted Library.

p. 111: Photo of Clifford Roberts and Bobby Jones, courtesy of Sidney L. Matthew Bobby Jones Archive at Emory University Library.

p. 121: Photos of Robert Hudson from the 1947 Ryder Cup, courtesy of Pacific Northwest Golf Association.

p. 125: Photo of Ben Hogan next to car, courtesy of the USGA.

p. 129: Photo of Ben Hogan by Hy Peskin, courtesy of the USGA.

p. 130: Photo of Mrs. and Mr. Hogan, courtesy of the USGA.

p. 131: Photo of Hogan's 1-iron, courtesy of Associated Press.

p. 142: Photo of Arnold Palmer and Jack Nicklaus, courtesy of the USGA.

p. 152: Photo of Hale Irwin, courtesy of the USGA.

p. 153: Photo of Sandy Tatum, courtesy of the USGA.

p. 156: Two photos of Lee Elder, courtesy of Associated Press.

p. 175: Photo of Jack Nicklaus, courtesy of Associated Press.

p. 181: Photo of U.S. Solheim Cup team, courtesy of Ladies European Tour.

p. 194: Photo of Team GB/Ireland by Popperfoto, courtesy of Getty Images.

p. 198: Photo of Tiger Woods, courtesy of Associated Press.

Acknowledgments

A couple of years ago, it struck me that Back Nine Press was creating the sort of books I enjoyed the most. I didn't own every volume this young, golf-centric company had produced certainly, but did have a few, and it was easy to identify a link common to all of them—these were books written and published by people who clearly loved the game.

When the idea for this book occurred to me, I thought of Back Nine Press first. While selling as many books as possible is obviously paramount to any new publisher, and attracting customers the primary concern of any small business, Back Nine Press seemed just as keen to promote the many great aspects of golf and conscientiously spread its gospel.

Jim Sitar, the founder and publisher, liked the idea and gave it the green light. And I can say with some confidence that, in addition to crossing the commercial 't's and dotting the legal 'i's, Jim's focus has been on creating as good a product as possible—easier said than done when your second child arrives in the middle of it all. Congratulations to Jim and his wife Molly, and thank you for letting me add to Back Nine's growing inventory.

There are plenty of other people whose contributions were essential and are much appreciated. Robin Dow at the Honourable Company of Edinburgh Golfers was generous with his time and knowledge, and for granting us permission to use the rare image of Muirfield's 1891 layout. Prestwick GC's Secretary Rob McGuire, and his predecessor Ken Goodwin, as well as the club's archivist Andrew Lochhead were likewise generous with time and images.

The insights of prominent golf historians Stephen Proctor, Roger McStravick, Mungo Park, Neil Laird at s*cottishgolfhistory.org*, and Charles Urquhart at *leith-rules-golf.co.uk* were invaluable, as were those of Hannah Fleming at the R&A World Golf Museum and Dave Moore at Oakmont CC. Sincere thanks also for images, advice, stories, and introductions go out to Erin Shields at Royal Liverpool GC, Stacy Schiff at the USGA, Tom Cade at the PNGA, Graham Park (author of *Golf's Greatest Gamble*), and Laura Baker at the Ladies European Tour.

Perhaps my greatest debt of gratitude, though, is reserved for Sidney Matthew, one of the game's great individuals who managed to combine being a prominent Florida lawyer with creating a huge private collection of Bobby Jones-dedicated media. Emory University acquired 86 boxes of photographs, newspapers, magazines, scrapbooks, correspondence, memorabilia, video recordings, and research files from Mr. Matthew in 2015, and he graciously read everything in this book relating to Jones to confirm its accuracy.

A Word about Using A.I. for Golf Research

Don't.

Before beginning research for this book, I'd imagined Artificial Intelligence might come in useful on occasion. Something of a slow adopter, I really wasn't familiar with the terminology, the scope, the capabilities, or the conversation surrounding AI. Like a lot (most?) of people, I just sort of knew what it was.

You get a quick tutorial on how to use it from a friend who's considerably more tech-savvy than you, and away you go, typing in your first question - probably something about the Open Championship. You already have quite extensive knowledge about the Open because you've been watching it and reading (a lot) about it for nearly 40 years. But you hope and expect ChatGPT will surprise you with a tiny detail you never knew.

And then it tells you something like Tom Morris won the inaugural event at St Andrews. You do a double-take, frown for ten seconds, and assume you've done something wrong. You've obviously worded your question incorrectly and haven't made yourself entirely clear. You apologize (without knowing who you're apologizing to), and then ask if it's sure that's really what happened.

It responds by saying you were right to doubt the initial answer and that, actually, this is the correct version of events. But that could be wrong, too, and you quickly realize you might know more about the Open Championship than AI. You secretly feel chuffed because you knew something AI didn't.

After several months of this, you learn how and when to use it, which is to say not very often. As with using Wikipedia, you get a strong sense of when a page is to be trusted and when it's best ignored. But even when you think it might be correct, you check with three or four sources you do trust.

In the end, though, you more or less stop using ChatGPT altogether because you know it isn't the friend you thought it might be. Not yet anyway.

—TD

INDEX

D

E

F

G

H

Wilson
Wilson Staff

32
15
4
17
11
1
13
36
20
10
45
46
19
9
33
8
29
40
3
23
38
21
47
31
35
41
14

50 TOURNAMENTS

About the Author

A former British PGA apprentice professional and member of the University of Liverpool golf team that played its home matches at Hoylake, **TONY DEAR** is an award-winning golf writer who has contributed to numerous publications on both sides of the Atlantic, including the *New York Sun, Sports Illustrated, The Guardian,* and *Links Magazine*. This is his sixth book, his two most recent being the *Golfer's Handbook* and *The Story of Golf in 50 Holes.* Dear grew up near London, but has lived in the United States for 25 years, and now lives in Bellingham, Washington.